THE NOISE

ROBERT DUNCAN

THE NOISE

NOTES FROM A
ROCK 'N' ROLL ERA

TICKNOR & FIELDS ● NEW YORK ● 1984

Library of Congress Cataloging in Publication Data
Duncan, Robert.
   The noise: notes from a rock 'n' roll era.

   1. Rock music — United States — History and criticism.
2. Music and society. 3. Popular culture. I. Title.
ML3534.D85   1984   973.92   84-8558
ISBN 0-89919-168-1
ISBN 0-89919-326-9 (pbk.)

Printed in the United States of America

P 10 9 8 7 6 5 4 3 2 1

Book design by Victoria Hartman

Acknowledgments

Thanks to all who so generously helped during the writing of this book. Special thanks to James Raimes, my editor and friend, and Barbara Lowenstein, my friend and agent.

Grateful acknowledgment is made to the following publishers for permission to quote from songs: "Gimme Shelter" (Mick Jagger and Keith Richards); copyright © 1969 ABCKO Music. "Cities on Flame" (D. Roeser, A. Bouchard, S. Pearlman); copyright © 1972 B. O'Cult Songs. "(Don't Fear) The Reaper" (Donald Roeser); copyright © 1976 B. O'Cult Songs. "The Next Big Thing" (Andy Shernoff); copyright © 1975 Sure Enough Tunes Inc. "I'm Eighteen" (A. Cooper, M. Bruce, G. Buxton, D. Dunaway, N. Smith); copyright © 1970 Bizarre Music, Inc., and Alive Enterprises; used by permission of Warner Bros. Music; All Rights Reserved. "School's Out" (A. Cooper, M. Bruce, G. Buxton, D. Dunaway, N. Smith); copyright © 1972 Bizarre Music, Inc., and Alive Enterprises; used by permission of Warner Bros. Music; All Rights Reserved. "All the Young Dudes" (David Bowie); copyright © 1971 Red Admiral Music, Inc., and Mainman Music, Ltd. "Sweet Home Alabama" (words and music by Ronnie Van Zant, Ed King, and Gary Rossington); copyright © 1974 Duchess Music Corporation and Hustlers, Inc.; used by permission; All Rights Reserved. "Anarchy in the UK," "Pretty Vacant," "God Save the Queen," "Seventeen," "No Feelings" (words and music by Johnny Rotten, Steven Jones, Paul Cook, and Glen Matlock); copyright © 1978 Warner Bros. Music Limited and Glitterbest Limited; used by permission; All Rights Reserved. "My My, Hey Hey (Out of the Blue)" (Neil Young and Jeff Blackburn); copyright © 1978 Silver Fiddle; used by permission; All Rights Reserved.

For Roni

THE NOISE

Prologue:
Do the Noise

My father always blamed it on the rock 'n' roll. The drugs, the sex, the faithless wild boys and girls obeying no authority and bearing no responsibility, playing havoc with America in a mindless quest for the good time they believed was owed them by the world. My father's not stupid.

A big guy, a tough guy, a football star from the days when, he will point out, they didn't wear all that sissy padding, a man from the days when men were men. A born cowboy, son of a cowboy sheriff, he's also not given to hysteria. But one night at dinner, back around 1973, when my mother had finished the latest gruesome tale of somebody's son or daughter going off to live on a commune or overdosing or otherwise rounding the bend, my father, stiff-backed and stoic as usual in his place at the head of the table, suddenly gave out with a burst of breath, forcing a nervous chuckle to cover it, and said with more bewilderment than I had ever heard from him, "What is going *on?*"

My father looked down the table at my mother and then left at his long-haired, would-be rock singer son, me, and then right at his pony-tailed, would-be rock guitarist son, my little brother, and then back at my mother. But for once there was nothing of the accusing or combative in his gaze, which seemed instead to take in a whole, long era that was finally, for the briefest of moments, breaking him down. I might have felt like smirking that we had at long last gotten through to the old man, gloating perhaps that we had him on the run. For one unique second my father had turned to really listen to this loud generation of mine. It was some kind of triumph, and I might have felt righteous and proud. But in his eyes there was a strange, sad glint, and all I could feel was bad.

. . .

Every victory is somehow Pyrrhic, I've learned since, and being right is almost always being part wrong. But at the time I wouldn't have believed it anyway because we were right and about to win. The boasts of the 1960s — that we, the sons and daughters of America, would bring down the corrupt world of our fathers and from the rubble would rise a place of peace, love, and total freedom — had begun in the seventies to gain the ring of prophecy, even as they were losing their luster. In 1973, as if by some magic nostalgia, the sixties were indeed coming true.

After a decade of war in Vietnam, the United States in 1973 was finally giving up, surrendering in effect, and as much to young dissenters and their allies at home as to the tenacious enemy abroad, this "peace with honor," as the administration's gloss had it, becoming the first military defeat in the history of the nation. Elsewhere in 1973, bowing to the arguments of young women in revolt, the Supreme Court of the United States concluded that abortion was in fact legal — and soon enough, through Medicaid, the government would have to begin paying for those abortions too. While homosexuals had been marching from the closet to demand their rights since 1969, by 1973, as if to confirm every father's fear of what homosexuals and rock 'n' roll both were all about, a young man named Alice Cooper, whose concert act

2.

featured black leather, whips, and a simulated hanging, was topping the charts and taking young America by storm, if not by force. On campus and in the schoolyard, too, sleeping pills were the drug of choice of the day, but everywhere, illicit drugs of all varieties had become the recreational norm by 1973. And through the efforts of a clean-cut and eminently respectable new young people's organization called NORML, the pot smokers' lobby, marijuana was on its way to being "decriminalized" across the country, literally from New York to Alaska. Lastly, in 1973 the government itself was actually starting to fall. After being charged with extortion, among other felonies, and copping a plea on tax evasion, the vice president of the United States, conservative Republican Spiro T. Agnew, was compelled to relinquish his post. And at the same time over on Capitol Hill, a Democratic Congress, to top it all, was busy greasing the way out for Agnew's Republican boss, the thirty-seventh president, Richard M. Nixon. But you didn't have to be "paranoid," as a pair of young *Washington Post* reporters would write that Nixon was, to believe that the demise of his administration had more than a little to do with the wild-eyed sons and daughters and a tumultuous era they defined.

There was more. And 1973 wasn't even the half of it. But simply add in the perhaps unrelated fact that this was the year that OPEC first shut off the gas, and it becomes not at all unreasonable to say that in 1973, in America, a world was indeed coming down. And it wasn't only my father's.

What *was* going on?

*I*t wasn't just fashion. A change has taken place in this country over the last fifteen years, a deep and broad change that may yet prove to be lasting. It is also unfinished. And I don't mean the swing to the right of recent years or the more profound and enduring swing to the left that preceded it. Such things, especially the two taken together, do say something about the highly changeable nature of the times. However, as we swing back and then back again, it becomes apparent that, like most matters of historical significance, the substance of this change resides not in politics but in an even murkier realm of psychology and culture. Essentially the change is in the American character.

The change is not entirely cataclysmic. In a sense, it's the culmination of a continuous effort by Americans to resolve the contradictions of their collective life, contradictions going back to the beginnings of the modern era, to the beginnings of the Industrial Revolution in America, to the Civil War, to the very founding of the country, contradictions addressed in the Enlightenment-era rational humanism that, by presuming the perfectibility of man, made such a founding possible. But ultimately the change can be nothing *but* cataclysmic because the ultimate contradiction of contemporary America is a cataclysm itself, the cataclysm that sundered the atom and so history. Pursuing his perfectibility, man has run straight up against his obsolescence and extinction. The flesh peers over the abyss of the spirit. Something has to give.

• • •

"You've got to do it all at once — change everything fast — the faster the better," Margaret Mead told an interviewer from *Psychology Today* in 1971. "This way each detail of the

4.

new life can support other details so one is not constantly reminded of the old ways." Margaret Mead was one of our most serious students of change, and this was her warning to a changing America. It was a warning she had first given voice to almost two decades earlier, in 1953, pointedly proffering as "food for the imagination of Americans" a new book about the Manus, the islanders she had initially examined in 1928 for *Growing Up in New Guinea*. Entitled *New Lives for Old*, this follow-up study, according to Mead's introduction, was "the record of a people who moved faster than any people of whom we have records." By this record, so hopefully concluded, Mead was trying to show her own compatriots that change can be good, appealing to a "precious quality which Americans have developed . . . a belief that men can learn and change — quickly, happily, without violence, without madness, without coercion, and of their own free will." In 1953, with Joe McCarthy and the House Un-American Activities Committee still hard at work purging the nation, Margaret Mead was particularly worried, as perhaps some are today, that "false prophets seek to change our priceless inheritance of political innovation and flexibility into some untouchable fetish of unchangeableness." The story of the Manus was her fable of a brighter future in America — a future, as she would later recognize, not at all unlike our recent past.

The Manus were a small, primitive, isolated society of fishers spread out among a few dozen villages set on stilts in the coastal shallows around Great Admiralty Island — also known popularly as Manus — northeast of New Guinea. Subject to Germany before the First World War and to Australia after, investigated by young Mead in the twenties and inveigled in the thirties by a band of Christian missionaries, the islanders managed nevertheless to remain relatively unchanged until the Second World War, when they were set upon first by the Japanese and then the Americans, the latter establishing amid these unsophisticated people the largest U.S. military base between Pearl Harbor and Guam. Indeed, the war would bring over a million Americans — accompanied of course by all the most advanced machinery of warfare and civilization — through the island, and inevitably, after several years of incessant, pervasive contact with Western styles and technology, Manus society began to undergo a fundamental transformation.

By Mead's account, to be fair, the Manus actually liked the Americans, finding their loose and open manner and, in particular, their great machines a source of profound fascination. And in many ways this was not simply the sad old story of the imperialists bringing syphilis and capitalist exploitation to the happy and innocent natives. A lot of the time, said Mead, the natives here were neither. In fact, while there was much to admire in their society, especially its gentle child-rearing practices, the Manus maintained as well some homegrown customs remarkable for their low nastiness — special mention going to the institutionally corrupt capitalistic economy, which demanded of the Manus breadwinner a talent for duplicity and a taste for raw rapacity unequaled outside the boardrooms of Big Oil. Thus did Mead argue that change might well be an improvement. Be that as it may, her basic point was that change had arrived and that the task of the Manus in the postwar period would be to deal with it. Which they did.

It's not surprising that by the end of the war certain of the Manus had already embraced the new and quite unceremoniously dispatched the old. These were the visionaries, an element in every society, and from their mostly young ranks emerged the visionary leaders who would seek to organize the change into what they called the "New Way" for Manus society. Establishment of the New Way was not, however, to be an uncomplicated undertaking. It seems many of the Manus—mostly the older generation—were not so blessed with vision as were the young. *They* saw only the decline of the good old way, not the rise of the new and improved. And so they clung to the old talismans, to the dogs' teeth and seashell money, to the traditional Manus garb, the grass skirt and loincloth, to the rubber-gum pottery and spears; they clung to the old ways — and very shrewdly, very much in keeping with one aspect of the old ways, they also clung to the talismans and native currency discarded by their New Way neighbors, hoarding these against the day that everyone was returned to his senses and a windfall could be realized in the ritual resupply business. But would *you* buy a used dog's tooth from these men? Evidently the burgeoning number of youthful New Way followers would not, not now and not later. While the old people were adamant about not changing, the young people were equally adamant about not changing back. Whereupon an impasse had been reached and change was stopped. Until the Noise.

The symptoms were various, but always loud. A standard case might begin with much excruciating moaning and whimpering followed suddenly by total collapse. Prostrate and shaking violently as in seizure, eyeballs rotating back, the afflicted might hear the dead speak or speak himself in the tongues of the dead, telling of dancing spears turned into paper money and many planes and ships bringing great cargoes to the Manus from God. And, invariably, he would begin to scream, sometimes far into the night, reported Mead, to very eerie effect; and then finally, still in the throes of loud seizure, and acting as well at the behest of ancestors and deity, the stricken one would exhibit the most bizzare symptom of all, frantically gathering together all of his old possessions in order that he might race down to the beach and cast everything into the sea. In order that he might wait. And wait. But for what? For the cargo, of course, the vast new riches that the voices said would be his just as soon as he had disposed of the old.

.7

"The Noise," as Margaret Mead translated the Manus expression, hit the island society in 1947 like a hurricane, and before the year was over, had just about leveled it. In one clique or village after another, someone would start trembling and shouting and then throwing all his old belongings away and soon enough a great caterwaul would have arisen from the whole group and the water of the lagoon would be gorged with pottery and spears. Word about this would travel on around the island, until eventually someone else would pick up the message that a cargo had actually been *sighted* and there and then a caterwaul would rise again. But in the village of Peri, abandoned some time before by a younger generation gone to pursue the New Way, the skeptical elders left behind received the *most* startling — and compelling — news of all. This time, in this place, wrote Mead, "the message was simply that the cargo had arrived; they had only to make the necessary preparations." And in a panic, they did. And so finally did the Noise come to that most staunchly conservative of Manus communities, not, the anthropologist explained, "as a mystical religious seizure . . . but as the practical preparation for the certain arrival of a wonderful cargo of European goods, which had already arrived elsewhere." But still it came, enveloping old now as well as young. In the end, to the holdouts of Peri, the Noise had seemed to be just good business sense.

So they waited. The religious, the idealistic, and the calculating, all of them waited. Some got mad: in one group the men killed the prophet who had first brought the word. Others tried, tried again, the Noise developing into a cult, a new religion, with screaming seizures a regularly practiced rite. Although the Noise, of course, failed to bring the Manus actual cargo, it succeeded in bringing another kind of cargo: change.

The Noise was the naked voice of the Manus. It was

the baring of the urge for new, for change — or at least the baring of a willingness to try. For those who resisted the New Way most vehemently, the rise of the Noise gave proof that they resisted against lengthening odds, and the Noise itself, like an inoculation, made the pain of their change mercifully brief. For the converted, the Noise provided solidarity, a deeper spiritual unity with all of their people and a new sense of the significance of their mission. Those on the fence on Manus island were pushed off. The Noise was an engine of change. "After the Noise," Mead concluded, "the people . . . were sufficiently in step with each other to be able to go forward in working out a new pattern . . ." And indeed, over the years (Mead checked again in 1964), to make that new pattern work out. As silly, as bizarre, as crazy and meaningless and loud and utterly irrelevant as it might have seemed, the Noise was a necessary total shaking up before total change.

. . .

Cargo cults, as the anthropologists have labeled such events as the Noise, now turn up regularly in primitive societies suddenly dragged forth into the modern world and great change. They don't always work out as well as the cargo cult, and the change, of the Manus. Without leadership, with only the utopian vision, said Mead, movements for change finally don't know where to go, or how, and so they go bad, slipping into stasis, defensiveness, and ultimately self-destruction. But of course what concerned Mead most was not the cargo cults Down Under, but those right here at home.

In 1953, while working on the Manus book, Margaret Mead had been worried that change in her own country might stop, that McCarthyism might become to the dream of America — a dream born out of a cargo cult we call the

Boston Tea Party — something like what Stalinism had become to the Russian dream. In 1971, with change in America at last come again, Margaret Mead warned us about what might come next. "Well," she replied to that same *Psychology Today* interviewer who had expressed his own concern, "no civilization is immune to apocalyptic cults or revolutionary or counterrevolutionary panaceas. We have quite a few around now, and some of them frighten me too. From one point of view the whole of history, particularly our own American history, can be seen as a struggle between those who wait for an easy utopia — they want a prophet or a party to usher it in with a supernatural event — and those who know how to shape our institutions and who work to renew them day by day." In 1971, with change come again, Margaret Mead was worried about the Noise that brought it.

The citizens, seized by a chemical trance, raised a caterwaul over the land. Moaning and primal screaming, Americans scattered to their shores to throw it all away — lest they be left out of the sexual revolution, the race revolution, the women's movement, the drug craze, the credit explosion, the information boom, or any of the vast fantastic cargoes of magic fruits of the new. Finally, not even the old men on the Hill could resist the demented siren's call. So, young and old, the citizens of America came together for an unprecedented leap of faith and there by the Potomac in 1974 dispatched Richard Nixon and the old; and then in 1976, in the most radical consensus in American political history, welcomed Jimmy Carter and the new — the unknown, even. A man who as governor of the great, largely unreconstructed state of Georgia had once reported the sighting of a UFO. Sober.

. . .

In the 1970s, the cargo arrived. It's fashionable to say it never did, to say that the realpolitik of the 1970s was where the ecstatic, visionary sixties finally ran aground. It's common wisdom these days — especially among those who had believed themselves to be the admirals of the sixties fleet. Another of their standard apologias arrived the other day, David Harris's sixties memoir called, of course, *Dreams Die Hard*. To which the *New York Times* book reviewer responded with a sadder-but-wiser aye-aye: "Neither the expectations that so many people in this book had for their lives, nor the hopes they had for a bright new world came to pass; the 60s were over and its easy promises had come unraveled." Such is the party line. You hear it, wistful yet chastened, from Jerry Rubin (*Growing Up at 37*) and Weather Underground refugee Jane Alpert (*Growing Up Underground*), as well as, in ascending degrees of vindictiveness, from Christopher Lasch (*The Culture of Narcissism*), Tom "the me decade" Wolfe, and such "neoconservatives" as Norman Podhoretz (*Commentary* magazine). "The sixties flopped" is the tiresome message. But mostly the Podhoretzes are writing about the Rubins, and the Rubins are writing about their anomalous, overinflated selves. For the greater part of America, the sixties did not flop in the seventies, nor have they flopped in the eighties. For a huge group, perhaps a majority, of Americans, the cargo did arrive.

In fact, for my money, the seventies *were* the sixties. Or, in the immortal words of demographic oracle Daniel Yankelovich, who offers a similar reading of the seventies in his book *New Rules*: "In the sixties cross-section surveys showed that the shifts in culture barely touched the lives of the majority of Americans ... By the seventies, however

... all was pluralism and freedom of choice: to marry or live together; to have children early or postpone them, perhaps forever; to keep the old job or return to school; to make commitments or hang loose; to change careers, spouses, houses, states of residence, states of mind." And it's true! In the seventies, the utopian visions of the earlier decade were absorbed at last into mainstream America and, for all the unavoidable dilution, gained new and enlarged significance, just as Margaret Mead suggested they would, as part of everyday American life. But of course the real cargo was the enduring possibility of change itself.

• • •

This then is a book about the American Noise. It's about a time of change and a new will to change. It's about a people's search for new values with which to confront the radically new circumstances of postwar technological life, a search for truth in wild speculation, indeed for permanence in change. And it's my own personal search, my own confrontation with new circumstances — including the most startling circumstance of turning thirty — and all the old questions of faith and love and sex and death. I'm sure it's a search because it has found me changing my mind — and then changing it back again.

Since nothing and no one is untouched — whether they are actually changed or changed back or simply compelled to make an effort to remain the same — this excursion into the American Noise must touch on a whole range of Americas and Americans, several of whom are sketched here in interviews — my versions of Mead's field reports, my transcriptions of a culture as I was discovering it. So this is a book about business and politics and religion and culture, about the mass media and technology; and it's about old as well as young, my parents as well as my peers. It's about the generation which sparked change and the generations which, all together, will have to make it stick. And finally, it's about the rock 'n' roll — as silly, as bizarre, as crazy and meaningless and loud and utterly irrelevant as sometimes that might have seemed.

· · ·

"*Womp-baba-loo-bomp-a-lomp-bam-boom . . .*" said Little Richard, and to a lot of young Americans that about said it all. Indeed, as silly, as bizarre, as crazy and meaningless and loud and utterly irrelevant as it was, so were the times. They were times of vast sunny prospects and bottomless dark dread; times of invincible rationality and inscrutable irrationality; of sobriety and of debauchery; of unparalleled affluence and of surpassing debt; times of freedom, but only as directed; times of piety and of sacrilege; of faith and no faith at all. The best and the worst as Dickens never could have dreamed, these were the times when humankind rose to the heights of its glorious powers and sank to the depths of its most abject powerlessness, when we mastered the very elements of nature and in so doing were enslaved. They were times of great progress backward, times of beginnings and of the end. They were times that made you want to shout ("Howl," if you were Allen Ginsberg and the beats), which is just what Little Richard and the rockers did. "*Womp-baba-loo-bomp-a-lomp-bam-boom . . .*" Somehow in such times it made a whole lot of sense.

In a unique voice, at once as broad as mass communication and as intimate and direct as the new transistor radios, rock 'n' roll was speaking to the contemporary contradictions. Born of the times, and ultimately inseparable from them, it was sense as well as nonsense, pleasure as well as pain, beauty as well as blight. It was primitive yet high-tech sophisticated; black yet white; macho yet "feminine"; individualistic and heroic yet highly social too. Like Pop Art, which would owe to it, rock 'n' roll was culture and the

.13

crassest commercialism. Like Dada, to which it would owe, it was humanity shouting to be heard over the machines and all the while cranking the machines up louder. And like any of the modernist genres, it was defiantly secular, even as it stood in for religion — but then rock 'n' roll came from rhythm 'n' blues, which came from backsliding gospel. It was complete freedom marshaled to a 4/4 beat. It was fun, but, like Richard's shout, of such a crazed intensity that it could come only from knowing fun's flip side. "Rock 'n' roll" — the term itself was contradictory. It was all for life and all for risking it. It was hateful and loving; exceedingly violent and wantonly sentimental. Margaret Mead once said that "parents have been raising unknown children for an unknown world since 1946." What Little Richard and Elvis Presley and Chuck Berry would seem to have done, then, was to speak in the unknown tongue.

And so rock 'n' roll turned out to be much more than just the latest sound, indeed much more than just the music. From it emerged new ideas of style, a new sense of beauty, new attitudes toward things in general, new values, even a new sense of truth; a new popular aesthetic that became something like a new popular ethos. Our own postwar age resonated with rock 'n' roll as Fitzgerald's never quite had with jazz. It was rock 'n' roll, in fact, more than opposition to the Vietnam War, more than support for civil rights, more than utopianism and mysticism and dope and left-over beatnikism, more than affluence and education and youthfulness — all of which of course were wrapped up with it — that defined the rebellion of the late sixties and was its essential spirit and vitality, its very heart. More than anything else, rock 'n' roll defined the rebellious generation, that plurality of Americans who began as the baby boom and wound up as Woodstock Nation and who in turn, more than anything else, have defined contemporary America. Which brings up one last contradiction.

If rock 'n' roll has been the heart of rebellion, it has also in a sense been the soul of conservatism. To some of the recent counterculture memoirists, that is precisely why the rock 'n' roll rebellion of the sixties finally failed. "Of course," explains Abbie Hoffman in his autobiography, *Soon to Be a Major Motion Picture*, "rock as revolution was one of the era's biggest put-ons. Its high energy got you wet all over. Got you horny and angry. Made you feel a part of something bigger. But it was not revolution. Revolutions are not engineered from the studios of communications conglomerates. . . . Mick Jagger can sing all he wants about fighting in the streets; he's gifted and outrageous. But he probably inspired more young people to become millionaires than to overthrow the system. . . . [Rock] was only 'revolutionary' because we said it was." Surely Hoffman's right that rock 'n' roll was not revolution. He may even be right about Mick Jagger and the young millionaires, rhetorically speaking, that is. But still, isn't there something to be said for getting horny and angry? For the renewing intensity of experience and the emboldening intensity of expression found in the best rock 'n' roll? For the sense of solidarity? And isn't there something to be said for thinking big? Isn't it just possible that wanting to be a rich and famous rock 'n' roll star can be the seed of a larger creative dissatisfaction, that the impulse to be a millionaire can be transforming in many unexpected ways, that it can actually turn out to be revolutionary? Introducing her 1981 collection of essays, *Beginning to See the Light*, feminist and rock critic — and leftist — Ellen Willis makes a relevant observation. Regarding among leftists a certain "puritanical discomfort with the urge — whatever form it takes — to gratification now," she suggests that "it is the longing for happiness that is potentially radical, while the morality of sacrifice is an age-old weapon of rulers."

Rock 'n' roll proposes no new political program, no flaming new ideology. Ultimately, it may well be conservative —

but in pursuing happiness, not to mention life and liberty, perhaps what it conserves is the *true* spirit of revolution. And if rock 'n' roll ultimately gathers its contradictions into its own version of that hair-trigger paradox called America, it's not complacent. At its worst, to be sure, perhaps at its average, rock 'n' roll can be as much an opiate of the masses as any old-time religion, as mystifying and manipulative as any old merchandising lie. At its worst then, it may be oppressive, cynically promising the audience: "Buy a new car, be cool, be saved!" At its best, however, rock 'n' roll proposes that we join forces and shake down the lies and make the false promises deliver: "*Jump* a new car, be cool, be saved!" And then, laying rubber off the lot, just decibels in front of the sirens, such rock 'n' roll laughs with Chuck Berry: "I'm so glad I'm living in the USA . . . Anything you want they got it right here in the USA." At its best, rock 'n' roll raises a caterwaul over the land and calls the bluff of the American dream. At its best, it's an American anthem that's also an American Noise.

And if the cargo never arrives, the cargo — more or less; for good and sometimes for ill — arrives anyway. Ask your dad.

16.

1

hud.

Suddenly it was the 1970s. A change that was gonna come had come. The generation of change had arrived. But what is it about cargo? Suddenly, *thud* . . .

The drugs had seemed to promise better. Back in high school in the sixties, I had looked forward quite moistly to this day when acidheads would rule the world. Through fixed, black Frisbee pupils, I glimpsed the dawn of a golden age, a paradise regained, the millennium, the halcyon epoch of LSD in which the hippie and the businessman, the longhair and the cop, the freak and the straight would stand hand-in-hand in one great silly circle, the universal acid experience having delivered us at last to a universal recognition of the absurdity of the modern predicament, all badness having been washed away in a sea of giggles like tribal artifacts in the South Seas surf. In the future, in fact, there would be no businessmen and no cops, no hippies or freaks either, all tribes enfolded into one. There would be no hate or war. There would be no money; there would be no poverty. For that matter, there would be no work, at least nothing hard. In a world conversant with LSD, neither would there be laws or jails or injustice. There would be no high school principals, no high school teachers at all — because ultimately there would be *no high school.* Yes, peace, love, understanding, and total freedom would be all the rubbery regulation. And if sometimes the planes didn't run on time, things would sure be a whole lot funnier.

A kind of instant, technological Noise all its own, biochemically amputating imagination from perception and so effect from cause, acid did lend itself to grandiose visions. Then again, when you come upon yourself "half a million strong," as the anthemizers put it, at Woodstock, that's pretty damn grand. At that point, an LSD paradise seemed not only doable, but half done already. There were, however, other forces at work. And things didn't exactly turn out as I had planned.

Oh, I got my acid world all right. The promise of the drugs may have been extravagant, but to an extravagant degree — for better or worse — it did come true. How else to explain Jimmy Carter, the Bob Dylan-quoting UFO-spotter with his Beatle haircut and his running here and there to hug guys with pigtails down their backs (and meanwhile, back at the White House: snort-snort, toke-toke — or so it was said), except as the acid president? How else to account for the Democrats handing over their party, lock, stock, and pork barrel, to women and blacks and hippies — who handed it over to George McGovern — as far back as 1972? How else to figure a dyed-in-the-wool red-baiting Republican like Richard Nixon jumping in the sack with Red China, not to mention abolishing the draft and growing his sideburns? And what about Nixon's shaggy young archnemesis on TV, the erstwhile White House correspondent Dan Rather, who on the eve of his accession to the throne of American broadcasting, the anchor's chair for the *CBS Evening News*, blithely admitted that he had ventured beyond acid even by getting himself shot up with heroin, just for the experience — for *kicks?* And what *about* cocaine on Capitol Hill?

In rebuttal you might point to Ronald Reagan. But who

really voted for him anyway? Not many, in fact; demonstrably not most. And for how many of them was such a vote actually an expression of disaffection for the incumbent, perhaps a rebellious expression of political disaffection in general? And for how many more was a celluloid fantasy of a president actually an ironic selection, just some sort of goof? Viewed most favorably, the election of Ronald Reagan may only mean that we've come to love change in this country; viewed otherwise, it may mean that we no longer give a shit.

In rebuttal I could cite dopers, pinkos, peaceniks, and crazies; hair long or green or mohawk short; hippie-ism, punkism, feminism, rock 'n' rollism — and not only on the media-politico fringe, but everywhere in the life and culture of this nation over the last fifteen years. Have no doubt, the Republic of LSD thrives among us. To wit: a trio of hirsute cops, joke-shop bee-antennae bouncing crazily above their uniform hats, boogies down to the rock 'n' roll at the big No Nukes rally in Central Park in June of 1982; a female colleague — an honest-to-god policewoman, I might emphasize, with a nightstick and a gun and everything, one of the thousands of her kind who in a few years have forever altered the face of law enforcement in America — laughs and claps time, setting *her* bee-antennae to bobbing, while an earth mother–type leftover from the sixties gyrates out of the crowd and, to the express delight of all concerned, enthusiastically joins in; marijuana smoke wafts over the scene, and nearby another group of officers surveys the signs and sign carriers and quite forthrightly informs the TV camera that if not for duty they'd be out there protesting too.

"Nothing is real and nothing to get hung about," John Lennon once said in one of those spacey rock 'n' roll songs that parents and public officials invariably decoded as an invitation to drugs. And perhaps on one level it was. Yet following Lennon's murder, the New York City Council fell over itself to enact legislation naming a patch of park land

.21

Strawberry Fields in honor of that very song. To go stand there, the suggestion would seem to be, is to sense the psychedelic dislocation of the times. Even my mother was struck somewhere deep on hearing the news of Lennon and called to say that in the end she felt it was her loss too. And so in that moment, maybe, the silly circle was completed, the hallucination fulfilled, the cosmic consensus achieved, and the cargo delivered. Nothing to get hung about. Nothing is real. Including the contrary life of the wild man who helped to conceive it. Everybody say *wow* . . .

What is it about cargo? Somehow it wasn't much consolation that John Lennon died for our sins. In fact, for me, what consolation there was arrived from the most unexpected of quarters. It came from that handful of bitter oddballs who turned up near the bottom of the tabloid tribute stories and on the letters pages in the weeks succeeding Lennon's death and who in the heat of his canonization had the temerity and the tenacity to continue to protest that, far from being saintly, this was really a reckless, faithless, drug-proselytizing megalomaniac of an evil rock star who got his. They consoled me, these cranks, because they made me realize that to honor John Lennon unequivocally is not to honor him at all. But more than that, they also helped me understand how the cargo that Lennon had so singularly invoked has seemed on delivery to fall flat with a resounding *thud*.

. . .

Yes, I have my acid world — but without the acid. And I'm not only talking about LSD. *Acid* is a metaphor here — in much the same way that *drugs* is so frequently a metaphor among high school principals and others of the unhipped powers that be for the otherwise unfathomable motives of younger citizens who stray from the straight and narrow. Acid (what the younger citizens today call simply "cid") is a metaphor here in much the same way that the *experi-*

22.

ence of acid, of LSD — a drug described in the clinical literature as a psychotomimetic, the effect of which, in other words, mimes psychosis, is *like* psychosis — can itself be a metaphor. When I say acid, I mean a whole new way of looking askance at the world; I mean a psychological strategy that can deal with the psychotomimesis of postwar America, a society whose claim to sovereignty over its citizens is ultimately based on its infinite capacity to destroy them, whose vaunted Judeo-Christianity and Protestant ethic and Puritanism are finally based on nihilism. When I say acid, I mean something like "*Womp-baba-loo-bomp.*" And by an "acid world" I mean a place where an intractable element of "un-seriousness" pervades the affairs of men and women, a place where the individual, highly subjective, even ridiculous point of view can always get a hearing. By a world of acid *without* acid I mean a place where such views are merely codified and etched in stone.

Acid without acid: it's a place with no particular geography. Sometimes you think you see it at a No Nukes rally; sometimes you just sense its presence while riding in a car. It's not unlike the place in Thomas McGuane's 1973 novel *Ninety-Two in the Shade* where a young hitchhiker named Tom Skelton, a recent counterculture dropout literally and chemically tripping his way home, discovers suddenly that the peace of the new decade may be even harder to take than the wars of the old.

> . . . He stuck out his thumb and thought, They won't see I'm insane until I'm already in the car. It is hot and when I get to Key West I'll borrow some money and order a beverage. I'll get a six-pack and take my skiff out on the reef. If they say in the car that I am insane, I will take over the wheel.
>
> No one said he was insane; neither the hardware salesman, the United Parcel driver nor the crawfisherman who drove the last leg into Key West suggested such a thing. When Skelton told the hardware salesman that the paint had just

lifted off the whole car in a single piece, the hardware salesman agreed with him about how Detroit put things together. This was the epoch of uneasy alliances.

It's a place where they name parks after songs by John Lennon, a dope-peddling megalomaniac they once tried to exile, a place where the Noise might well be heard on the Muzak.

Taking drugs was at one time a way of stepping outside, both of oneself by the effects of the drugs and of one's society by the fact that the drugs were desperately illegal and hopelessly immoral. And if it's still a question whether drugs functioned more as a rite of passage to change for the young people of the sixties than as a catalyst, the shared experience of stepping outside, that external vantage point held more or less in common, certainly became a large part of the glue of their aptly named counterculture. The mystical nature of those drugs fostered a certain cultishness; their prohibition made secretive, cultish language and behavior something of a necessity. Of course, in the long run such exclusive behavior — as well as the inescapable fact that the psychoactive drug experience, in the way that it plays to our most idiosyncratic fears and foibles and fantasies, is always basically undertaken alone — would divide and weaken the counterculture as much as it had once served to bring it together. Again from *Soon to Be a Major Motion Picture* Abbie Hoffman inadvertently offers up a case in point, pausing in the midst of his revisionist excoriation of rock 'n' roll to draw a rather odd line in the dirt. "Loving dope," he announces with no little macho swagger, "makes you an outlaw; [but] loving rock music," he adds with no little contempt, "just makes you a good consumer." (It should be noted, however, that the outlaw Abbie Hoffman may have subsequently experienced a change of heart, becoming, under the terms of his work-release from prison, a conspicuous convert to antidrug do-goodism — if not necessarily to rock 'n' roll.)

24.

Of late the most striking illustration of the power of drugs to foment rancor and distrust is provided by those ubiquitous, runny-nosed whirling dervishes the cocaine cultists, whose particular fanaticism always seems, most distressingly, to entail the usurping of the bathrooms at big, crowded parties. Furthermore, as to any intrinsic subversive properties of LSD 25, ponder, if you will, the career of Timothy Leary, gone from scientist and Harvard professor to guru to jailbird (however unfairly) and fugitive, to stand-up comic to disk jockey and most recently to geek, paired off with Watergate convict G. Gordon Liddy in the lecture circuit's equivalent of a sideshow, in the twenty years since Henry Luce first brought him and psychedelics to our attention in *Life* magazine. On second thought, maybe Leary is less a victim of acid than of Luce. In any event, if taking drugs is no longer an impetus to revolutionary solidarity, stepping outside has become more like stepping in. When the marijuana crop in Tennessee is estimated to be second only to cotton and in California, the nation's largest agricultural producer, second to none, then it could be that loving dope just makes you a good consumer. Or it could be that the revolution of the sixties has succeeded de facto, in spite of itself.

Actually, in the years that have ensued, the words most often used to describe the revolution of the sixties have been sixties-era epithets like *co-opted* and *sell-out* — if not simply *defeated*. As we have seen, some of the sixties-era revolutionaries who use such words appear almost to rejoice in them. Of course, having had their revolution sold out from under them, or just beaten, probably came as a relief to some, especially to those who had most obviously and thoroughly painted themselves into a Day-Glo corner. Titling a chapter in *Motion Picture* about the early seventies "Bummed Out on the Movement," Abbie Hoffman details his own discomfort with what he had wrought, especially a younger, renegade Yippie faction which undertook to harass Abbie and his partner, YIP cofounder Jerry Rubin — mocking, for instance, the latter's pronouncements about not trusting anyone over thirty by presenting him a well-publicized "media cake" on the occasion of *his* thirtieth birthday. For other counterculturists, perhaps defeat better satisfied a romantic impulse; victory, after all, implied certain mundane responsibilities. Still others may have mistaken personal disappointment for generalized disaster, looking on with addled anticipation, as one tide carried off the drab detritus of a past way of life but the next did not return a rainbow. Then again, maybe Margaret Mead was right that in order to change successfully we must change everything, fast, and maybe the changes that emerged from the sixties were just too little, in proportion to the changes that were necessary, or came too late. But the most puzzling fact of the matter is that by the beginning of the seventies, in the face of almost unimaginable, nigh-hallucinogenic successes, Woodstock Nation had already been beset by a distinct sense of failure.

Vietnam, Nixon, racism, sexism, and the displacements of postindustrial capitalism. I wouldn't deny that there were some lacerating setbacks and bloody failures, or that sometimes it looked like a total loss. But it seems that the greatest failure of our maturing opposition movement was not a failure to implement change, but a failure to take heart from less than complete success and then to press ahead. And ultimately there's an arrogance in such a failure, especially for a movement that in its democratic rhetoric and bluesy pretensions took pains to identify itself with "the people," because ultimately it's a failure of faith in them. In McGuane's novel, Tom Skelton, like so many real-life counterparts, was seeking an answer in a world increasingly without any to "the question of his conviction or his courage." But in returning home to Key West, he was finally just surrendering to the status quo, to an old-fashioned America of machismo and force and deadly "free enterprise." Thus, going along, Skelton winds up

26.

with a shotgun hole in his chest, a man of pointless conviction and cartoon courage. As the narrator tells it: "It was the discovery of his life." One is reminded of the antiwar Weathermen (named, of course, from a lyric in Bob Dylan's "Subterranean Homesick Blues") blowing themselves up in Daddy's home on West Eleventh Street. What Tom Skelton and the despairing devotees of apocalypse failed to recognize is that the best hope resides in the million small and comical "uneasy alliances," in McGuane's phrase, that those uncool folks at the No Nukes rally and my mother shedding a tear for Lennon can be a renewal, that others buying in does not have to mean your own selling out — not if yours is the true courage to *live* a conviction.

But beneath the surface of the disillusionment, the despair, and the resignation some would have as characteristic of the 1970s were numerous subtler currents. And Strawberry Fields was not, in fact, the cemetery of change — if some people gave up in the seventies, improbable others were just getting started. Our Noise, too, has many movements. Even in the embrace of nihilism there was hope.

But first, the despair.

ock 'n' roll lore has it that the sixties crested at Woodstock in August of 1969 and crashed barely four months later at Altamont. Woodstock, of course, was "half a million strong" and all that glorious stuff from the Crosby, Stills, Nash, and Young hit of the Joni Mitchell anthem: "We are stardust," it continued. "We are golden." Woodstock was the apotheosis of *wow*. Altamont, on the other hand, was solid, unalloyed *thud*. At Altamont, the rock 'n' roll–style

.27

anarchy of the 1960s was exposed for the dubious proposition it had always been — flukey Woodstock aside — as human nature unbridled was revealed to be not tolerant and peaceful but authoritarian and murderous. In the archaic argot of LSD, if Woodstock was the counterculture peaking, Altamont was the counterculture heavily bumming out.

But rock 'n' roll lore does not necessarily reflect the facts with any great accuracy. The Woodstock Music and Art Fair was a capitalist enterprise conceived in arrogance, implemented in negligence, and quite conveniently couched in hippie transcendence ("Three Days of Peace and Love" promised the ads). It returned millions in profits, after the sale of film and record rights, to its young promoters, who were rescued from total disaster only by the extraordinary, even transcendent, good will of their patrons and the heroic efforts of various state and local agencies, local volunteers, and Wavy Gravy's visiting Hog Farm commune, which served food, transmitted messages, and retrieved bad trippers. And still, despite that, while there was indeed a birth at Woodstock, there were also injuries and two deaths — one a heart attack, the other a young man run over by a bulldozer while asleep in the mud in his sleeping bag. Which brings up another fact, that much of the time, to the discomfort, if not danger, of everyone, it also rained. Peaceful and lovey and full of great rock 'n' roll music (Jimi Hendrix, the Who, Joe Cocker, and CSN&Y, among many others), Woodstock was indeed a singular phenomenon. But it wasn't entirely the carefree idyll it has been cracked up to be.

Nevertheless, if Woodstock wasn't as good, Altamont — the Rolling Stones–sponsored day-long festival at Altamont Speedway near San Francisco — wasn't as bad as we tend to believe. Most, if not all, of the famous violence there was carried out within a small area in front of the stage —and in front of the cameras — by a small group of hostile outsiders,

Hell's Angels hired (for a reported five hundred dollars' worth of beer) to handle "security." And if the anarchy can thus be said to have failed, it did so only in part, and then only where it emulated the "responsible" authoritarianism of the society at large. Compared to other Saturdays in other American cities with populations over three hundred thousand, but even compared to idyllic Woodstock, the death toll at Altamont — two by accident; one by murder, in a fight — was not so very drastic after all.

To look at the trio of undiapered blond cherubs frolicking in the cover photo of the *Woodstock* LP is to immediately understand that what the *New York Times* first headlined as a "Nightmare in the Catskills" was surely more in the nature of a dream, a huge collective wish. Woodstock's significance lies in the realm of the lore and legends and myths that truly knit us together. Woodstock is the myth of the sixties, the latest myth of eternal youth and, indeed, of cherubic innocence triumphant. If sometimes it was cloying, the myth of Woodstock was also big enough and expansive enough to accommodate an entire "nation," to many of whom it will always remain a light. But it was Altamont, in fact, that showed the way into the post-Woodstock era, and Altamont was a dark little myth called *Gimme Shelter*, a wish of another kind.

Intended more or less as a simple documentary of the Rolling Stones' 1969 tour of the States, including the culminating free concert at Altamont, *Gimme Shelter* became, in the hands of filmmakers Albert and David Maysles, the maggoty underside of the acid utopia, a countermanding anti-myth to Woodstock's myth of innocence: "Oooh, a storm is threatening," Jagger warned in the title song — with a powerful appeal of its own — "Rape! Murder," Jagger continued, "It's just a shot away . . ." *Thud*, indeed, but no less the glorious for it.

.29

Ultimately, of course, events offstage gave the film its special focus, and the action of *Gimme Shelter* turns not on the actions of the Stones, who are basically passive, but on the actions of the Hell's Angels and a young black man named Meredith Hunter. The next in that continuing line of pivotal strangers in American life and history, Meredith Hunter, for reasons yet obscure, made his way from a California ghetto that weekend to Altamont and then through the three hundred thousand to a choice spot near the stage, and the Hell's Angels too. In his shades and black shirt and green sharkskin suit, he was a throwback to a bygone era of hip, though not unlike some flashy street dude perhaps in a song by the Rolling Stones. He was also as thoroughly out of place as could be amid the sea of mostly white, T-shirted hippies. And when he drew his pistol, according to the Angels who killed him, he was aiming at the stage and the Stones. In his moments of glory, Meredith Hunter fulfilled enough irony to give even the most ironic fabulist pause.

An afternoon of storied California bands — the Jefferson Airplane and Flying Burrito Brothers among them — comes and goes, and as the darkness deepens and Hell's Angels wax ever the more indiscriminately security conscious with the butt ends of their cuesticks, the Rolling Stones tentatively occupy the stage. As Jagger minces and prances, shucks and jives — flaming cautiously here in the presence of an obviously warming powder keg — the group runs down its modern-blues-for-mister-charlie set and is launched into "Sympathy for the Devil," a Satan's autobiography of infamy and terror, when the joint begins to blow.

As the club-wielding Hell's Angels detonate incomprehensibly among the hippie crowd, Jagger cuts the song off and, hands to hips and the schoolmarm's tapping toe in his voice, demands to know, "*Who's* fighting? And *what* for?" A curly-haired postadolescent boy at Jagger's feet looks up and, with a touching, saucer-eyed seriousness of purpose, makes

30.

the only real attempt to explain. He is drowned out. The situation here is as far beyond explanation as it is beyond earnest saucer eyes. The violence continues to ebb, and mostly to flow, with its own unfathomable rhythm, and as quickly as the band starts up the devil song again, another dusty melee down front compels them to stop. Soon Jagger is flailing at his crowd-control buttons, even working against image to essay a little peace and love and implore: "*Peee*-pul, if we *are* all one, let's *show* we're all one." And though they eventually muddle through to the next number, "Under My Thumb," Mick's phony peace and love is all in vain. The camera catches Keith Richards crossing himself. The powder keg reaches critical mass.

"Guy out there's got a gun and he's shootin' at the *stage*," an Angel barks in Jagger's ear up on the big screen. "Can you roll that back, David," says Jagger, now in the editing room. And so, as the film's climactic scene progresses in grainy close-up and freeze-frame through the Steenbeck, we watch as Mick Jagger watches as Meredith Hunter apparently casts his bid for the Satanic mantle as rock 'n' roll's first assassin. "There's the Angel, right *there*, with the knife," says David Maysles. And indeed, after a moment's study we can see it too. With the editor rolling the footage back and then forward, stopping and then starting over again so that Jagger can sort out the confusion, we all watch as a sad Hunter named Meredith gets captured — again and again and again — by a shiv-plunging Hell's Angel, this jungle's more ruthless and calculating game.

"Where's the gun?" asks Jagger. "I'll roll it back," says the codirector, "and you'll see it right there against the girl's crocheted dress." Sure enough, there's the gun. Cut to: the girl in the crocheted dress, now on the big screen. Some minutes have passed. She is sobbing into the chest of a boyfriend, who holds her awkwardly. They are young and clean and pretty: a pair of teenage cherubs. "Don't let him die," she wails. "They *won't* let him die," he says with all the quiet, young-man bravery he can muster. "Look, they're gonna put him in this whirlybird here . . ." And indeed like some awful spinning ride escaped from a nightmare county fair, the helicopter, lights blinking red and bright white, rotors loudly flaying the night, descends, and paramedics load on what is already the corpse of Meredith Hunter. "But they can't hear his *heart* . . ." the girl protests hopefully to the boy. But they can't. Another chopper spirits away the Stones. In the eerie spotlighted dark, the people begin to leave (or are they actually arriving, as some very sharp-eyed critics parsed this footage?). Music up: ". . . If I don't get some shelter, oh yeah, I'm gonna fade away."

Altamont was the myth of *Gimme Shelter,* and *Gimme Shelter* was the myth of the end of the sixties, of growing up and old, the myth of the getting of wisdom and of cherubic innocence's death. You could see it in the boy's eyes as he struggled to explain to Jagger or in the tears of the girl by the helicopter or in the freeze-frame of the exhausted face of Jagger himself as he walked from the editing room for the last time: the face of a generation that had fought the good fight — or so went the glorious myth. For those of us who had none, Altamont was our Weather Underground, our Khe Sanh even. "Out on the street," wrote Michael Herr at the end of *Dispatches,* "I couldn't tell the Vietnam veterans from the rock and roll veterans." Altamont was the myth of our finding our courage amidst our rock 'n' roll convictions. Indeed, while Jagger was shrunk to a silly, scrawny schoolmarm (never completely to recoup), rock 'n' roll was swelled with the knowledge that someone had died for it, *because* of it. Danger, seriousness. We were playing with live ammo after all. Altamont was the glorious myth of defeat. It was at once validation and relief.

. . .

32.

"The war primed you for lame years," Herr continued, "while rock and roll turned more lurid and dangerous than bullfighting . . ." No matter if Altamont and *Gimme Shelter* weren't your particular cup of meat, the *thud* of falling bodies, that music of death and defeat, was everywhere in those years.

There were the *actual* deaths: of the Stones' Brian Jones in summer 1969, just before Woodstock, and of Sharon Tate and friends at the hands of Manson and Family in summer 1969, just after; of Jimi Hendrix, Woodstock Nation's black hero, and Janis Joplin, its heroine, little more than a year later and a month apart; of four at Kent State in spring 1970; of Jim Morrison in 1971; and on and on — not forgetting the assassinations of 1968: another Kennedy and a King. There were the defeats, the symbolic deaths: the "police riot" outside the Democratic Convention in Chicago in 1968 and the obstructing of peace candidate Eugene McMarthy and his "Children's Crusade" inside and, later, the indictment of Abbie Hoffman and Tom Hayden and the rest of the Chicago Seven on charges stemming from the convention protests; the closing of the rock 'n' roll temples, the Fillmores East and West, in 1970 and 1971; the commercialization, both licit and otherwise, of Haight-Ashbury and the East Village and hippie ghettos across the land; the hippies-to-the-slaughter finales of the movies *Easy Rider* (1969) and *Joe* (1970); the idea of hippie movies in the first place — not to mention Broadway's execrable *Hair*, also 1969; and finally and especially, the dissolution in 1970 of the Beatles. It was a high time for falling. And there were plenty of corpses, of one sort or another, to go around.

But apparently not enough. Indicative of silliness, but a silliness of the times, was the strange new version of Beatlemania that converged on the Beatles' penultimate release (but ultimate recording), *Abbey Road*. No less happily hysterical than that of 1964, the Beatle frenzy of 1970, however, fixated on Paul McCartney and the blunt fabrication that he had died. Tracking the phantom evidence, poring over Fab Four photos and the runic margins of LP designs, spinning Beatles records backward and straining to hear the promised secret words "I buried Paul," Woodstock Nation remained on the giddy edge and in thrall for several days. (But eventually we buried John, of course — and just imagine the younger Mark Chapman, intent under the headphones, alone in his room, gathering in all that publicity and stashing it somewhere subconscious, where it could remain for ten years, ticking.)

Happily, Paul yet breathes. In the meantime, handicapping the terminal cases had become high sport around rock 'n' roll, especially after the record companies got hip to the marketing possibilities inherent in an untimely demise, the death "hook," if you will, most strikingly demonstrated by the posthumously platinum Jims — Croce, that is, and the more recently resurrected Morrison. That nothing is a sure thing, including morbidity, was probably best exemplified by the case of poor Baby Huey of the Babysitters (Who? See what I mean?), ignominiously put to death twice, once in real life and once thereafter in the marketplace as rock 'n' roll's greatest posthumous flop. But as far as the pure sport is concerned, I guess no handicapper, professional or amateur, will ever understand how Keith Richards survived: with his patented "elegantly wasted" look — the paradigm for a whole generation of would-be rock stars — he was always at the top of our lists. Keith does seem bent on proving that it's quite enough to live fast and leave a good-looking corpse; that you don't necessarily have to die young (and by most measures he no longer is), if at all, to do so.

Suddenly, *decadence* had become the word of the day — cropping up often enough that the literary critic Richard Gilman would eventually be provoked into setting us all straight on its derivations and meaning in a petulant little tome entitled *Decadence, the Rise and Fall of an Epithet.*

34.

But whatever it *meant* to most people — generally something in the vicinity of excess, self-indulgence, and immorality — the *pursuit* of it, of decadence, was fast replacing the pursuit of peace-and-love. And if it thus appeared that we were renewing our unseriousness, our sense of the absurd, that was not always the case. People could be as dogged and intransigent about decay as about flowers. As countless photographs from the Stones' 1972 tour of the States can attest, Keith Richards was dogged about decay. Except Keith Richards, of the rotted teeth and heroin stupor, a practiced English romantic, managed to wear that decay with a truly Byronic flair — indeed it was during this most decadent period that Keith and the Stones produced their transcendent, tubercular masterpiece, *Exile on Main Street.* However, Keith Richards is an original — and perhaps never more so than when at the end of the seventies he finally kicked junk to come back stronger than ever. Most of our rock 'n' roll consumptives were neither so original nor so innately blessed with style, and mostly they just produced more decay.

What was developing here in these first post-Woodstock years among certain despairing post-Woodstock Nationals had now gone beyond that distinct sense of failure into a real taste for the shit, an habituation to the *thud.* And what was developing in the cultural realm seemed very much to mirror it: an aesthetic of the grim and gruesome; a formalization of the despair; an aesthetic, no less, of death.

* * *

If the music was less literal than television (e.g., *That's Incredible*) or the movies (e.g., *Snuff*) it was no less formalized and despairing.

NY TIMES, 7/4/81, OAKLAND, CA — The boy, shirtless, blue-jeaned and barefoot, had that tanned, muscular blond look that is quintessentially Californian.

But his brown eyes were wide and darting and he was frightened...

"I felt like I died out there, I really feel like I'm dead," the boy said, making it clear that he thought he might in fact be dead and that perhaps this was what dead was like...

The boy had been brought into the improvised hospital in the Oakland Coliseum, where rock bands like REO Speedwagon and Blue Oyster Cult were hammering the summer air on July 4 with thundering riffs of heavy metal music. A sheepish friend explained that the boy was sick and terrified, pursued by demons loosed by an overdose of the hallucinogenic drug LSD.

But the boy was actually suffering from what one doctor ruefully dubbed "polypharmocopia": a little bit of everything.

...The boy conceded that he "ate a whole bunch of stuff," and began ticking it off: "Uh, I took two yellow jackets, I smoked some hash, and uh, acid, I ate a whole lot of acid, and there was some wine, and some hard stuff, some whiskey..."

"It's a one-way ticket to midnight," sings Sammy Hagar in his eponymous tribute to the music he loves the best, "Call it heavy metal."

Heavy metal: pimply, prole, putrid, unchic, unsophisticated, antiintellectual (but impossibly pretentious), dismal, abysmal, terrible, horrible, and stupid music, barely music at all; death music, dead music, the beaten boogie, the dance of defeat and decay; the *huh?* sound, the *duh* sound, *thud-thud-thud-thud-thud* about the extent of it; music made *by* slack-

jawed, alpaca-haired, bulbous-inseamed imbeciles in jackboots and leather and chrome *for* slack-jawed, alpaca-haired,
downy-mustachioed imbeciles in cheap, too-large T-shirts
with pictures of comic-book Armageddon ironed on the
front; music made for (need I say it?) money, too, and out
of not too cleverly concealed — or by any stretch *entitled* —
contempt; music of the machine, by the machine, for the
machine; not just music, a whole spaced-out subculture, a
sub-subculture, a walled-off, dammed-up, blacked-out sub-
society; a perversion of the rock 'n' roll dream so grotesque
that the sixties-experienced "survivor," no less the thinking
and adult, must recoil in complete moral disgust, the thought
of reading about it more repellent perhaps than the utterly
repellent thought of listening to it or, God forbid, seeing it,
smelling it; the music on which the music biz of the seventies founded its far-flung success, the very spine of the era in
which rock 'n' roll revenues surpassed movies and TV; the
paradigm of the counterculture into the mainstream; shit.
Heavy metal, mon amour, where do I start?

Start with the basics, I suppose, which in heavy metal is
bucks. The fact is, Woodstock's "half a million strong" was an
accountant's epiphany too. As Woodstock Nation impresario
Bill Graham once put it, comparing his two-thousand-plus
capacity Fillmores with the later festivals, "I think Woodstock, despite all that's been said and written, was the start
of a new mass production in rock 'n' roll." And, indeed, for
all the noise, the music business of the sixties was a mere in-
fant — squalling perhaps, but tiny — by comparison with the
brute of the post-Woodstock seventies. In the seventies, in
fact, the music business finally grew up — like some kind of
thyroid case — to become the music industry.

Judged strictly by their sales figures, the heroes of sixties
rock 'n' roll — the Doors, the Jefferson Airplane, Jimi Hendrix, Big Brother, even the early Rolling Stones — could have
hardly got arrested in the truly go-go market of the seventies.

selling consistently less than the million dollars' records that *used* to be the standard for the Gold vard, a group like the sixties-era Stones might well ...d itself back on the club circuit. *Everybody* went gold in the seventies — even with the standard raised to half a million *units* sold and the price of that unit, the LP, nearly doubled, from around $5.98 in 1969 to around $9.98 in 1979. In fact, in the seventies almost everybody went *platinum* — marking a million units sold — with maybe a dozen of the most commercial bands pushing double-, triple-, and quadruple-platinum (as the indecent sales multiples were conjugated) and beyond. According to the industry trade association, record companies shipped (less returns) some seven hundred twenty-six million records and (more expensive) tapes at a peak in 1978, down to six hundred fifty million in 1980, the year they first cried poverty while continuing to outstrip Hollywood. That's *billions* of dollars worth. Estimating conservatively, even accounting for inflation, the music business ballooned over the last fifteen years by a not-quite-Exxonesque ninety to one hundred percent.

Which doesn't account for the carefully nurtured and highly profitable ancillary market in T-shirts, belt buckles, books, posters, and the like, hawked at live shows, head shops, and malls near you; nor does it account for concert ticket sales — and the three-dollar seat at Graham's modest Fillmores became in the seventies eight to twelve bucks at mammoth Madison Square Garden, and more for one of those multiple costar circuses that could induce eighty thousand into Oakland Stadium of a summer afternoon. And until the bottom began to fall out late in the last decade, it was on their forty to eighty (and more) date tours of the nation's, and the world's, stadiums and arenas that post-Woodstock rock 'n' rollers — as opposed to their record companies — were making most of *their* money. Which is exactly how the expression *arena rock* came to be (literally) coined. And

38.

arena rock — that is, rock 'n' roll for arenas and other over-sized places — was (and is), for the most part, heavy metal.

Heavy metal sounds like its name: very heavy bass and drums and pig-iron guitars. The name itself was gleaned from the William Burroughs novel *Naked Lunch,* a favorite text among rock 'n' rollers (several groups, including the Soft Machine, Steely Dan, and the Senders, have raided it for their names), and all ominous and explosive associations with "heavy water" and nuclear physics are completely welcomed. Heavy metal music is achingly ominous. It is frighteningly explosive too.

If rock 'n' roll is loud, heavy metal rock 'n' roll is loudest and then some. And since those heavy metal forerunners, Blue Cheer, made their sole claim to fame in the late sixties as the group with the most powerful amplifiers, the genre's practitioners have been obsessed — even more blatantly than the rest of us — with the technological phallus, with sheer decibel volume and the size and quantity of their "equipment." But *loudest* is not only the best and most important part of the heavy metal style, *loudest* is also why this style was so suited to the cavernous, sound-devouring arena and so to the economy of scale that would be the linchpin of mass production rock 'n' roll, just as it has been the linchpin of Henry Ford's Detroit. And it's no coincidence that in the opinion of many rock 'n' rollers the city of Detroit is the heavy metal capital of the world.

Like most categories of popular music — of twentieth-century music, for that matter — heavy metal is a somewhat elastic description. Almost any rock 'n' roll that is loud-unto-distortion might be heavy metal — but not necessarily. But if its ultimate definition is imprecise, it's still fair to say that heavy metal, even more than the rest of rock 'n' roll, is directly traceable to the loud, hard, electric-guitar-based city blues that came together down the road from Detroit on Chicago's South Side and that was embodied for all time by the molten masters, Howlin' Wolf and Muddy Waters. Beyond the fact that heavy metal rockers have always liked to play the blues, the electric blues permeates heavy metal. It can be heard in the instrumentation; in chord progressions and song structures; in some of the majestic (when not plodding) tempos and simple, deliberate rhythms and boogie-ish rhythm guitar riffs that heavy metal favors; in the growling, sexually insinuating vocal mannerisms of the singer and the stutter-and-wail virtuoso lead-guitar technique. It can be seen in the hypermasculine — and both electric blues and metal are largely the province of male performers — down-and-dirty stage posturing that complements the vocal attack.

And even heavy metal's popular foothold in Detroit can be traced to the groundwork laid by blacks and black bluesmen, up from Chicago and points south, and so, as well, its connection with the lower classes, and the assembly line. As Amiri Baraka (then LeRoi Jones) related in *Blues People*: "It is interesting to note that there are a great many blues written about the Ford company and Ford products. One reason for this is the fact that Ford was one of the first companies to hire many Negroes, and the name *Ford* became synonymous with Northern opportunity, and the Ford Model-T was one of the first automobiles Negroes could purchase — 'the poor man's car.' " And though heavy metal may be white contemporary rock 'n' roll, it is still demonstrably poor man's, or at least working class, music.

Still, heavy metal is not blues and not solely blues based. For one thing, the black electric blues — including rhythm 'n' blues, its slicker, faster derivative — from which heavy metal developed was actually passed down to it, mostly, by white, English musicians, such as the Yardbirds and John Mayall's Bluesbreakers, who fronted the electric blues revival of the midsixties. And, much as Elvis and the early rockers had mixed country with r 'n' b and blues to get rock 'n' roll, these latter-day white boys mixed rock 'n' roll *back* with the blues to get heavy metal.

Exactly where and when white blues-rock became heavy metal is as hard to say as what exactly heavy metal is. Jeff Beck (a Yardbirds alumnus) played loud, distorted, big-beat blues with his group (including Rod Stewart), on the late sixties LPs *Truth* and *Beck-Ola*. Cream, the first pumped-up supergroup (with Eric Clapton, a Mayall-Yardbirds grad), perhaps came even closer to heavy metal by playing loud, distorted, big-beat blues in arenas for the millions (of people *and* dollars) — if size of venue and commercial success are any measure. An old r 'n' b hand himself, Jimi Hendrix certainly liked to get heavy, and he was the emperor of distortion — but his extensive forays into nuance and subtlety would seem to militate against him as a bona fide heavy metallist. Rock critic Robert Palmer recently put forth the Kinks and their early hard-rocking hits, "You Really Got Me" and "All Day and All of the Night," as the prototypes. And what about Blue Cheer anyway? Or the grotesque Iron Butterfly with their epic sludge-fest "In-A-Gadda-Da-Vida"? What about Vanilla Fudge (too much keyboards?), whose whole weird point, long before heavy metal, was to slow down and heavy up — to *imponderate*, if one could do such a thing — Motown hits for a white audience?

But if it's impossible to really single out *the* original, it has become widely accepted — and with good reason — that heavy metal as a genre began in earnest with ex-Yardbird Jimmy Page and his band Led Zeppelin. Releasing their first two albums in 1969, Page and Co. — along with the heavy metal style they came to stand for — were promptly crowned as the new conquering horde when in 1970 they vanquished the Beatles from a nigh-permanent slot atop British *Melody Maker's* annual readers' poll. And throughout the ensuing decade, in the polls and in the marketplace, both at home and even more so abroad in the States, Led Zeppelin would continue to rule the heavy metal kingdom, if not quite the whole rock enchilada.

Shucking the lighter pop elements, as well as the old blues numbers, of the initial LP, the band emerged with the first full-blown heavy metal on *Led Zeppelin II*. On that second album, Page, who served as producer, cosongwriter, guitarist, and guiding light throughout the group's eleven-year career, fused the coded essence of contemporary rock 'n' roll with blues grit and r 'n' b drive into a technological juggernaut that would be some sort of ultimate, *scientifically* compelling — and commercial — rock 'n' roll. That is, he took the free-form electronic noise jam popularized by psychedelic bands — and made most expressive by Hendrix — cut it short, and arranged it around a not-so-free 4/4 beat; he presented a truncated, steadier version of the extended drum solos established as the heavy drummer's civil right by Cream's Ginger Baker; he thickened up the phlegmy distortion of the guitars, careful to keep a bright, trebly edge, and flayed the rhythm home with slashing power chords — those syncopated, chordal accents that remain the Who's trademark — at the same time bringing the bass to the fore; he jacked up tempos and kept the boogie riffs pithy — like machine guns — and suffused John Bonham's elemental drumming with a heavy artillery echo (military metaphors entirely appropriate to heavy metal); with overdubbing and more echo, he augmented Robert Plant's blues squawking and bird orgasm simulating; and lastly he recorded it loud, orchestrating the dynamics as meticulously as everything else, achieving in the end such a controlled, directed explosion of sound that it might well have come out of a machine. Which, in fact, it did: the modern, post–*Sgt. Pepper's* recording studio, a-blooming with more knobs and levers and cryptic lights every day.

If Jimmy Page's basic intention with *Led Zeppelin II* was

42.

unstoppable drive, "Whole Lotta Love," the album's first and best known cut, would seem to be that intention's vindication. But for all its driving insistence, there is something to "Whole Lotta Love," no less than the rest of the record, that doesn't grab — or grabs mechanically: Page's dirty blues feeling more like an assignation with the Auto-Suck than a roll in the hay. Like so much of the heavy metal that was to follow, it's efficient, but it's cold. Which may be one reason it so often arrives preheated with hype (and, indeed, Led Zep call their song publishing company Superhype). But then basically it's fake: the electronic fuzz box and the purposely destroyed speaker cone are not much more than a musical equivalent of the pre-ripped T-shirts Macy's would later market to the punks. And it's remarkably faceless too: those quirky, personal narratives of the blues are hardly very quirky or personal in these high-gloss environs. It's almost as faceless, in fact, as the faceless, hyped-up graphics of so many of the heavy metal album packages. So, I suppose, to say that heavy metal is slick, modern, commercialized, soulless blues — another instance of black culture suffocated in white bread — would not be inaccurate. But neither would it be inclusive, certainly not as far as Led Zep is concerned.

Heavy metal skidded up and down the scale — rougher to smoother, better to worse — from the archetype of Led Zep II, as did Zep themselves, who made a point of being the genre's most artistically adventurous group — and, granted, an anomaly — after becoming its most commercially successful. Having set down the archetype, and then cemented it with Led Zep III, they set about pulling it apart, unveiling the results on their fourth LP in 1971. This time, in one of those believe-it-or-not cultural cross-pollinations that keep culture alive and kicking, they married their new Chicago blues to ancient Celtic folk music, the South Side to Stonehenge, producing a semiacoustic prepsychedelic blues — "Druid Rock," as one admiring critic described it — that yet retained the compelling qualities of heavy metal. The LP wound up as Zeppelin's — and reputedly heavy metal's — best seller to date.

Zoso, as the disk is known, the actual title being etched in indecipherable pagan runes, runs a wild gamut from heavy metal to country blues to British folk. But it is the album's eight-minute centerpiece, "Stairway to Heaven," wherein the band puts the gamut all together, that is the definitive statement of *Zoso*, if not of all of heavy metal. A heavy metal madrigal, drenched in Druidisms — and yet the "most requested" radio song of the seventies — "Stairway" opens gently with acoustic guitar and a chorus of ancient flutes and bird-man Robert Plant at his most melodic and subdued. Almost imperceptibly an electric guitar steps in for the acoustic, quietly picking the arpeggios, now lightly strumming a jazzy chord into the song's bridge. Always building slowly, as if actually ascending that stairway, the song achieves both majesty and tension, now working in Bonham's rock bottom drums, driving through a revived Plant's tastefully aching Audubonisms to a regal seventh-chord guitar flourish and everybody pulling in tight until — an acid rain of solo notes from Page at his most incisively brilliant and a sock-it-out heavy metal finale. The music offers one of those superb melodramas that only rock 'n' roll can bring off with impunity.

The words, however, inscribed with due reverence in olde calligraphy on the album's inner sleeve, are something else.

Reflecting Jimmy Page's fascination with black magic — a fascination that would prompt him to open a black arts bookstore in London and purchase Satanist Aleister Crowley's old manse in the suburbs — the lyrics to "Stairway," to most of *Zoso*, are of an apocalyptic, faerie tale nature that would become characteristic of Led Zeppelin and too many of its heavy metal inheritors. Not specifically Druid but creepy nonetheless, "Stairway" is a call to spiritual arms couched in a prayerfully muddled allegory of "a lady" who's trying to buy her way to salvation. It invokes "the May-Queen," and "white light," and prophesies a bad time that will precede a good time when wood nymphs will laugh again. It concludes by confidently marching off banality's White Cliffs of Dover in a couplet promising salvation "When all are one and one is all/ To be a rock and not to roll." And if one frequently forgives rock 'n' roll its words on account of its music, the Day-Glo paganism herein makes it simply impossible. So in venturing to find a new place for rock 'n' roll within an Anglo-Saxon heritage, Led Zep often ended up retrieving the empty from the faked. (Still, that solo . . .)

. . .

Heavy metal is a song of the pit. Another cultural microcosm of the social and psychological currents of the post-Woodstock era, heavy metal paralleled the draining of hope in its flood of giddy gloom and false hope and paralleled the draining of meaning in its filling up with exotic, empty meaning, in its defensively ornate fantasies of a *Star Wars* apocalypse, and in its inflation of rock 'n' roll pretension and — literally — volume. In its devotion to recording studio precision — a devotion it shared with most seventies rock 'n' roll — heavy metal paralleled the insidious creep of technology at large. In its macho stance — including the lumbering, egoistic aggression of its live sound — it paralleled the reaction to the "feminine" manners and fashions of the sixties. In its business sense it paralleled the return to business as usual.

Like so many of our hit movies and bestsellers, heavy metal, for all its Sturm und Drang (and it *is* Wagnerian), is basically conservative, cautious, rigid — which might account for another part of its popularity with the traditionalist white working class. But then heavy metal's ultimate appeal has much less to do with the daring of rock 'n' roll, which it almost parodies, than with the reactionary impulse to escapism. Even tarted up with an exculpatory sheen of mystic profundity, it remains as determinedly out-to-lunch as the *Superman* movies or such of its fellow profundities as *Jonathan Livingston Seagull* (movie, pamphlet, and Neil Diamond operetta). And beneath the sheen, the essence of its escapist technique is just as simple, just as reducible, because again the vital essence of the heavy metal style — and so the essence of its appeal — is its loudness.

Certainly it was loudness that appealed to those concert promoters who were now stuffing their pockets as never before as they stuffed ever larger arenas that, more than any recording could be, were home to this noise. And of course it was loudness that appealed to the fans. Now rock 'n' roll had always liked *loud,* in part because *loud* was unlikable and in part because *loud* could hold its own in the cacophony of modern city life. But mainly rock 'n' roll liked *loud* because *loud* meant passion, *loud* meant the pent anger of the age, and loud rock 'n' roll thus became an acting out of that anger and so some sort of return to the senses in the time of the rational, the technological.

Yet paradoxically, getting loud also meant getting technology, louder, even more; and as rock 'n' roll expanded, seeking new depths and ranges of feelings as well as new fans, there would be two kinds of bills to pay. And sure enough, today all sorts of rockers must make their accommodations with the technology (and the business), piling on the electronics they've come to need and love in order to get human again in the arenas they've come to need and hate — while at the same time Jonathan Richman is scoffed at for using acoustic guitar and stand-up bass and the house PA system (just like the early Elvis) at Town Hall in hip Manhattan and is rightly deemed the rankest weirdo, but for all the wrong reasons. But of all rock 'n' roll it was heavy metal that would pay dearest — and gladly — to buy the cybernetic tail that would wag its dog. Because heavy metal wanted loud*est.*

46.

If *loud* meant passion and acting out, there was a line it crossed and a balance it tipped as it coursed the circuits and tubes of the Marshall amp stacks, and when the loud*est*ness of heavy metal came out the other end, into the arena, it was a series of sonic body blows, true violence and trauma, and finally something quite the opposite of passion. In fact, the loud*est*ness of heavy metal was a deadening of passion, a deadening of the senses, of the laughing irrational, no less than the rational, a deadening, period. With heavy metal there was no acting *out*, just the being acted *upon*. Nothing really to do but hold tight and take it: mass Auto-Suck, total escape. So where rock 'n' roll had once been a catalyst for fuck-it-all anarchy, heavy metal rock 'n' roll was anaesthetic. And unto them the resemblance of *loud* to *'lude* was at last revealed.

. . .

Recently, in a back issue of *Creem*, I came across an interesting photograph of Jimmy Page from his heyday with Led Zep. He's seated onstage, tucked in behind a pedal steel guitar, laughing to someone just out of camera range, while the cowboy shirt he wears casually unbuttoned flops open to expose a T-shirt with an image of a large, bisected disk across the chest. On the disk is printed the word *Rorer* and beneath that the number 714. And if that doesn't mean anything to you, it's a fair bet you never liked heavy metal in the first place.

The Rorer 714, as any righteous heavy metal fan could tell you, is (or was, until the patent was peddled to Lemmon, who until recently produced a Lemmon 714) a human horse pill of a sleeping potion comprised of a substance called methaqualone hydrochloride and better known by its brand name, Quaalude. First marketed in 1965, Quaalude is one of a group of drugs classified as sedative-hypnotic, whose effects are to induce gaping stupor, loss of motor control, loss of memory, and even, if you must, sleep. As any righteous heavy metal fan could also tell you, sopors, as the pills are sometimes called (from soporific), and heavy metal go together like hand and glove; where one is, you will likely find the other. Mixed with booze, which drastically, synergistically potentiates Quaalude's effects, they were perhaps the ne plus ultra of post-Woodstock's aesthetic of death — in any case they'd get you dead, or thereabouts.

Though doctors find it impossible to specify from among the downs panoply, rock 'n' rollers have no doubt that the night in April 1975 when she met destiny, Karen Ann Quinlan washed down her gin-and-tonics with some 'ludes. And so rock 'n' rollers, in their darkly humorous way, have claimed her as their own. Indeed, a band called Starz was even inspired to song by her predicament, diving into the midst of the controversy with a merry metal ditty entitled "Pull the Plug," which is what some people also wanted to do to Starz, who are anyway since defunct. But the case of Karen Ann Quinlan did finally bring the issue of death in the technological society to a head. "The Right to Die" was how *Newsweek* slugged its April 1976 Quinlan cover story, and inside, a physician from Georgetown assured us, "Technology has advanced so that no one really has to die, so we have to make a choice." But no matter what he said, the choice of course was not *whether* to die, but *how,* and the discussion of *how* to die was nothing less than an attempt to formulate an aesthetic of death.

As good and decent and noble as the campaign for Death with Dignity and the Right to Die is, it is also fraught with dangers. In a sense, the idea of *death* with dignity demeans life. Indeed, the whole idea of setting aside a portion of life as the doomed portion, as death, whatever else it might do, invites resignation, if not morbid fetishism and cultism and true decadence. Everyone, of course, must die, and no one wants particularly to do so without dignity. But what most people observe as the indignities of death today are really the indignities of technology as it is manifested in the modern hospital. But at the same time the indignities of the modern hospital are in many ways a manifestation of the supreme value assigned by our civilization to life. In any event, the effort to make it nicer to die does summon to mind the critic Walter Benjamin's warning to the First World War-era Futurist movement about its own obsession with the deadly. "The aestheticization of war," he wrote, "is the ultimate . . . in man's self-alienation."

One thing that should certainly give us pause is how well our increasing concern with death correlates with culture's increasing debasement of life. We might wonder if the Right to Die movement is in any sense just fashion. And is there a connection between our new attitudes toward death and the incidence of suicide, especially among young people, for whom it has come over the last fifteen years to be the second most common cause of death? What to make of an aptly short-lived rock 'n' roll club in New York that called itself Youthanasia? Not too much, perhaps. But what to make, for that matter, of that sloppy, sleepy, deathlike, and sometimes deadly category of drugs called downs — among which we might include Valium and Seconal, as well as Quaaludes — that was the drug group of choice in the post-Woodstock era? What of the extremely fashionable heroin? Booze? Or could such self-obliteration actually be a solidly offensive defense, in the age of nuclear weapons and the obliteration of the species?

"Just give me a sopor for the weekend!" went the hook line to the seventies teen anthem, "Weekend," by the proto-punk group the Dictators. For the best of the old psychedelic groups there had at least seemed to be *some* idea of looking beyond the drug itself: LSD at least *seemed* to open up. And if a legion of acid casualties is muttered testimony to the fact that acid could shut you down — not dead perhaps, but crazy — as well as anything could, at least the acid experience *seemed* to be a new perspective and thus to represent at least *hope* for change. But Quaaludes couldn't even pretend. Quaaludes were nothing whatsoever but the drug of *thud*. Unequivocally decadent. Lest acidheads be tempted to gloat, however, there is still that nagging notion that without the drugs of the sixties that Abbie Hoffman so loved, the drugs of the seventies and eighties could never have been, that far from bringing us closer to utopia, LSD-25 brought us to Rorer 714.

· · ·

It's not surprising, considering that the audience was predominantly male, that heavy metal and its death trip boogie arrived all bound up in the new machismo, then resurgent across the land. But heavy metal had its own special vision of a new macho ideal. And while one thinks of Robert Plant, that ideal was actually more of a cross between Plant's sexual — that is, genital — exhibitionism and Jimmy Page's black magic aura. Metal's macho ideal, in fact, was a Teen Beelzebub with a sock in his pants; a contemporary rebel without a cause pumped up with psychedelia and a peculiarly psychedelic sadism; a wild one, if you will, of the rack rooms of the intergalactic night. With various incongruous trappings lifted from science fiction and biker movies, from horror movies and from Christian apocalyptic lore and ritual (crucifixes were popular), and from those original death trippers the Nazis (sometimes secondhand by way of sadomasochism), the heavy metal rockers looked to be the true embodiment of the Woodstock-era epithet — invented by the underground press to describe Manson-like cults — "psychedelic fascism." In any event, it was (and is) a long way — but all in good fun, mind you — from Howlin' Wolf and blues machismo. Or was it?

All in good fun, groups named Black Sabbath, Judas Priest,

Scorpions, AC/DC (electricity, that is; no sexual ambiguity *here*), and the Godz (now defunct, of course), not to mention Blue Oyster Cult and Led Zeppelin, decked themselves out in jackboots and studded black leather and California Highway Patrol–style mirrored shades and titled their albums *Masters of Reality, Paranoid, Sin after Sin, Tyranny & Mutation, Technical Ecstasy, Houses of the Holy, Heaven and Hell, Back in Black,* and *On Your Feet or On Your Knees.* All in good fun, Led Zeppelin (whose name itself was a punchline) called the record company they founded with their profits Swan Song, with poor Icarus as the logo. But no one seemed to get it. And while Blue Oyster Cult certainly started out with satire on their minds, if not in their hearts, in such songs as "Before the Kiss, A Redcap" (i.e., Seconal), they wound up scoring their first big hit with a more straightforward soft rocker called "Don't Fear the Reaper": "Don't fear the Reaper/ We'll be able to fly/ We can become like they are/ Baby, don't be afraid . . ." Macho mystical. Or so it was taken. Because no matter the bands' intentions, good fun was basically antithetical to the determinedly propped-up decadence, the pumped-up power mongering, the sealed-off escapism of heavy metal, at least as the fans had come to love it. Besides, true machismo is too laughable ever to let itself laugh. But another question: what does it mean that machismo in this latest post-Hemingway incarnation had become *inviting* death (but not pain), *loving* it, as opposed to welcoming it when it comes and facing it and damn the torpedoes? Perhaps one clue is that Hemingway himself, after all, was a suicide.

• • •

One more thing about heavy metal. In the post-Woodstock years the music business, as befitted its new status as an *industry,* took to calling records *product,* a term that many of the artists themselves even adopted as part of the hip argot.

And foremost among rock 'n' roll genres that's what heavy metal was and is: product, with all the implications not only of an art stripped of its uniqueness and magic, but an art that is no more than another link in a production-consumption-production chain. And while critics in the seventies coined the phrase "corporate rock" to refer (derisively) to a certain homogenized, quasimellow sound — of, say, Journey or even the Eagles at their most insipid — it was nonmellow heavy metal that was the *real* corporate rock. And it's the heavy metal grind circuit performers, each pulling down his eighty to a hundred thou a year, brushed aluminum attaché case in hand as he jets — business class — from Cleveland to Detroit to Kansas City (to Manchester and Birmingham, UK) and back again — before returning home to Greenwich, Connecticut, or Grosse Pointe, Michigan — each, in his satin warmup jacket or leathers, as indistinguishable from the next as a Gray Flannel Suiter amid his Westchester commuter chums — it's they who are rock 'n' roll's first corporate managers. Only incidentally do they get up onstage and play music; and being in the recording studio is pure research and development, just like they do at Bell Labs for AT&T. One thinks of Bachman-Turner Overdrive — or BTO, as they were known by logo — singing their satirical semimetal hit: "I'm just takin' care of business everyday/ Takin' care of business . . . And workin' overtime." Funny thing is, they were.

. . .

Still there remains something irresistible about heavy metal — for all its gross sensationalism, for all its mindless escapism, for all its painful volume and blatant commercial calculation. To a great extent, heavy metal is the last bastion of the rock 'n' roll believer. In the ways that it doesn't pretend to be anything *but* masscult, teenage rock 'n' roll — while so much of rock 'n' roll (for better and worse) strains to be "adult" in one way or another, whether by rockifying spoon-

52.

june-moon pop (as the Doobie Brothers have done most successfully) or by speaking to the troubles of Woodstock Nationals as they slip toward middle age (as Jackson Browne has done most successfully), or by getting artistic (or anti-artistic), some sort of highbrow, even *difficult,* as is the case with the proliferating avant-garde, experimental, new wave, no wave, jazz-rock, jazz-funk, fake jazz, funk-punk, and neo-punk groups who are, some of them, so *serious* that they're in danger of becoming *respectable* — and in the ways that heavy metal pretends with a vengeance that rock 'n' roll is *everything,* the be-all and end-all, as perhaps *you* once believed (ca. the Beatles) and as perhaps succeeding generations should have a chance to believe, and then goes on to make Madison Square Garden literally shudder with the proof; in the way that it's gratuitous and pretends not to give a shit and so at least mimes lashing out at the machine; in the way that it's violent and assaultive and so overwhelmingly loud that maybe it does in its best moments cut through the bland domination of the technology and its economic system; in the way its unretiring loudness and its posturing makes it seem like us against them again: in *those* not negligible ways heavy metal preserves the true rock 'n' roll spirit, and so, if one is willing to suspend disbelief briefly — and sometimes to be duped — heavy metal is a place to go feel that exhilarating spirit just one more time. And then keel over — *thud* — stoned unto death.

Imagine gigantic drums — *bam-bash-bam* — and a great echoing voice:

> My heart is black,
> And my lips are cold,
> Cities on flame
> With rock 'n' roll;
>
> Three thousand guitars
> They seem to cry . . .

.53

Let the girl rock 'n' roll . . .
Cities on flame now
With rock 'n' roll!

And that's the point: you don't have to like Blue Oyster Cult
to feel that sometimes they sure do hit the spot.

I remember standing in a little knot of fans off to the side
of the stage the last time Black Sabbath played the Garden.
When, during a guitar solo, I pivoted to leave, I found myself face to face with Ross the Boss from the Dictators. A
punk, but with obvious roots in heavy metal, Ross seized me
by the shoulder. Shooting his other hand out to point at the
stage, wild-eyed and grinning, he shouted above the din:
"D'ya *hear* that?!? *That's* rock 'n' roll!" Not much on Black
Sabbath (I'd come to see the openers, BOC), I looked skeptical, but Ross just grinned and moved closer to the noise. Turning his pointing hand into a fist salute, he shouted again,
louder, "*Heavy metal,* man!" and shook the fist with glee. And
somehow it was too ingenuous to be corny (and he too smart
for it to be just dumb), and as the soloing screamed back into
my consciousness, for a moment I felt the electricity. And in
that moment I envied Ross the rest of his evening. It may be
bad and it's no doubt bad for you and that may very well be
part of what makes it irresistible. *Heavy metal,* man. One
thing I'll guarantee: your parents will never like it.

Baraka, again in *Blues People,* said something about rock
'n' roll — this was back in its infancy — that would seem to
apply today to heavy metal. "To be sure," he wrote, "rock 'n'
roll is usually a flagrant commercialization of rhythm & blues,
but the music in many cases depends enough on materials
that are so alien to the general middle-class, middle-brow
American culture as to remain interesting." The materials he
was talking about were the Chicago blues — again the parallel to heavy metal. "Rock 'n' roll," he went on (and we might

read instead heavy metal), "is the blues form of the classes of Americans who lack the 'sophistication' to be middle brows, or are too naive to get in on the mainstream taste; those who think that somehow Melachrino [Blondie? Doobies? Talking Heads?], Kostalanetz [Paul McCartney?], etc., are too lifeless."

So I'll take death?

> I used to shiver in the wings,
> But then I was young,
> I used to shiver in the wings,
> Until I found my own tongue;
>
> Now I sock 'em everywhere that I sing,
> 'Cause you know, baby,
> I'm the Next Big Thing . . .

He styles himself "Handsome Dick Manitoba," after the "bad guy" wrestlers he has always admired. He is twenty-eight years old, husky and square of build and not handsome, not in the conventional sense, and he does not come from the Canadian wild. He comes from, and has now gone back to, the Bronx. Although his real name (which, as a token gesture to the discretion he would never be bothered with, I will not be using here) is in fact Richard, no one ever calls him Dick.

> We knocked 'em dead in Dallas,
> Though we didn't pay our dues
> We knocked 'em dead in Dallas,
> They didn't know we were Jews;

I sock 'em everywhere that I sing,
'Cause you know, baby,
I'm the Next Big Thing . . .

He used to sing, after a fashion, with the Dictators, the first punk band, after a fashion — at least the first to make an album, releasing *The Dictators Go Girl Crazy!* in the spring of 1975, a full year before the Ramones' debut. *The Dictators Go Girl Crazy!* contained such noisome instant classics as "(I live for) Cars and Girls," "Weekend" ("Just give me a sopor . . ."), "Master Race Rock" ("We're the members of the master race/ Got no style and we got no grace"), a remake of the sixties surf anthem "California Sun" (remade again by the Ramones), and Handsome Dick Manitoba performing a duet with co-lead singer and songwriter Andy Shernoff on the old Sonny and Cher hit "I Got You, Babe." The Dictators themselves contained, in addition to Manitoba and Shernoff: Ross the Boss on lead guitar; Scott Kempner, a.k.a. Top Ten, on rhythm guitar; Stu Boy King, replaced by Richie Teeter, on drums; and when Andy moved to keyboards, Mark the Animal Mendoza on bass.

The Dictators Go Girl Crazy! sounded like heavymetalsurfpunk. It was a kind of novelty music with a kind of soul. It was funny, but touched with the angry and sad. It was teenage, but at the same time knowing that the teens end. Or maybe not. In any case, it was a masterpiece, and as far as rock 'n' roll is concerned, it has by now stood the test of time. At the time, back then, some people went crazy for the Dictators. But not a lot.

Now I won't be happy,
Till I'm known far and wide,
With my face on the cover,
Of a TV Guide;

I sock 'em everywhere that I sing,
'Cause you know, baby,
I'm the Next Big Thing . . .

The Dictators made two more albums over the next three years, one, *Manifest Destiny,* that emphasized their heavy metal side, the other, *Bloodbrothers,* that leaned more to punk, both of which tried too hard to make up for the commercial failure of the first record and thus failed themselves. However, the band toured extensively — as an opening act in arenas, as a headliner at the punk clubs that were sprouting all across the country in the late seventies — and the legend of the Dictators grew. Live, they were sometimes rough, sometimes almost polished, always unpredictable, exciting, and very loud. Indeed, at least once at a New York club, a Ross the Boss guitar solo made a girl's ear bleed.

Handsome Dick Manitoba himself was an Andy Shernoff song incarnate. He was infantile and proud and funny and vibrant and charming, and occasionally he was all that and much more. He also had a rare and true gift for projecting such qualities of humanity from a stage. But I bring him up here not primarily as a performer, as some kind of representative of heavy metal or punk — though he is that, too. I bring him up here as a familiar if not representative figure from my generation and from the changing times, as a prologue of sorts to them. He may not have any of the answers, but he certainly covers a lot of the questions — he *is* a lot of the questions. Verily, Mead's post-war unknown child. The Noise incarnate, too. And as special as his life might be, I find much of my own life in it and suspect that you'll find some of yours. Which doesn't mean I'm proud of all of it, of the excess and degradation he describes. Which is not to say I'm ashamed. In fact, to my mind, the decay was often the liveliest thing going.

.57

I sock 'em everywhere that I sing,
'Cause you know, baby,
I'm the Next Big Thing.

Nevertheless, he wasn't. And neither were we.

. . .

In return for a command recital of the saga of Handsome
Dick, I have promised him a meal at my local Mexican restaurant — not that I have to coax. He meets me at my house a
mere twenty-four hours late and accompanied by a girlfriend
— all of which is both unexpected and expected at the same
time. Thinner than I have ever seen him, indeed almost *thin*,
Manitoba wears black boots and black pants and a black
leather jacket. Almost thin myself, I wear brown boots polished to black, black pants, and a black leather jacket. Punk
has been finished everywhere but Los Angeles for some time
now, and as we clomp off toward the restaurant, our trusty
chicks at our sides, we suddenly remind me of nothing so
much as those middle-aged mothers from the sixties in their
miniskirts and white vinyl go-go boots, or maybe a couple of
swinging singles in platform shoes and chains. The kindly
woman in the restaurant seats us all the same. We order margaritas and commence to wallow in Manitoba's past. Our
chicks suffer long.

"A bunch of friends of mine used to hang out in this college town, New Paltz, up in New York," he says. "I used to
go up there on weekends and stuff and hang out. Andy Shernoff was going to the university at New Paltz, and I guess one
day everyone got bored with what they were doing and decided the best thing in life to do would be to be in a rock 'n'
roll band. This must be seventy-three, seventy-four.

"We knew this real good guitar player, Ross, who used to
play with this band called Total Crudd — with *two* d's," he
clarifies in his gruff deadpan, "C-r-u-d-d — and he used to

58.

like to smoke pot and play music. So Andy talked to Ross and then to Scott. Scott came from the Bronx. I met Andy at New Paltz — I used to call him Rock 'n' Roll Andy. It was all a matter of mutual friends. Everybody kind of knew everybody, and everybody was into rock 'n' roll. Andy, Ross, and Scott basically got together and said, you know, 'Let's start a band.' So they rented this house in a town called Kerhonkson, New York — I ain't gonna spell it for you," he offers, gruff again, "look it up on a map — on the other side of the mountain, fifteen, eighteen miles from New Paltz. I was out of high school, and I dropped out of college after about a term and a quarter — college was Lehman [of the City University of New York] . . . You know, it's Harvard, Yale and . . . Lehman. Lehman was just an extension of high school. My first term I had a 2.6 average. I went out with about a 3.0. But you know what I failed? Guess. . . . *Music.*

"It was ridiculous. Going to college was just like taking a different bus to high school. I couldn't take it. Thirty-seven books to read in the first two weeks. More than I ever read in my life! So I got a job in the post office; I bought a car; and weekends, I'd drive up, take Quaaludes — we all took Quaaludes — and hang out in New Paltz.

"So I would go up there to party," he continues in his heavy, and in part studied, Bronx accent, "and these guys were broke. They told me they were eating, like, M&M's and *spaghetti.* So I would go up there, and we'd go to a store and buy two dollars' worth of stuff and then steal — we'd walk out with breakfast sausages down our pants and stuff. And I'd come home and cook breakfast. I was the breakfast chef of the Dictators.

"It wasn't the Dictators, at first. It was a hundred thousand names we thought up: Tommy the Truck, Fireman's Friend, Beat the Meetles. We thought up all these names and decided that the Dictators had the right ring to it. A real funny name — a bunch of Jewboys called the Dictators . . . you know, *ha,*

.59

ha. . . . So basically that was the origin of the band. If this was Marvel Comics, that would be the Origin Issue."

• • •

Next, the nascent Dictators sought help from rock writer Richard Meltzer, a friend with whom Scott had first corresponded as a fan and whose influence on the style and even the wrestling substance of the group was extensive. Indeed, on the first album they would credit him (as "Borneo Jimmy") for "Inspiration." Meltzer had also been a key contributor to Andy's legendary but short-lived fanzine, the *Teenage Wasteland Gazette,* which was "the literary equivalent of the Dictators," according to another contributor, Handsome Dick. "I wrote two articles for it," says Manitoba. "I was, like, the cub reporter. I wrote an article called, like, 'Downs Are Good for You.' Those were crazy days." Another famous *TWG* article was Meltzer's about a famous Handsome Dick Manitoba party.

"Okay," Manitoba begins. "My parents went away on vacation. It was a Friday night. I was working in the post office, and I had my car, and I drove around to all the playgrounds in the Bronx, stoned out on 'ludes, and said, 'Everybody come to my party.'

"Now I had a reputation for being a party buster. I would go to people's houses and take, like, a jar of pickles and throw it out a seven-story window and then take a thing of cottage cheese and smear it all over everyone's carpet. So people kind of said, 'Well . . . we're not gonna hurt the guy on *purpose,* but when there's a party there, we're gonna let ourselves a little loose . . .'

"So I went around to every playground in the Bronx just screaming, 'Everybody come over to my house for a party!' Playgrounds where there were, like, a hundred people. Friends and others. . . . So I got a bag of a hundred Quaaludes. There were a couple of bottles of booze, about twenty cases of beer.

And whatever there *is* was at that party. . . . There were guys fucking girls, girls fucking girls — I don't *think* there were any guys fucking guys. I *know* there were girls fucking girls and guys fucking girls, and I know that the security police from the housing project we live in came up, and I know that the real police from the city of New York came up.

"I know that about eight hundred dollars' worth of jewelry was stolen from my parents' bedroom. Pillows, shopping carts, were thrown off the twenty-sixth-floor terrace. One of my friends just fell flat on his face — where normally your hands would go out instinctively to protect yourself, he fell flat on his face and broke his nose. There was blood all over the floor. He went to the hospital. My other friend, Cliffie, was totally naked, and got locked out of the apartment on the twenty-sixth floor, and when the cops came up, he hid in the stairway naked — while I was dressed in a jock strap with red lipstick swastikas drawn all over my body. I was in bed with some girl, and all of a sudden the door opens, and it's the New York City police and 'What the hell is going on here???' And I said — and I'm stoned from, like, a *billion* Quaaludes — I go, 'It's okay, it's okay.' And I swear to God I remember this, the cop took me aside and said, 'Eh, I wanna tell ya somethin'. The next time you have a party like this, you better invite me.'

"Cops kept coming up. Security cops came up twice; regular cops came up once. And Meltzer was being . . . quite obnoxious. He knew this trick where you can take pencil lead and shaving cream and write on the walls and it won't come off — it's *ingrained* in the wall. And he wrote *Fuck you, asshole* all over the walls. . . . There was a total amount of about three hundred people went through the house at one point. Someone stole the rest of the Quaaludes, everything . . .

"The next morning I could only talk, like, 'Duh-guh-duh. . . .' and it took us eighteen hours to scrub the floors and try and scrub the walls. And then my parents came home. My parents come home, and there's *no jewelry* and *Fuck you, asshole* written all over the walls and half the house thrown off the terrace. They had just moved from the city housing project to the world-saving Co-op City. And I had said to them, 'I'm gonna have *one* party in this house.' Better than ten shitty parties, right, I'm gonna have *one* party that people are gonna remember forever — a *legendary* party. And a few months after that my parents went on vacation, and I had the party . . .

"And people remembered it forever."

But what about his parents?

Don't be ridiculous, his expression tells me. "So what could they do to me?" And then, with just a tinge of rue: "Ah, but it was my fault. I shouldn't have been living there in the first place."

Of course, now he is living there again.

·   ·   ·

Not long thereafter, Meltzer introduced the Dictators to his friend Sandy Pearlman, a rock critic turned manager and producer of the Blue Oyster Cult.

"Sandy came up and liked Ross's guitar work. They'd just been fooling around a couple of months. I wasn't in the band at the time, not at the beginning. I was cook. I was gonna be the roadie. I was gonna do whatever job hadda be done.

"So Sandy saw they got a great lead guitar player — Sandy's into great, heavy metal lead guitar players. He saw Andy was a talented songwriter — Andy had written, I think, 'Two Tub Man' around that time and this song called 'Fireman's Friend,' which is based sort of on Superman. And he saw everyone loves rock 'n' roll and had a great spirit, and on gut reaction he liked the band, and goes back to New York and gets the band a deal with Epic Records. The band plays no gigs, maybe one gig. I'm roadying. A little while after that, I think it was seventy-five, we went in and made *Dictators Go Girl Crazy!*"

Manitoba slows now to make clear a most crucial point. "We're all big wrestling fans," he says. "I was the *big* wrestling fan, but everybody was into it, too. They appreciated a good use of wrestling. And so we called me the Secret Weapon.

"The bad guys in wrestling," he instructs, "used to pull a secret weapon out of their trunks and hit the good guys — a half dollar or something. Or a broken pencil — that's the Sheik. The Sheik used to do that, throw fire and a broken pencil to crack your face open." Once again, he's not laughing. But then wrestling fans don't. And I suppose that's the fun. "So I was the Secret Weapon.

"I wasn't really the lead singer, but they figured, 'Hey, we gotta utilize this guy somehow...' So I would do things like be sitting around getting restless, and there was this little ramp in the studio that went down from behind the control room and through a door into the studio. I would take this chair and roll down the ramp and smash into the door. Then I'd go, 'I'm bored,' and go out to the Blarney Stone, where you could get this shot of scotch for, like, ninety cents or eighty cents, and I'd have ten drinks and make friends with this alcoholic, some degenerate sitting next to me, and we're buying each other drinks — and I'd come back into the studio *totally* smashed and they'd tell me, 'OUT! Get out of the studio! We're not paying a hundred dollars an hour for you to mess around.' And so — you know when you drink too much and get real sick? — so I went into the bathroom and lay down on the floor because the cold tile felt good on my face, and they found me sleeping on the floor of the bathroom..." He leans forward to the pocket tape recorder propped up between a margarita pitcher and a beer bottle on the table between us. "This is for my future job references," he says, and then, finally, he laughs. Except now he doesn't mean it.

A serious undertone is audible on and off as he resumes.

Pride sometimes; sometimes defensiveness. "I think the first album was one of the least pretentious things ever done. There was no self-consciousness. It was so much fun making that. Just a bunch of guys going crazy. We're in a studio, and we'd never been in a studio before. Played maybe one gig or zero gigs. And I was just sort of doing the sound effects for the album. Grunts and groans. I sang 'Two Tub Man.' I sang certain lines — I sang the line 'I'm the Next Big Thing.'

"I got in the band because they knew they had a personality on their hands — the *story* was that I'd lost all the equipment, so it was cheaper to put me in the band. I think I lost an amp head. So that was the going joke at the time. Everybody in the band wasn't a hundred percent sure about me being the lead singer. Murray [Krugman, the co-manager] and Sandy were. I loved the idea. I guess they thought they needed a more aggressive personality up front. Andy is not the most outgoing, aggressive person on that level, the level to be seen in front of people. I'm kind of like a ham. I like attention. I'm sort of the greaser with the heart of gold. So everyone finally decided I was the lead singer.

"Not the lead singer in terms of a Rod Stewart type of lead singer," he clarifies. "I was still splitting a lot of duties . . . and pee-pees." Everybody gets it about a second later. It is *not* the serious undertone. It's the kind of goofy aside that is just part of the flow of his speech. It's not certain if he even notices. "I was going to be the front man," he says, rushing on. "That was basically it. It was more for live purposes at first than recording."

If not a great deal of time elapsed between obscurity in New Paltz and a modicum of fame, that was part of the joke of the Dictators — and, indeed, almost the *definition* of punk. But it was also, Manitoba can see in retrospect, part of the problem. "Things came pretty quick to us," he says, the undertone resurfacing. "That might've been bad in a way, that we didn't pay the dues. We wound up making our mistakes and going through the growing pains of being a band in front of the public. The only one in that band who'd ever played in a band before was Ross, in local yokel bands.

"We confused the fans, I think. Different people, I think, bought each album. Not *many* of 'em, but . . . we were searching for an identity. But our identity was our first album. When it didn't do well commercially, we got scared and jumped into something else. I'm disappointed we did that. You know, you stick to your guns and you live or die with what you are. What kind of band that's going in to make their second album has no idea what they want the album cover to look like? No idea how they want to be dressed, no idea of what kind of image they want to present? I mean, we were *something,* something *definite* on the first album, and we didn't realize it. We didn't realize what we had, and we got scared because of commercial failure."

Part of what they had was *funny,* a quality they seemed to grow uncomfortable with over the years, as if *funny* was not what they had really intended, as if *funny* had somehow sunk beneath them. I ask Manitoba.

"Well, we always wanted there to be a humor within the music," he answers, "but we wanted to be taken as a *band* too. I mean, not serious musicians like Joe *Pass,* right?" He chuckles. "But we wanted to be — 'Hey! These guys got *chops!*' That kind of stuff. And the humor part would be what would maybe give us personality. We thought that would separate us and get us a lot of attention."

How did he see his own role?

"I was, like . . . just *me* turned loose onstage. . . . Well, it wasn't all of me. I was never . . . there were certain parts of me . . . if I would talk about being sensitive, or something like that, I would be laughed down. So it's just the outrageous part of me. Which is part of me. But that's the part they wanted to push. They didn't want to hear about anything else . . ."

An awkward moment. Manitoba picks up the thread. "In the beginning we were playing this place in Queens called the Coventry, getting our chops together in front of seven people a night. This was the tail end of the glitter era. The New York Dolls were on their last legs. Seventy-five or late seventy-four. I'm twenty, twenty-one years old. We used to buy White Castle hamburgers and bags of french fries and throw the french fries at the audience. They didn't know how to take it. Now I didn't expect people to get up and go crazy and say, 'Yeah! I realize this is the Next Big Thing!' But it was like: '*What* are these guys *doing?*' And four years later, when the Sex Pistols are telling you that you're fucking assholes, and people are cheering them to death, it caught on. Murray used to call it antitheater. But we didn't go home and think, 'If we throw out White Castles, this'll be the reaction, and it'll be good because of this . . .' We *felt* like doing it, and we *did* it.

"We didn't care really when they didn't react, because when you hang out with a bunch of guys . . . You ever go to Nathan's? Or any hangout? There's always a clique, and every clique thinks that where they come from they're cool. Their sense of humor is what's happening. They're cool. We thought everything we did was *so* cool, and everyone in the world was gonna crack up and say, 'This is the coolest thing I ever saw in my life! This is great!' And we realized that doesn't necessarily go over when you're talking in terms of millions of people, or even . . . *tens* of people . . ."

• • •

Periodically through the evening, Manitoba gets up to use the phone and does so now. Sometimes his girlfriend gets up with him and goes to the bathroom; sometimes she stays behind and wonders how much more I could possibly want to ask; sometimes she remains asleep. Manitoba returns. He is having trouble reaching his party. From rumors, I have an inkling who that party is, but I don't pry. In fact, I don't really want to know. I ask about his first experiences with rock 'n' roll.

"When I was a little kid, rock 'n' roll always made me feel *cool*," he says, stretching out the last word. "I listened to the Beatles and stuff like that. I always liked the Rolling Stones. I had an older sister, and she was sort of middle-of-the-road musically. She'd have stuff like Dion in the house, which I loved, too. But then in the fourth grade I met Scott — we were in the smart class; I'm a genius." He mugs. "Untapped potential, you know.... Scott would keep me cued in on what was happening.

"When I was fifteen or sixteen, I went downtown to the Village to buy a jacket, and I bought this blue suede dungaree jacket — it *looked* like a dungaree jacket, except it was blue suede — from Paul Sargent's. And with the fifty-dollar jacket they'd give you a free album. I looked at the albums and I never heard of any of 'em. So I said, 'Scott, pick me out an album.' And he says, 'Here, take this one.' And it was Velvet Underground, *White Light/White Heat*. And I'd go home and listen to it, and I was listening to these songs about drugs and about . . . like . . . ah . . . mostly about drugs . . .

"Me and Scott would go back to the first album, too, with the banana on it. We'd go over to Scott's house and put tin foil over a kazoo and punch holes in it with a needle and smoke hash — you could do it with the cardboard that came on a hanger, too. We'd smoke hash and put on a red light and listen to the Velvet Underground. And then I'd walk into my building and all the kids I grew up with, the kids in my neighborhood who I used to play football with, *tackle* in the streets, they'd be there. I'd come in with these records, and they'd say, 'Flamin' Groovies? Velvet Underground? Holy shit! What the hell is *that*???' Or 'Suzy Creamcheese' from Frank Zappa — they couldn't relate. And that was the first time I realized that was great. Even if I didn't like this music,

I would carry the album around because I'd feel great to be disassociated from them. This," he adds earnestly, sounding like his own psychiatrist, "was part of the quest for attention."

And, indeed: "Now the first record I remember — if this is like a psychiatrist's office, you go back to your childhood — was 'Tom Thumb' by Russ Tamblyn, the guy from *West Side Story*. I think that was the guy. And then I had this album with all the theme songs from shows like [sings], 'Wyatt Earp, Wyatt Earp, brave, courageous, and bold/Long live his name and long live his story . . .' Now the first album I remember *buying*, as a record collector, was Jefferson Airplane — no, it was Jeff Beck, *Beck-Ola*, with the apple on it *and*, I think, a Jefferson Airplane album. I hated it. But I remember when I was fifteen, I went up to the country, and I'd already tried smoking pot a little, and I listened to the first Led Zeppelin album, smash-your-head-against-the-wall kind of music." He grins. "And Johnny Winter. Those were the albums I *bought* . . .

"There was a period when the hippies first came in," he goes on without prompting, "that I was really scared of them. I was like thirteen, fourteen years old. I used to go upstate with my parents to a bungalow colony, which is a place guys send their wives so they can stay in the city and fuck their girlfriends. When I came back from the country this one summer, the whole culture had changed. And my friends — I had *different* sets of friends. There were the regular guys I played football with, and then my *friends*, my real closest friends, who were always a little bit more intellectual. And I come back and everybody's hair is a little bit longer than allowed, and they're wearing big bell-bottoms and listening to all these new groups. I called Scott and said, 'What kind of groups you like?' He said, 'They got this new group called Canned Heat that're real good.' I guess this was about a year before Woodstock. And then the next year was Woodstock, and I was indoctrinated.

68.

"But at first I had a hard time deciding whether to run back to my old friends — because these new guys were even getting too weird for *me*. But when I ran back to them, I had nothing in common. The guys around the block were, like, *football*. The other guys were, I guess, hippies. Except," Manitoba specifies, "me and my friends were never into laying in the mud and backpacking around the country and being dirty. We tried tripping for a while, but it didn't take over our lives. I was really never comfortable with the hippie scene. I always felt like a caboose of that scene. In the new wave, I was more like the leader."

So he *wasn't* a hippie?

"I *was* a hippie. I became very politically oriented. I marched. I was like the white leader at my high school. We left my high school one day and marched up Gun Hill Road in the Bronx and, like, a thousand of us, we walked around half the Bronx and marched from one high school to another, a distance of about ten miles total. I was a hippie, but I just didn't feel comfortable with it all the time."

If some of the time Manibota is only pretending, some of the time he's pretending so well that you can't be entirely sure. But if he is not actually regressive and infantile, he has an eye for the details of childhood that would surely be the envy of any novelist. He's telling me about summers in the late 1960s. "The big thing up in the bungalow colony was the words to 'Satisfaction,'" he says, now muffing the words as he sings: "'When I'm travelin' 'round the world, tryin' to make some girl *pregnant*.' We used to listen to it slow and stuff like that. We used to pull our hair so that — 'Look! It's just over the top of my ears!' And then your parents'd make you get a haircut. And I couldn't go to a late show at the Fillmore East yet," he continues, and I reel with the recovery of a memory. "But then somewhere around fifteen or sixteen, it was, 'I'm *not* getting a haircut. I *am* going to a late show at the Fillmore East.'" *A late show at the Fillmore East!* I'm thinking. But Manitoba, like any voluble child, has already gone ahead.

"And I think I was eighteen," he is saying, "when I took my first Quaalude. I was in the country, standing in Main Street, USA, and a guy came over and says, 'Hey, you wanna try one of these?' I knew the guy. He gave me an orange one, one of the old ANS sopors — that's why sopors is in 'Weekend.' And this thing was great. I was, like, gliding; I was so smooth. And this guy comes up to me and says, 'You want a job?' I said, 'Yeah.' So I started working. That was my first night. I worked up in the Catskill Mountains as a dishwasher in a Chinese restaurant."

When he was a kid, did he want to be a rock 'n' roll star? I ask Manitoba.

"When I was a kid," he replies, "I wanted to be a lot of different things at different times. . . . I wasn't a big record collector, you know. Scott was *totally* into rock 'n' roll, every aspect. I *lived* rock 'n' roll. I was a living embodiment of rock 'n' roll, my whole culture, my whole lifestyle — the craziness of it anyway. I was a *music* fan, just not . . . I was actually more of a *sports* fan. I'd buy an occasional rock 'n' roll magazine, but I read the sports pages religiously. When I was a kid, I wanted to be a *great* relief pitcher. I wanted to be a Goose Gossage. I wanted to come in with sixty thousand people in Yankee Stadium, with one out, men at second and third, in the ninth inning, and, like, two *feared* hitters, and strike 'em both out with my heat. And go: '*Yeah* . . .' So I got to kind of do that, in my own way. The nights that it was good, it's the greatest feeling in the world. The nights that you go over good onstage and the fans are digging it, you want to stay there forever."

• • •

Phone call. While he's away, I order more drinks. Beer for me. Margaritas for everyone else. When he returns, I change the

70.

subject. "After *Girl Crazy* was finished, then you went out for your first tour?"

"*Tour?*" he asks back. "The *tour* consisted of a long drive. After we played a show in the Bronx Halloween night, we drove to Winnipeg to open up a show for Nazareth and a band called Hudson Ford. I don't know how far it is — fifteen hundred miles? New York to Winnipeg? And in these shitty little cars that Sandy told us were good. You hit sixty miles an hour and the car would do figure eights on the highway. So we drive up there, bought a quart of Johnny Walker Black duty-free, got there, and I got my stage outfit on — first time I'm wearing it: red sequined jacket, black tights, white boots, white *wrestling* boots; it was a wrestling outfit, custom-made, a *bad* guy wrestling outfit. It was tights, with trunks over the tights, and down the side of each leg it said HANDSOME in white on black, and on each cheek of the tushy it had a star, and then it had a little Olympic-type tank top and a red sequined jacket with HANDSOME DICK MANITOBA and a map of Manitoba on the back, same as on the album, and HDM on the boots in red on white. I designed it. It was expensive, boy. I still have the red jacket; *that* I'll *always* have — and one boot.... So we drive up there and get ready and Nazareth says something like they didn't know we were on the tour. They wouldn't let us go on. So we drank the whole bottle of Johnny Walker Black and went home the next day."

Not a very happy experience, I suggest.

"I don't remember ever being particularly unhappy about it," says Manitoba sincerely. "I remember saying, 'Good. Fuck them.' Listen, here's a bunch of guys never did anything before, given money, given rent-a-cars, hotels, driving around the country, and...we *wanted* to play, *yeah! Shit!* we wanted to play. But if we didn't play, we didn't play. We said, 'Well, we're here, let's have a good time.'"

Soon, however, as Manitoba describes it, their problems changed. "For the second album, since Sandy and Murray were managing us and they also managed Blue Oyster Cult, we were gonna thrust into the arenas, be an arena rock band. More heavy metal, which *was* a part of us. But I think that crushed us," he continues with only a hint of regret. "I think that really destroyed us, going out into those big arenas, not knowing *what* the hell was going on. Standing in front of twenty thousand people, opening for Kiss . . . you know, like, 'What the hell am I doing here???' A certain part of the audience would be cheering maybe, but when *Kiss* came on, it was *overwhelming*. And when we were up there, there was always a guy standing up, you know, doing this: fuck finger. Or there would be a bunch of guys in a clique going, 'Boooo! . . . KISS-KISS-KISS!' One concert in New Jersey they threw chairs and stuff, and our roadie had to go out in the audience and keep watch. One guy picked up a chair and was going to throw it at me, so I got down on my knees like a bad guy wrestler and, you know, I *dared* him. . . . I think we should've tried to build up an audience more, instead of going from CBGB's to playing for twenty thousand."

The Dictators eventually departed from the Kiss tour. The rumors had it that they did not jump. Handsome Dick explains the relationship of the two groups. "We were a pain in the ass to Kiss. I would be at the airport at seven in the morning — we'd be rolling each other around in wheelchairs in North Dakota at seven in the morning — and Gene Simmons is Jewish, and his real name is Hyam Klein, and he changed it to Gene Klein, and then changed it to Gene Simmons, and I would say, 'Gene?' and talk to him in Yiddish. And, like, we'd act obnoxious. Paul Stanley, or one of them, called me a rock 'n' roll Totie Fields or a fat Fonzie, something like that. . . . Every time we'd crack a joke to them, they'd come back with something like, 'Well, ah, ah, when we walk in the bank, they don't laugh . . .' They didn't exactly *say* that, but . . . If they did throw us off the tour, they were lousy. But from what I hear, I don't know. And when I went into the studio to make a demo tape, Gene sent one of his flunkies down with a bunch of songs and said, 'Use a song.' It was a nice thing to do. You know, he's not looking to make a million dollars off of *me*. So I thought it was a nice thing to do. I don't really have any bitterness towards them. They were the bosses. If *we* were the bosses and we were playing in front of twenty thousand people and we thought these guys were assholes — in terms of what would've been assholes to the Dictators — *we* might've been nasty to *them*. I don't know how I would've reacted if I was a millionaire rock star."

Manitoba almost sounds resigned. Suddenly, another voice is heard to croak: "Did ya get to *Bloodbrothers* yet?" It is Manitoba's girlfriend momentarily returned to the land of the living. Manitoba reaches for cheeriness and tries also to pick up the tempo.

"We did a tour, it was great. With the Ramones, Widowmaker, the Nuns, the Dictators, and someone else. . . . Got in a big fight at the Whiskey in LA. We heard that one of the girls got hit, so after the show all of us came running down the stairs and challenged the whole city of Los Angeles to a fight: 'We're *bad* New Yorkers, you don't fuck around with *us*, you Los Angeles assholes!' I hated LA. I thought it was terrible.

"A couple of writers got thrown out of our shows for starting fights. That's what I like at our concerts," he says, slipping tenses, perhaps meaningfully, "when there's fights or riots. I like that. I've never seen no one get mashed to death or anything. But when they got into that kind of spirit," he now says, slipping back, "they didn't just come to see a show, they were gonna have a *good fucking time;* and the Dictators were gonna be *part* of their time. *That's* when I really dug it."

.   .   .

One more phone call. I can see across the room that he reaches somebody. He comes back and I steer the interview

.73

toward *Bloodbrothers,* the last album, and maybe some sort of conclusion.

"After the second album," Handsome Dick explains, "after *Manifest Destiny,* we figured it was time to get back to what we were, or at least similar. I don't think we got back enough. We were still too serious, so we made a *new wave* type of album. There still wasn't enough humor. I think the Dictators always had a personality crisis, an identity crisis. One album we were 'superstars'; one album we were regular downhome kids from the Bronx, which is what we *were* and what we *should've* been. You know what Popeye said: 'I yam what I yam and that's all that I yam!'

"From Andy's point of view, the *Bloodbrothers* album was, 'Let's give Richard a chance. This is *Richard's* album.' Let's give *me* a chance to be the lead singer of the group and take some control. It was *closer* to *Girl Crazy,* but it's like Andy said: he wrote *Girl Crazy* when he was nineteen, twenty years old, whatever. And I guess he's a real writer and can't just spew out things. He doesn't want to write, like, 'Yeah, we're taking Quaaludes and having these parties . . .' — going *back,* you know . . ."

There's something that Manitoba feels he must tell. I'm not sure why. I'm also not sure, once again, that I want to know. A mention of drugs is his excuse. "Yeah, everyone in the band smoked pot," he says casually, "but I was the only one who did, like, *drugs.* But I partied with them; I smoked pot for many years. In *those* days I partied with them. Then these different drugs came along and different people, different things . . ." He looks to his girlfriend. They share one of his more private laughs.

"To this day," Manibota resumes, "I'm still good friends with all of them. Scott's still a very close friend. But, you know, drugs have a way of drawing boundaries between cliques. In the Bronx it's like that. You know, whoever does dope — it's not cool to hang around people who do dope.

74.

But the people who *don't* do dope will eat like ten Quaaludes in a week. And *that's* okay, 'cause it isn't dope. And they smoke a ton of pot, and *that's* okay. And maybe it is, I guess, because you're not gonna die or get hepatitis or whatever, or die in *two minutes*, from being on Quaaludes. But you *can* die from dope."

It's not exactly that I don't want to know; it's that I don't want to believe. But he goes coolly on: "It doesn't pay to get into it on a long-time thing. I'm not a doctor, I don't know. But for one, I don't think dope — well, according to people like William Burroughs, it's not something that destroys your vital organs. I mean, the *pure* shit. I'm not talking about milk sugar. And it's not necessarily like speed or cocaine or those kinds of drugs. I think if you do cocaine enough it affects your nerve endings, your synapses and stuff like that. But I'm very hypocritical about drugs. I'll take a lot of different kinds of drugs. Theoretically, intellectually, I believe drugs are bad for you. They're *really* bad for you. The proof is in the pudding: Jim Morrison, Brian Jones, Jimi Hendrix, Janis Joplin — I mean, you can go on and on . . ."

"Mama Cass?" I venture, trying to goad him to humor, engage a more recognizable Manitoba.

"No, ham sandwich," he tosses back unenthusiastically, persisting with an uncharacteristic doggedness at his increasingly dubious point.

"I believe drugs *are* bad," he says. "I think they can pretty much destroy a marriage; they can destroy a band; a team; they can destroy anything, *any* drug that gets out of hand, I don't care what. And it doesn't pay to be self-righteous, like, 'I do *these* drugs, so I'm okay.' I think drugs are wrong. I think they're bad for you, and theoretically, I hate 'em. Emotionally, I love 'em . . ."

Does he think I know something? Is that why he feels he must explain?

"It's not like I *have* to do drugs every day . . ."

.75

Is it just bragging?

"But I'll be going out, and we're partying, going downtown, going to a club, and I'm gonna try to get a 'lude or try to get drunk or take . . . something else . . ." The laugh again. "It really destroys things in the long run, but it's fun while you're doing them."

Maybe the margaritas have something to do with it.

"But I've got some really good friends," he says, suddenly bitter, maudlin, "who, *whatever* I do, I know they're still gonna care about me."

Hearing him now, I feel guilty I haven't called Manitoba in six months, that perhaps *I* didn't care enough. But then, suddenly again, his mood brightens — after a rather dim fashion. "It's funny," he says. "I always walked a tightwire on that, about getting *too* fucked up. But then when I did start getting a little *too* fucked up, I stopped. Or at least stopped enough *not* to be too fucked up. But never stopped enough to be totally *not* fucked up. So it's like bouncing off the walls, back and forth. And at this point, who knows what's gonna happen tomorrow. At one time I never thought I'd stop smoking pot. I never thought I'd stop taking some pill. When I was seventeen, eighteen, I used to buy Quaaludes and Seconals and Tuinols — I think I did drugs more *times* in those days, to *more* excess . . ."

He bounces off the wall: one more sudden shift. And I realize now that he's telling me all this at least in part because he is preaching. "There are certain things you want to talk about that the society doesn't want to hear," he instructs, draping himself in a fine, hip sanctimony. "The old taboo. But it *does* feel good. It *is* a temporary relief. You know, I saw a picture at my friend's house, *Fort Apache*, and there's this Puerto Rican chick who was a mess, and she said, 'You don't understand what junk's about.' And he says, 'Nah . . .' whatever. And she goes: 'To me, it's three hours of floating on a raft in the Caribbean.' So . . . you *could* work eight months and stay home at night and watch TV for eight months, saving up enough money to float on a raft in the Caribbean for a week. *Or* you could do junk . . . you know, fifty times or something, and do all your floating on a raft in the Caribbean and not go away."

Until he says it outright I don't quite believe it. Maybe I do suffer from a narrow, bourgeois view of heroin. I argue with him for a few minutes. I think narrow, bourgeois things like, Will this be the last time I see Handsome Dick Manitoba? Finally, I can see that arguing is less than useless. Indeed, he agrees on every point. I move along to one last necessary question — even though the answer seems obvious. "How did the breakup happen?"

"One night," he says, "Ross, Scott, and Andy came over to my apartment and said, 'We're dissolving the band.' So I said, '*You're* dissolving the band?' But in essence they meant that I was being pushed out. And I said, 'You can't be the Dictators without me, 'cause I am the living *embodiment* of the Dictators.' And I am! I'll take blame for things, but I'll fucking hell take credit for things too. Andy was the intellectual, creative force behind the Dictators, but I was the physical, up-front force, the Dictators' image, or whatever you want to call it. I said, 'You can't be the Dictators without Handsome Dick.' So they were gonna change the name and form another band, but that sort of fell apart and they all got into their own things and that's it . . .

"I went and got a couple of jobs here and there. I got some music jobs, made a lot of connections in the music business, made a demo tape, nothing ever happened with it. I guess if I busted my ass I could easily get a band back together. I still got a name in this town. But it takes a lot of energy and a lot of time. And I'm not a songwriter. I could get musicians, but I think you need a writer. I would work with Andy again — I mean, as a writer. He's trying to do a lot of different things now. He's playing; he's writing; he's working.

.77

"Funny thing is, with all the big dreams and plans, with all the bands they've all been in at this point, the Dictators were still the biggest thing that ever happened in any of our lives. The most fun. There were guys who worked for us, who could've made *ten* times as much money working for other bands, who say to me, 'You know, if you guys got back together again, I'd be hard pressed to think whether I'd want to leave the band I'm working for, because it was so much fun and such a camaraderie — such a great feeling.'" Manitoba fondly considers these tributes.

"Funny, that kind of business is the type of business you're always supposed to be worried about 'cause you don't know if it's gonna be around the next day. I never worried about if it was gonna be around. We'd stick together, no matter what, until we made it. And if it was up to me, I would have; because it's still the most fun I ever had in my life and the best way to make a living.

"We went to Europe; we toured America numerous times; we made *three albums* — that's farther than ninety-nine percent of bands get! We got to where, I'd say, the bottom of the top. I'd've liked to seen us get to the top of the top. Even if we got to the *middle* of the top, that would've been okay. I never thought we'd sell millions of records. I never wanted to be too safe, like the Bee Gees — like, have the housewives in middle America go out and buy a Dictators album while they're doing their wash. I'd rather sell three or four hundred thousand albums and have a real strong audience, so I could make a real good living for a long time. Not be *filthy* rich, but comfortable enough where I could retire and have a place. You know, Handsome Dick's Broadway Bar and Grill, whatever — I just wanted to call it Broadway Bar and Grill.

"I just wanted to play music for as long as I wanted to. I would have been very happy doing that. I wasn't shooting for Rolling Stones — if it happened, it happened. I never thought I'd redo the Beatles. But our fans were very strong fans, the fans that we had; they really were."

As we await the check, somehow we get on the subject of Nixon and the draft and the draft lottery in which both Manitoba and I were not-quite-willing participants back at the start of the last decade. Naturally, inevitably, I tell *my* lottery number (211, fairly high), and Manitoba tells *his* (very low). Manitoba's girlfriend, who has perked up, so to speak, at the prospect of leaving, now volunteers: "My brother was three-eighty." Manitoba smiles at me. And then plainly, almost gently, but absolutely without contempt or malice, a Manitoba we know and love explains to her that a draft lottery number could never be higher than the number of days in the year. And then he gets up one last time to use the phone.

You could take it back to the Beatles and their long hair. You could, for that matter, take it back to Elvis and *his* long hair, to Elvis, the truck driver with the curvy, vampy pout, the lady-killer revered for the kind of swivelly hips that once we admired only in ladies. You could take it back to Jerry Lee Lewis, who took a thirteen-year-old cousin as his child bride. Or to Chuck Berry in stir on a Mann Act rap. Or to Little Richard and *his* pancake makeup. Indeed, something or other has been wrong with the boys of rock 'n' roll in the sexual department since there's *been* rock 'n' roll.

Of course, before pot or acid or Quaaludes, it is sex that is the basic high for rock 'n' roll. And unlike Tin Pan Alley — or Madison Avenue — rock 'n' roll has never been content to serve merely as come-on or foreplay. With its irreducibly emphatic backbeat, rock 'n' roll is fundamentally physical music, music that makes you move, sway, gyrate, hump, dance music, with all the ancient rhythmic and dance traditions of Africa behind it. And with its roots in the gospel music and Pentecostal ceremonies of southern Protestantism, rock 'n' roll has an even more immediate connection with the realms of the ecstatic and apocalyptic — indeed, with the orgasmic. Furthermore, as a cultural form that is at least half black, rock 'n' roll partakes of all the myths — fostered by age-old segregationist propaganda — of black male sexuality, myths of extraordinary size and potency that in fact rock 'n' rollers, black and white, have been only too happy to play up — even when, for the sake of someone's parents or Ed Sullivan, they have tried to play them down. Rock 'n' roll is drenched in sex. Rock 'n' roll — the name means it; even the '*n*' means it: *unh!* Rock 'n' roll *is* the sexual revolution — and for all their macho posturing, the boys of rock 'n' roll may have ultimately been the shock troops of the sexual revolution's most dramatic and enduring triumph: the women's movement. Still and all, what is wrong with the boys of rock 'n' roll in the sexual department is basically not sex but rock 'n' roll.

. . .

My father always blamed the drugs on rock 'n' roll, but he also always blamed the sex. Like I said, he's not stupid. I remember his comment when *Life* came out with its famous hippie extravaganza, the issue from June 1967 with the Airplane and some of the *really* long-haired guys from Big Brother on the cover. "Fags," said my father, a little amazed, but already a little nervous too. And, again like I said, my father's not the nervous type. "Fags," he said, looking down at all those boys with all that long hair, and it may be that he chuckled then too, to cover himself. But I could see that he was also mad. And so when he walked off, I promptly gathered up the magazine from where he had let it fall and over the next several days burned holes in it with my eyes. I didn't *want* them to be fags — and, God, that hair was *long*. But in the end I could have nothing but admiration for their bold new style. It worked.

Discussing the hippie-police confrontations of the sixties in a profile filmed for French TV not long after he surfaced from underground in 1980, Abbie Hoffman himself had some germane observations. "The hippies," he said, "were challenging much of the macho mystique of the police. It was an affront to them just for men to grow their hair long . . . It was all very psychological, very sexual. The remarks that would pour out from the police were *all* sexual." It wasn't *only* long hair, of course — for one thing, these kids were draft dodgers; for another, they were coddled college kids. But it was *mostly* the long hair. Long hair happened to be the most immediately apprehendable distinction and the handiest symbol. And to "straights" — which was the term we used for non-hippies, but which also is the homosexual term for heteros — it mostly symbolized fags. Heavy metal was in part a reaction to this, an assertion of a hippie machismo that would eventually make the male long-hair the seventies version of the greaser. Another reaction to the "men's problems" of the seventies was glitter.

• • •

If an open and free sexuality was some kind of antidote to the decay elsewhere in the culture, that is not to say such sexuality wasn't decadent. Certainly rock 'n' roll would do its damnedest to make it so. Which brings us right back around to glitter.

Even more elastic a rubric than heavy metal, glitter rock encompassed a wide variety of musical styles — from bright, melodic Beatlesy stuff to opaque heavy metal — but mostly described a new verbal and visual pose. The salient characteristic of this pose — which could range in its final effect anywhere from campy or femme to wise-guy tough — was that it usually came wrapped in some kind of trashy drag, sometimes sprinkled with glittery fairy dust, and always played to the worst imaginings of dads and cops, glorying in their accusations that we were spoiled brats and probably queers.

Perhaps the first, no doubt the most famous, of glitter rockers was Vincent Furnier, a minister's son from Arizona by way of Michigan, whose whole career was almost as improbable as he had hoped it would be. His band was called Alice Cooper, but the audience, misunderstanding, thought he alone was she. Eventually, dumping the band in order to make his lunge for solo immortality, Furnier would be able to capitalize on his identification as *the* Alice Cooper — and craftily forestall anyone else, specifically his old bandmates, from capitalizing on it — by legally changing his name. If by usage the name was more his than theirs, the move to grab it reeked of naked greed and ultimately may have proved Faustian — a characterization Vincent/Alice might have welcomed, badness monger that he was, in the days before his deal actually went down. In any case, there was good reason to fight for that name. As far as the Alice Cooper phenomenon was concerned, the name in fact was just about the whole game. It was premise and punch line and fundamental gimmick: a *man* (or men) named Alice. And if it was also not much to build a career on, show business careers — and this most definitely was *show* business — have been built on much less.

The show they did finally build on and around this slim — but undeniably winning — bit of effrontery was by far the most elaborate and theatrical in rock 'n' roll at the time, not to be frequently surpassed in the meantime. And the theatricality served to mask an essentially unmusical talent — though in the early days it wasn't always clear that there was much talent of any variety there. Indeed, the first time I saw Alice perform, back in 1970 on some syndicated "rock festival" TV special (another dubious legacy of Woodstock), he was trying to hypnotize a great stadium full of people with a little tiny pocketwatch — which demonstrated balls, especially with the crowd heaping assorted unpleasant missiles onto the stage, but also a rather dim sense of proper theatrical scale. But over time, continuing to draw on similar nightmarish effects from bad surrealism and scary B-movies, the show developed impressively to include Alice presiding over live boa constrictors and dismembered baby dolls and giant dancing toothbrushes (set upon by Alice as "Mr. Tooth Decay") until the climactic moment when he would be "executed" on stage — on one tour, by "hanging"; on another, by "decapitation" in a life-size guillotine.

Alice eventually became good enough and notorious enough at his own bad surrealism to entice for a moment the *king* of the bad surrealists, Salvador Dali, from his lair, whereupon amid much ballyhoo at New York's Museum of Modern Art the master unveiled his holographic portrait — *Alice Cooper with Snake.* Despite such highfalutin, press-agented goings-on, I should stress that Alice himself never pretended to have anything more than humor in mind. And while he may have gotten a bit pumped-up about his theatrical abilities and that humor's success, nevertheless in spurts it *was* funny. From his 'umble beginnings as a glitter rocker named Alice, Vincent Furnier grew up to become a master in his own right, the king, as some critics labeled him, of shock rock.

· · ·

If Alice's theatrics masked an unmusical talent, it was nonetheless that same unmusic that made the leap to costly, grand-scale theatrics possible. And actually, when the band stuck to the sloppy, drunken heavy metal arrangements it seemed best equipped for, the music had some real heavy metal appeal. It was the thumby attempts at subtlety and complexity, and later the slick production, that made the music sound fake — heavy metal with needless, insupportable mainstream show biz pretensions, as opposed to the merely synthetic sound of Led Zep. Alice himself was possessed of one of the fakest voices in rock 'n' roll — which is really saying something when from Jagger on down rock 'n' roll singers have almost all been faking (usually black blues) to one degree or another. Meant to suggest some sort of congenital rottenness and menace, his nasal plaints and growls came off hammy, monotonous, *too* theatrical, but mostly just unfelt, insincere. Indeed, there was something about Alice Cooper — in his attitude and theatrics, as well as in his music — that was practically the definition of third-generation (that is, post-Elvis *and* post-Beatles) rock 'n' roll: he was playing the rock 'n' roll *star* rather than playing the rock 'n' roll. But my point is, it was finally his rock 'n' roll, his *music* that got him into the Top Forty and made him a star, improbable though that once might have seemed.

It was after two musically and commercially disastrous albums for Frank Zappa's Straight Records — Zappa having signed them for the obvious nonstraight reasons and, according to Alice, because their early performances at Los Angeles' Whiskey-A-Go-Go were known to clear the house in something under two minutes — that the band took the *Love It to Death* LP to Warner Bros. in 1971 and came up with the first of several improbable hit songs.

"Life's foam on my face and hands," Alice mewled over some bluesy arpeggios,

> Life's foam on the up and down,
> I'm in the middle, the middle of doubt,
> I'm a boy and I'm a man . . .

And then with the guitars fully cranked for the chorus, he shouted home the punch line:

> I'm eighteen! I get confused everyday,
> Eighteen! I don't know what to say . . .
> I'm eighteen — and I *like* it!

From the self-indulgent, self-pitying, spoiled brattiness of the lyrics to the earnest warty-handed amateurishness of the music, what Alice achieved with "I'm Eighteen" was the first third-generation anthem — literally, a Battle Hymn of the

88.

Jerkoff. But then as Dave Marsh, scoffing at the notion that rock 'n' roll is about fucking, would write in the rock criticism anthology *Stranded*: "The real truth is that rock was invented by teenagers with pimples, and acned adolescents are mostly getting it on with their fingers."

Alice followed up his first big hit with a song about stardom. Of course. "She asked me why the singer's name was Alice," he could be heard to whine this time. "I said, 'Listen, baby, you really wouldn't understand.'" And somehow "Be My Lover" (from late 1971's *Killer*) still managed to capture hipper-than-thou even as it indulged in it — managing as well to make that commercially all-important leap to the charts. But it was Alice Cooper's third time out that really worked the charm.

From the title — which Alice said came to him via a Bowery Boys movie — on down, "School's Out" (from the 1972 album of the same name) contains nary a wrong move, totally tapping into the anarchy to become Alice Cooper's greatest hit and one of the *all-time* terrific teen anthems. His most slickly theatrical recording to date, if it was not Alice's *least* faked, it was his *best* faked. And indeed we even believe it when, at the end of a rocking litany of "we ain't" that and "we can't" this, the singer finds himself too carried away to calculate and tosses off: "We can't even think of a word that rhymes." We even enjoy it. But the crux of "School's Out," as it should be, is the chorus, in which glitter's own Mr. Chips leads a dirty-faced, Lord-of-the-Flies kids' choir into rebellion. "No more pencils/ No more books," the children sing quietly at first, with Alice barely mouthing the words, over a tensely restrained backing, "No more teachers' dirty looks . . ." Until suddenly, comes an ominously martial pounding from the rhythm section — and release:

> School's out for summer!
> School's out forever!

And in the end, Alice sneering:

School's been blown to pieces!

Whereupon an explosion is heard (and here we even excuse Alice's literalness) and gangs of kids cheering into the fade-out. And no matter if you haven't been in school for twenty years, you can still get that tingle. Rock 'n' roll's life-as-adolescence metaphor was never more aptly or expressively couched — and, alas, not by Alice Cooper either, who followed up his most expressively produced LP with *Billion Dollar Babies*, his most expensively packaged. Which figured.

But if *Billion Dollar Babies* wasn't worth much as tunes, Alice of course was always mostly pose and packaging, and that was really his greatest talent and — to me at least — remains his greatest significance. And that gets us back to the point. Because while I still swear by the anthems, it was the unmusical (and nonstarring) Alice Cooper of 1970 who with *Easy Action*, the second of the disastrous Straight LPs, changed my life. And it had nothing to do with listening, nothing to do with ears at all.

Asses.

I first became acquainted with *Easy Action* in the high school bookstore, which in 1970 was experimenting with stocking rock 'n' roll records. The rock 'n' roll record in question was propped alongside a dozen other disks in an out-of-the-way rack — the experiment evidently halfhearted, no doubt on moral grounds — and I just caught a glimpse of it as I stepped out the door. Asses. I pivoted. But then I was seventeen and locked away in a boys' boarding school in the wilds of New England and maybe a little sensitive. Then again, what red-blooded son of Adam wouldn't have been just a little sensitive to something so excruciatingly fine as this big, bright, full-color snapshot of five sequined and micro-skirted asses all in a heartstopping row? And legs. And asses. As I approached, however, the album cover surrendered new meaning.

At it turned out, the girl on the left of the line wasn't a girl at all — and he proved it by twisting from the hips to leer back at the camera. I mean, it was girls' legs and asses — but this one here was a guy. But they weren't *all* guys, surely . . . "Alice Cooper," of whom I was uninformed, read the name over the photo. What about those asses? Those pert, those insolent asses? Those asses presenting oh-so-seductively? Those backs arching and silky legs spread beggingly? But the girl on the end was a guy . . . I seized the cover from the rack and flipped it over. A front shot: leering, laughing, mocking. Indeed, all guys — and ugly, to boot! I flipped it back. But those legs. Those asses. And, God, what I wouldn't have done for some female asses, *one* female ass, the wondrous taut globes in my aching little palms, one female *anything* . . . But these were guys — but, my God, what *asses!* "Life's foam on my face and hands." Did it make any difference? "I get confused every day."

But I was seventeen and I liked it.

I did. I really liked it. But not like *that,* or not exactly. Granted, a good ass is a good ass is a good ass. But in the end I liked these because I laughed. I laughed at myself. And I laughed at everybody else. It wasn't really a nice laugh. I liked *Easy Action* because I liked the *fuck you* of it. And I meant *fuck you* both ways, *either* way: sex *or* violence. And here, like in my fondest fantasies, Alice Cooper had blended the two, the sex and the violence, to such devastating effect that all I could do was cackle in abject admiration. Offering at first glance some easy action, offering in principle to fuck you, they promptly turned it around — just as you reached out — into "fuck *you.*" Here might be the policeman's taunts ricocheted back in his face. Here was certainly all your parents' fears about long hair terribly fulfilled and then some. Here was something that could really hurt dads and cops, maybe even reduce them to glints of tears.

An Alice Cooper was not something the authorities were entirely equipped to deal with in 1970. You couldn't call out the riot squad to put it down — although during my first week in college, later in 1970, when a group of militant gays occupied the main building, our college president would do just that. But realistically, this was beyond politics and government, beyond college presidents, beyond mom and dad. This was disgusting. "Gender fuck" we called it. "I said, 'Listen, baby, you really wouldn't understand.'"

So when they took the high school yearbook photo of our rock 'n' roll band, I squeezed into a girl's jumper and puckered up. And if it wasn't unique, it was unique enough for there and then. My little friends thought it was funny — we laughed, *this* would shake 'em all up. My friends liked *fuck you*, too. But the younger kids in school called us "those homos." And the principal's wife suggested sadly (and sotto voce) that one or another of us might be afflicted with an unspecified "problem." In other words, it worked — just like the guys in *Life*.

And make no mistake, this was no Princeton Triangle routine either. Its fundamental intent was not to amuse, and amusement was generally not its effect. Besides, varsity drag, for all its jollity, was really much sexier (look at that famous photo of Fitzgerald in drag at Princeton). Varsity drag was horny dilettantes teasing each other. In a jumper I meant sex as violence. Actually, I didn't mean sex at all. "School's been blown to pieces!"

92.

Being homosexual, or at least *seeming* homosexual, was the new way to be black in rock 'n' roll. To seem homosexual was the new way to be different, cool, special, a romantic outlaw (and in this case, truly a *romantic* outlaw). Not that it was all right actually to *be* homosexual — at least it wouldn't have been comfortable — just as it wasn't really all right or comfortable anymore to be black in the white mainstream of rock 'n' roll. So that stalwart of the genre, the white rocker in blackface, was now joined by — and sometimes combined with — the hetero rocker in homo drag. Thus, in order to wink at us about his homo connotations, did Alice Cooper make a big macho point of drinking lots of Budweiser (whence, he would later confess in *People*, his alcoholism). Thus, in order to hedge their bets, did some rockers — hetero, homo, and otherwise — let it be known that they were now *bi*.

Actually, in the decadent world of post-Woodstock sexuality and dazzling glitter rock it was *bi* rather than *homo* that was really where it's at. And with Elton John officially in the closet until later in the seventies and Alice expanding into shock rock, chief among bisexual rockers — and ultimately king, as well as queen, of glitter — was David Bowie.

Like Alice Cooper, Bowie founded his career on the radical sexual pose. Also like Alice, this flamboyance bespoke a strong bent for the theatrical in general — and the grand, ruined, futuristic, Metropolis-like set that surrounded Bowie and the band on the *Diamond Dogs* tour was surely the match of most of Alice's creations. But then as an actor la Bowie has easily surpassed the accomplishments of la Cooper, having starred now in several movies and on Broadway — to thoroughly respectable notices — in the challenging *Elephant*

.93

Man, and today is heard to make noises about retiring from rock 'n' roll altogether to devote the whole of his attention to thespianism.

Despite his successes on screen and on the boards, however, and *un*like Alice Cooper, Bowie has made his greatest claim to fame with his achievements — singing, songwriting, and producing — on vinyl. With "Changes" and "Is There Life on Mars?" on the *Hunky Dory* LP in 1971, he demonstrated a minor mastery of a melodic and haunting, mid-Beatles-style rock 'n' roll. The following year, on *Ziggy Stardust and the Spiders from Mars,* a rock opera of sorts, he pretty much defined the limits of glitter rock, both as sound and attitude. On *Pin-Ups* (1973), with his peculiar robotic remakes of British Invasion classics, he not only anticipated certain six-ties-revival aspects of punk and new wave, but more impor-tantly, paved the way for new wave robots like Devo — which is not to mention that along with Bryan Ferry of Roxy Music and Lou Reed he practically invented the overbred and overwrought vocal style of the new wave. On *David Live* (1974), cut with Philadelphia's premier black studio band MFSB, and on *Young Americans* (1975), which in-cluded the Lennon-Bowie r 'n' b hit "Fame," he anticipated the resurgence of black music, especially black music as disco, to preeminence in the pop world, and along with the Bee Gees, spurred it along into white neighborhoods. And on *Station to Station* (1976), which included a rollicking love song to a machine ("TVC 15"), he put it all together, robotics with soul, for his most original, if not quite best, record to date.

David Bowie's best record, however, was not a David Bowie record. David Bowie's best record in fact was Mott the Hoople's *All the Young Dudes* — specifically the title song, which David Bowie produced and wrote but which Ian Hunter sang. A thrilling synthesis of heavy metal and pop, with the most mesmerizing refrain since "Hey Jude"

94.

and ironic, sometimes bitter, lyrics worthy of a rock 'n' roll John Osborne, "All the Young Dudes," released the same year as *Ziggy Stardust* and complementary to it, might have been the era's great anthem — capturing the post-Woodstock period, the third generation, as Osborne's *Look Back in Anger* captured the postwar and the "Angries" — if its writer didn't at the same time understand — and if it wasn't true — that the time for anthems had more or less passed. This then was an anti-anthem for an anti-time.

"Billy rapped all night about suicide," Hunter tosses off in his bleakly cheery British Dylan voice, "How he'd kick it in the head when he's twenty-five." And then he dismisses it. "Speed jive . . ." he says. But the dismissal becomes additional testimony to a third generation sunk — not unhappily — even further into decadence, into apathy and resignation. "And my brother's back at home," sings the young narrator,

> With his Beatles and his Stones,
> *We* never got it off on that revolution stuff,
> What a drag,
> Too many snags . . .

He sneers the last word, scoffing at the idealism of his older sixties-era brother. As for himself, like any heavy metal poly-pharmacopiac, he'd just as soon get fucked-up —

> Well, I drunk a lot of wine
> And I'm feeling fine —

and get fucked, he adds, any way I choose —

> Gonna raise some cat to bed . . .

A *sexual* polypharmacopiac too, it seems. Shouts the kid in triumphant conclusion: "I'm a dude now!"

And then with Hunter running alongside, exhorting, "I

want to *hear* you!" and "I want to *see* you!" and finally, in the
fade, "I want to *kiss* you!," the band, clapping and swaying
to the beat, links voices for the refrain:

> All the young dudes,
> Carry the news,
> Boogaloo, dudes,
> Carry the news.

And maybe it's a long way from "We shall overcome" — and
the seventies, like they say, a long way from the sixties — but
then again maybe it isn't.

There were some at the time who claimed this was a gay
song, that "young dudes" in fact was a euphemism for gays
and "boogaloo" referred to dancing at gay bars, that this was
a hymn to the gay life and a call to come out of the closet —
to "carry the news." And considering the composer and the
nature of the glitter aesthetic he largely defined, it would
probably be odd if there weren't something of gayness in
there. But there is also something more.

In fact, I would venture that the ambiguity of "dudes"
here is precisely the point, that actually "All the Young
Dudes" is a kind of *generic* anthem: one size fits all. Indeed,
it's a song for the *misfit* (whoever or whatever he or she
might be); a song of disengagement for the disengaged, of
group solidarity for the ungrouped; an anarchists' anthem and
a nihilists' hymn — and so, of course, yet another song of the
times as well. And for all its bitterness and desperation —
the "news" of its subtext: that anthems are finished; groups
and movements dispersed; Woodstock Nation kaput; that
now is the time of the dudes, those lone wild boys (and girls)
hunting the good time, coming together in spite of themselves, doing the boogaloo till they drop — "All the Young
Dudes" does remain sweet, truly an anti-*anthem,* an exalta-
tion (you can feel it in a certain inexplicable, and surely un-
toward, pride that will still well in the chest or tingle on the

96.

spine whenever that refrain billows out of a radio or juke-box), the statement somehow of something noble: the good-ness of the bad, the morality of the immoral, the dignity of the undignified, and the humanity — shared on a sweaty dance floor as well as any place — of us all.

Thus did David Bowie put forth a decadence that was in fact healing.

. . .

Down in the sequined trenches, however, the young dudes themselves, while not necessarily disputing the theory, were somewhat less refined in its practice. "And if I'm acting like a pig," David Johansen barfed out, "that's because I'm a hu-man being . . . a riff-raff human being!" But then if Bowie had most accurately described the life, it was Johansen and the New York Dolls who set out to prove it could actually be lived. Which it couldn't — not really, not for long, certainly not to the max. A corollary of decadence as healing would be failure as success — a concept self-limiting in the extreme. And so by the time they went into the studio to record their first album, the Dolls had already lost their drummer to a downs overdose and were well on their way to a (short) career chock-full of decadence and failure, a career which in that sense was a very big success.

If the Dolls were not merely an impersonation of young dudes, that is not to say they weren't self-conscious. And per-haps self-conscious is too moderate a term. Where Alice Cooper and David Bowie at the start of glitter were third generation, the New York Dolls at glitter's high-water mark were fourth — post-Bowie. Where Bowie, no less than Alice, played the rock star as much as the rock 'n' roll, the Dolls seemed prepared to dispense with the rock 'n' roll altogether. They seemed prepared even to dispense with the rock star-dom, playing instead "rock stars" from yet another distance, "*glitter* rock stars." But not unlike the double-negative movie-within-a-movie of *Gimme Shelter,* finally it worked. The quotes-in-quotes, all that self-consciousness laid on self-consciousness, somehow served to make the Dolls about as genuine a rock 'n' roll band as turned up in the last decade. And their records, which by rights should have been the most perfunctory ephemera, stand out even today as among rock 'n' roll's most enduring.

The New York Dolls were very much the product of a scene that flourished along with them for about two years in the early 1970s and was situated in and around a place called the Mercer Arts Center. Located in Manhattan near Bleecker Street and Broadway in the DMZ between East and West Villages, the Mercer was only one part rock 'n' roll club. In addition to the Oscar Wilde Room, the cabaret from which the Dolls and Teenage Lust and the Harlots of 42nd Street and Eric Emerson and his Magic Tramps held forth, the Mercer enclosed in its magical rabbit warren of reclaimed urban architecture a legitimate theater (long-time home to the satire *El Grande de Coca-Cola*), a clothing boutique, art gallery space that mostly emphasized the new arty television called "video" (and would, when the Mercer closed, move downtown and open up autonomously as the Kitchen), and of course a bar. The place was slick, hip, chic — and inordinately influential. Indeed, in fashion and interior design and art, no less than in music, so much of what punk and the new wave would encompass — for better and worse — at the end of the decade was already encompassed at the beginning here at the Mercer Arts.

To a certain extent, the Mercer was a performing annex to Max's Kansas City, the now-legendary (and defunct) bar/beanery/cabaret farther uptown, across Fourteenth Street. Max's — or at least the back room at Max's, the back room which *was* Max's to those in the know — was clubhouse and internecine battleground to the various New York artists, writers, actors, musicians, and the like, who made up the bloodied remains of the American avant garde of the fifties and sixties. But Max's, the back room, was dominated — in spirit and sometimes in numbers — by Andy Warhol and his Superstars and satellites, who worked, most notably in those nonhalcyon days on movies and aphorisms (*In the future blah-blah-blah . . .*), at Warhol's famous studio, the Factory, located since 1968 within shouting distance of Max's, diagonally across Union Square Park. And in a way just as he dominated the back room, from where he or his emissaries or stand-ins would sally forth to dominate the Mercer and daub the Dolls and, by extension, glitter with his cachet, Andy Warhol was the true eminence grise behind much of seventies and eighties rock 'n' roll, indeed behind an exceedingly large portion of contemporary American culture, pop and otherwise.

Next to Warhol, needless to say, Alice Cooper was just another Midwest hayseed, a hick. But on occasion even David Bowie would journey to the back room to sit at the master's feet — and finally be moved enough to write "Andy Warhol" on *Hunky Dory*. Of course, Mick Jagger — probably as responsible in the long run for the new decadence as Bowie and Cooper combined — was enough smitten with Andy to induct him as a full-fledged rock 'n' roller by commissioning him to design the famous crotch-shot cover — which opened by means of a real zipper to reveal . . . underpants — for *Sticky Fingers*, the première release in 1971 of Jagger & Co.'s Rolling Stones Records. And while it's true that, since the Beatles, many of our most prominent rockers, including Bowie and Keith Richards, have come from art school backgrounds, it wasn't Warhol's art that attracted rockers to him. It was something much more elusive, much more intangible, mysterious, uncommon, and ultimately perhaps dangerous. It was him. And the arty, pan-sexual, decadent, demimondain, infantile, ultrahip hurricane of which he was the invisible placid eye. Andy Warhol was a perfect adaptation in a self-conscious age: everything he touched was effortlessly subsumed into an Andy Warhol movie — including Andy Warhol. He was the film. (Which may be a couple of steps down from Christopher Isherwood's being the camera, but then neither was this Berlin.) In other words, not even "Andy Warhol" existed. There was only " ."

But if Warhol was the philosophical father, the theoretical sperm-bank depositor, to glitter and the Mercer and the Dolls and eventually the new wave, it was Warhol's boy Lou Reed who actually put a dick in it. I say he's Warhol's boy because Warhol, attracted in his increasingly less inscrutable way to the power, money, action, and boys of rock 'n' roll, lent his fame and bankroll to Reed's band back in the sixties, installing them in the Exploding Plastic Inevitable, his happening *cum* avant nightclub on St. Mark's Place (on the site of what would shortly be the original Electric Circus). But the truth of the matter is Lou Reed was then, as now, his own man, his own true original. And if his connection to the Dolls' music is less obvious than his connection to the music of, say, Richard Hell, it would be hard to imagine them without him. So excuse a digression.

His band was called the Velvet Underground after the title of a paperback about sadomasochism. As the name suggested, unlike other psychedelic era bands, the Velvets were grounded not in folk music, but in stranger and harder stuff: on the one hand, the avant garde electronic music of John Cage and LaMonte Young (to whom Velvets' second banana John Cale had served an apprenticeship); and, on the other, formulaic trash rock from the early-sixties Brill Building, where Reed had been a staff songwriter. The band had absorbed bebop and the Beats, and at Syracuse University where he had been an honors student and promising poet, Reed had been taken under the wing of the poet Delmore

Schwartz. All these disparate interests and influences showed through in some of the most deceptively literate, coolly modern and hopelessly awkward rock 'n' roll ever played.

Deceptively literate because the main songwriter's lyrics — which posited a desperate world, a life of compromise in the shadow of ideals, a world of longing for love and waiting for drugs (and then longing for drugs) that could itself have been described as a velvet underground — were so plain and his phrases so often curt, and frequently he didn't rhyme when you wanted him to or rhymed too plainly or too soon when you didn't want him to at all. All this while the trend at the time was toward the purple, and the steadily rhyming run-on, toward "rock poetry" that might express the acid and put its writer up there in literature with Lennon and Dylan. It was coolly modern rock 'n' roll because, for one thing, the main songwriter was also the main singer, but not much of a voice, which was OK, except his phrasing was as jarring as his rhyme schemes (and much weirder than Dylan's) and when he wasn't trying to sound hiply affectless, he was trying to sound passionate, which instead sounded like a masturbator about to get over (which may have had not a little to do with the amphetamines that fueled the endless movie of the Warhol galaxy in those days). Where other rock 'n' roll singers faked blackness, so did he — except he sounded like he was faking humanness: a coolly modern android. And it was hopelessly awkward rock 'n' roll (if you still need proof) because on top of all this — and (worse) underneath it — everybody from the drummer to bassist Cale (who tripled on keyboards and on screaming electrified cello) to the songwriter, who also played guitar (and who kept it switched to a bassy, unadorned jazz tone that was odd in contemporary rock 'n' roll, yet somehow matched his vocal timbre), seemed bent on fucking with the beat, turning it around, rushing it, reaching (in "Sister Ray") for some sort of rhythmic white

.101

noise, ignoring rhythm altogether, *sometimes* by design. In short and in sum, the main songwriter of the Velvet Underground was Lou Reed and the songs were an open window to his soul.

The Velvet Underground was not very popular. And they were probably most widely known, not for their music, but for the Warhol cover of their first album, *The Velvet Underground with Nico* (1967), which sported a peel-off banana sticker, a joke (maybe Warhol should have been a comedian — maybe he is) on the brief banana-smoking craze (a joke itself) that followed on Donovan's hit single "Mellow Yellow." I, for one, hated the Velvets when I first heard them; as, for another, did the guy from whose record collection I purchased the banana album for a dollar; I thought they weren't rock 'n' roll. And they weren't. In songs like the driven, febrile "Sister Ray" on the one hand, and the gloppy, spooky "I'll Be Your Mirror" on the other, in the fresh lyrical acuity of their now-classic hard rockers, "Sweet Jane" (in which "Jim he is a banker/ Jane she is a clerk"), "Waiting for My Man" (uptown, to score, natch), and "Rock 'n' Roll" ("Her life was saved [from the suburbs] by rock 'n' roll"), and especially in their death-rattle signature piece, the still-troubling "Heroin" ("It's my life/ And it's my wife"), which is Jim Morrison's "The End" made sickly flesh, the *real* End, and demands we face our most insidious compromises by selling one to us — in these and others they were assaulting the emerging rock 'n' roll orthodoxy, as much as anything else, and, if nothing else, they pushed the limits of what rock 'n' roll could say and how and with what kind of weirdo voice. David Bowie, Brian Eno, Bryan Ferry, Richard Hell perhaps, and the New York Dolls were listening. The rest of rock 'n' roll would begin to catch up when Lou Reed unexpectedly hit the Top Forty in 1972 with his second solo album, *Transformer* — not coincidentally, a Bowie production — and its wistful acoustic single, "Walk on the Wild Side," about Holly

102.

(Woodlawn), who "plucked her eyebrows . . . shaved her legs and now he was a she," and about Candy, who "in the back room . . . was everybody's darlin'."

Which brings us back to the Dolls, not unknown to Max's back room themselves.

Though the cover of the Dolls' eponymous first album, released in 1973, showed them posing and puckering in high drag, you never could have mistaken them — or not for long — for just another glitzy clot of Warhol Superstars. And it wasn't just that lead guitarist Johnny Thunders looked a little too genuinely greasy in his heavy metal shag-cut black hair and maybe a little too rough; nor that the platform-booted, tousled blond bassist Arthur Kane — described by rock writer Tony Parsons as "a drunken haystack in drag" — was too much the slob. It was that they were not capable of taking it seriously — not rock 'n' roll, not rock stardom, and especially not the back room. Nihilism on nihilism, and before it inevitably imploded, it served to keep them honest — and us, too. By which I mean, it kept us all laughing.

"Personality crisis," Johansen spat, mocking the determinedly screwed-up who gravitated to Max's and the Mercer and the Dolls, "you got it while it was hot." Off the rack, so to speak. Elsewhere, pulled over by a couple of overeager cops who want to know "where do I come from," the singer turns to us and, with a matter-of-fact *self*-mockery, says: "With this junk on my face/ It's so easy to see/ I come from Babylon." A tidy, regional double entendre (from these thoroughgoing regional chauvinists) referring not only to the Biblical city but to the Long Island town named for it. Still elsewhere, Johansen and the boys climb a fence to paint a mocking smirk on Lou Reed's "Heroin" in their own "Looking for a Kiss" ("not a fix," they add), mocking the "beautiful" trendy junkies who are, regrettably, "so obsessed with gloom." Always laughing — in particular at the scene around them — always with an edge. Indeed, sometimes it wasn't really laughing at all — and so just the kind of laughing I, for one, could dig.

Still, playing with fashion — and the Dolls at the Mercer were eventually right there in the thick of hip fashion — was surely more dangerous than playing with fire. The Dolls risked becoming merely the latest in fauve chic and finally tame. And mocking fashion, they risked becoming the court's jesters, fools. Sometimes they came close — sometimes during his wanderings in the rock/fashion desert, after the demise of the Dolls and before he signed a solo deal, Johansen — or his publicist — went over, what with his incessant posing with the stars. But finally the Dolls, at least, managed, remaining untamed and untameable.

The true source of the Dolls' untameability, their ferocious dignity, when all other acts of outrage — including their lyrical taunts — failed, was their truly ferocious music. And if you thought heavy metal's *too loud* was hard to take, the Dolls added *too fast*, the heavy metal disintegrating under the impact, throwing off lethal shards of guitar as it wheeled crazily around the room on the rims of its out-of-control rhythm section. That all of them — especially the rhythm section, but including vocalist Johansen — had a way to go before they mastered, before in some cases they *learned,* their instruments had a lot to do with their fundamental and inviolable alienation from the civilities of both square and hip — basically, if you weren't meant to like these sounds, you hated them, chic or no. Detroit's MC5 and Iggy and the Stooges (whose breakthrough LP, *Raw Power,* was produced by Bowie) had preceded the Dolls into this noisy far territory of rock 'n' roll, and they too died the commercial death. But the Dolls passed away not just because the world wasn't ready for them, which it wasn't — but then it wasn't any *more* ready for the Ramones or the Sex Pistols, who emulated them, four years later. It was that, taken as a whole, in sum, the New York Dolls were impossible. Their center could not hold.

Around the middle of summer 1973, the Broadway Central Hotel, a nineteenth-century grande dame gone flea-bag near Bleecker and Broadway in the DMZ between East and West Villages, fell over, landing on the Mercer Arts Center, which abutted it to the west. The Central could not hold either, literally. And though the Dolls would go on to spread the faith abroad, touring Europe and Japan, and in the next year, 1974, record their second (and last) album, aptly titled *In Too Much, Too Soon* — and Johansen would go on, albeit a decade later, to his first semi-hit with the *Live It Up* solo album — the collapse of the Broadway Central also proved to be the collapse of the golden and silvery age (such as it was) of glitter.

. . .

But could I really lay glitter and rock 'n' roll sex to rest without saying something more about the Stones? I mean, if together Warhol and Reed were glitter's father, what does that make Mick Jagger? Its grandfather, I suppose — because *before* the really long-haired hippie bands from San Francisco, *before* Lou Reed, *before* Alice Cooper and David Bowie and the New York Dolls (and, in some cases, *after* as well) there was Mick Jagger, rock 'n' roll's foremost androgyne, Woodstock Nation's leading homo-hetero. As far back as 1965, when "Satisfaction" was topping the charts, I remember the questions about Jagger. I remember a kid at summer camp that year telling me that my favorite lead singer, Mick Jagger, had slipped off to Sweden for a sex change. I remember *believing* it too. I remember my disgust and, finally, my profound chagrin. Indeed, everyone has known there's something wrong with Mick Jagger in the sexual department since there's been a Mick Jagger. Where Keith Richards has served us as the paradigm of the new mortality, Mick has represented the new sexuality.

Of course, Jagger has long been our leading black-white

too. And having mined black *music* for his repertoire in the sixties, he went on in the seventies to explore blackness itself, in such songs as "Brown Sugar" and "Sweet Black Angel," and "Some Girls," while taking up with the newest black music, the r 'n' b of the seventies, disco. And it may have had more to do with pride than with either a sense of responsibility or a desire to avoid protracted litigation that Jagger was so quick to capitulate back in 1973 when a black woman brought suit in Britain to designate him as father to her mulatto child. But my point is that, as with many of the rockers to follow, issues of race and sex obviously merged in Jagger's mind and in his rock 'n' roll. So in *Gimme Shelter*, watching some especially torrid footage of Tina Turner, the black acetylene-torch singer who opened for the Stones on the 1969 tour, we hear him comment wryly, self-mockingly: "Nice to see a *chick* for a change." But he might as easily have said — and perhaps he meant to (surely he thought it) — "Nice to see a *black* for a change." Because to the white kids he was that too. And perhaps it's worth noting that while some observers have pointed to Jagger's thick, sensuous lips as the salient characteristic of his pan-sexuality, others have cited those same lips as characteristic of his negritude.

When you put the two together do you get something like the myth of black lust cubed?

There was a renewed concern with blackness throughout glitter rock, whose practitioners were borrowing much more extensively from black music and black style, contemporary as well as traditional, than anybody else in white rock. The word *dude* itself, which Bowie put in another context, was borrowed from black street dialect; so was the name of the company that managed him, Mainman. More importantly, Bowie was one of the first established white rockers to write and perform disco — though it was Elton John, oddly enough, who in the midseventies broke through to black radio as perhaps no white rocker before or since with "Benny

106.

and the Jets." The Dolls also went to black music, sixties soul, for songs and moves, covering Gamble and Huff's Philly soul chestnut "(There's Gonna Be a) Showdown" on the second album, but also Sonny Boy Williamson's "Don't Start Me Talkin'" and the Cadets' 1956 novelty hit "Stranded in the Jungle," *still* in Johansen's act. So are the moves he borrowed from James Brown and Wilson Pickett and Little Richard — as well as (and, in part, via) Mick Jagger, to whom the similarly be-yapped Johansen might be the mulatto son who got away. Of course, as far as the white rock view of blackness and sexuality is concerned, Lou Reed probably put it most succinctly in a song that shocked some of us on first hearing it in Detroit circa 1976, but whose inflammatory irony seems almost quaint now in the post-punk years. "I Wanna Be Black" the song was called, and in it Lou told us why: "I wanna . . . Shoot twenty feet of jism/ Have natural rhythm."

But as for the Stones: from the very beginning of his two-decade rock 'n' roll career Mick Jagger has tried to embody not only a black-white, but a masculine-feminine synthesis as well — and today at forty, which as everyone hastens to point out is old for a rocker, having reached into himself for the hardest Stones albums (*Tattoo You* and *Undercover*) since *Exile on Main Street* in 1972 and a tour whose peaks rivaled 1969 and *Gimme Shelter* days, he would seem to be making the successful stretch for a youth-age synthesis too, proving teenagehood as the eternal season. Biracial, bisexual, and ageless, this British-born adopted American — he's also binational — subsumes into his supremely imperial self not just the disparate strands of rock 'n' roll, from blues to glitter and beyond, but something of the disparate, contradictory whole of postwar American culture, from A-bomb nihilism to latter-day utopianism to show-biz professionalism.

Finally, however, Mick Jagger's obsessions, the rock 'n' roll obsessions — sex and youth and blackness and danger — as

.107

silly, bizarre, as crazy and meaningless and loud and utterly irrelevant as they might sometimes seem, bespeak a deeper seeking: an obsession with true soul — that is, with finding one's own in a time so soulless that soullessness becomes a cliche, with finding an authenticity of experience and of self that might supercede laws and categories and so rise above the predictions and manipulations of the technology and its minions. And if the search sounds Nietzschean — and such a self would seem to be superhuman — that's only because it's so rare these days to come across a real — in the Johansenean phrase — "riff-raff human being."

The question now: where has the rock 'n' roll search led?

"With the 1960s emergence of a strong women's movement and other vocal activist groups," begins a 1980 issue of *Galaxy*, the house organ of the Gillette Company, "many companies wondered if a lasting shift in the country's values had taken place. If so, they wondered how this societal change would affect the manner in which they did business." In their wonder, Gillette, along with a number of other corporations, turned to the market research firm of Yankelovich, Skelly, and White, and together, corporate clients and researchers, came up with the *Yankelovich Monitor*, a report appearing regularly since 1970 that tries to identify and dissect social trends and tip its business subscribers. Basically, according to *Galaxy*, "the *Monitor* provides 'background music' for Gillette's marketing efforts." With, they do not add, a rock steady 4/4 beat.

Indeed, while certain heavy metal journeymen, commuting around their markets via business-class jet, were becoming the first corporate managers in rock 'n' roll, certain of the sharp corporate managers were becoming the first rock 'n' roll stars in business. In fact, soon enough there were corporate managers who, in some sense, could play circles around most rockers. And as far as sex was concerned, where rockers labored to present us with a bold new image of gender and sexuality, unisex, as some would have it, the corporateers managed almost effortlessly to turn us into it. But then it was the corporateers that gave us the pill, our license to license, in the first place.

As one of the oldest and largest American firms in the cosmetics and "personal care" field, the Gillette Company has always been concerned at some sort of basic level with sex. More directly perhaps than most manufacturers, Gillette makes and sells things that are sexual. And while you might argue that deodorant, such as Gillette's Right Guard, or shampoo, such as Gillette's Earth Born, or, for that matter, the Gillette Trac II razor are necessities of life, I would argue back that owning a plain bar of soap and wearing a beard, I've gotten along just swell. Of course, neither is an automobile a necessity of life — but you'll go a lot farther without a can of Right Guard in Los Angeles than you will without a car. In any event, there's no denying that for every ounce of necessity we buy in such "personal care" products we get at least an equivalent in sexy dross. And though Gillette also makes and sells Flair pens and Cricket lighters and Braun household appliances, and lately, Liquid Paper (invented, incidentally, by the mother of ex-Monkee Mike Nesmith) and markets the Welcome Wagon "community service organization" (those suburban body-snatchers), the sexy dross items continue to be the mainstay of its product line. So it should not have been surprising that when in the early seventies Gillette became one of the first of the *Fortune* 500 to get hip to rock 'n' roll, its first greatest hit would be with horny stuff, indeed a product that would come to represent the zenith of sexy nothingness and a truly great move in the American corporate boogie. But dig the context:

Imagine an American, a true-blue US male. A defensive lineman, say. College, Pac Ten. Imagine that the famous final days of the thirty-seventh president have arrived in the land, and football, a blood sport that president prefers, is again in session. As dawn's early light staggers up over Los Angeles, our lineman stirs in his too-small bed and realizes he did it again.

Again he broke training. Again. But, oh, for that one savory moment . . .

A pitcher of suds in each fist like the grips of a Harley and those happy tears at the corners of the eyes are like riding it without a helmet straight into the wind. Roaring through the frat house night, suds and sopors, sopors and suds. Jukebox screaming: "Call me the tum-buh-lin di-i-i — " Hey, that was my song! And then the Harley wipes out: dawn, and the lineman opens his eyes at last, giving in to the radio by the bed playing awful echoes of the night before. He snaps the sheet aside and before he loses the will, swivels to let his feet drop to the floor.

There, on the edge of the bed and pain, he sits, cradling his gigantic leaden head. Finally he pushes up and off and, wobbling slightly under the all-too-familiar cranial tonnage, careens toward the bathroom, hairy bottom popping out above the white waistband of his red cotton bikini briefs. In the shower he begins to feel almost subhuman. He chuckles. As he washes, he starts to sing like a fat Rolling Stone. He steps from the shower and towels off and slides into a nearly fresh pair of bikinis from the top of the hamper. He watches the pale, puffy thing in the mirror, now splashing on ice-cold water in hopes of startling the face back to life. He feels not at all terrible finally and tries to hold that feeling, brushing his teeth so vigorously that toothpaste foam rushes over his lip and down his chin like a symptom of cleanliness rabies.

110.

He shaves, and then laying the razor back in its indentation in the hairy, soapy, caked-on residue at the edge of the sink, he takes up a gunlike black plastic object from atop the toilet tank, running one hand partway down the length of its electrical cord to make sure it's still plugged in.

His right hand holds a comb. His left hand, he sees in the mirror, points a gunlike object at his temple. Unconcerned, he slips his left index finger along the butt of the gun until it catches and trips the trigger. The little tiled room fills with the noise. But this gun does not spew destruction. Instead, and quite to the contrary, this gun gives forth with something of the very essence of life on earth. And while his father had been happy just to breathe it — deeply and proudly — as a free citizen of this, the greatest country on the face of the earth, and his grandfather had struggled mightily for just a whiff of it in the rank lower decks of an Atlantic steamer, blithely now the young defensive lineman blows it at his head. For twenty dollars cash and only pennies a month electricity, this gun shoots air.

In 1971 the Gillette Company introduced the Max portable hair dryer. "That was probably the first attempt at getting men to have their own product," the Gillette public relations man tells me. "There was research that indicated at the time the product was introduced that men were using their wives', girlfriends', mothers' hair spray. Once that look began to develop — a dryer look, the 'Dry Look,' basically (and I think that those men who did not have normally straight hair also wanted to attain that look) — again, get 'em away from the female users' product and establish or develop a market of their own." And so in 1971, having already brought American greasers approximately up-to-date and out-of-the-closet with Dry Look hair spray for men, taking off from wild-eyed and, most especially, long-*haired* rock 'n' roll, Gillette then proceeded to take this idea of a masculine-feminine synthesis to the American masses on a scale that Alice and Andy W. and

.111

Lou and the two Davids (Bowie and Johansen) and even Mick, for all his calculated mass appeal, would never have imagined possible.

The Gillette Company is headquartered in Boston's Prudential Tower, a late-fifties, scenic-restaurant-capped high-rise and vintage American Bauhaus mistake, which is the centerpiece of the Prudential Center, the simultaneously misbegotten conglomeration of office and retail space that sits atop a vast semiunderground garage on Boylston Street and was once to have been the centerpiece of modernized downtown Beantown. Not strictly postindustrial — in that it does for the most part manufacture goods rather than provide services — the Gillette Company today, eighty years on, is nevertheless deep enough into the business of weaving fantasy — of selling images, literally, and sometimes, literally, of selling air — that it can still be accurately located within the broad mainstream of postwar, postindustrial, postuse American corporations. And, of course, as everyone from Tom Wolfe to Johnny Carson has observed, the hair dryer for men, popularized, if not quite conceived, by Gillette with the best-selling Max line, can be located right in the thick of it. By which I don't mean to suggest that men wearing blow-dried bouffant hairdos is important in and of itself. What's important is that Gillette's Max is a sign of the times and of the change.

Specifically, Gillette's Max represented post-Woodstock America and the assimilation of the counterculture and rock 'n' roll, the styles but ultimately the ideas as well. The Max represented that juncture where the corporation, to put it plainly, put it to the counterculture: you can fuck with sex, but don't fuck with markets. The Max represented corporate America getting on the putatively anticorporate bandwagon. The Max was the corporation learning to rock, and all that that implies. Actually, all that that implies was just what I was trying to find out when I visited Gillette one afternoon

112.

some time back and asked about marketing. Not that it answered.

I should probably mention that as far as corporate bad guys go, Gillette isn't, not really. Still, like most corporations, like most gangsters too, oddly enough, Gillette doesn't like to talk much — leastways not to outsiders — and usually does so only through its mouthpiece. Actually, it's probably harder to get through to a responsible executive at a large American corporation than it is to get through to a Mafia capo — or a rock star, for that matter. The corporation's mouthpiece — his shyster in the court of public opinion — is his public relations department. Ask to speak to a marketing manager, as I did at Gillette, you get the PR guy, the mouthpiece. Ask to speak to a research and development manager, as I did at Gillette, out comes the PR guy, the shyster. Sometimes, at some corporations, you're *lucky* to get the shyster. Just as its risk is limited, so, it appears, the corporation believes is its accountability. In a company such as Gillette, with its thirty-five thousand employees (ten thousand of them employed Stateside) and nearly two billion dollars in yearly sales, such a notion seems rather high-handed. In a company like Exxon, with eighty billion in sales and two hundred thousand employees, such a notion is dangerous. But, of course, buck-passing is part of the beauty of the corporate economic machine, part of the beauty of capitalism itself: it doesn't depend on people doing good or being good — anticipating, even, that they will be bad — for good to be done. All of which is a rather gruesome way of bringing out Doug Kenney, who is the PR guy at Gillette with whom I visited for part of an afternoon just before Christmas 1981, and who is not, by all appearances, a gruesome sort at all. The PR guy is distinguished from the promotion and advertising guys by the degree of subtlety with which he sells: he is not really supposed to be selling at all.

The PR guy might argue that he is only part of the efficient division of labor in the modern corporation, that his job is simply to free the managers of the profit end of the business from such tangential chores as answering criticisms, complaints, inquiries, and the miscellaneous cranks that accrue to any large business venture and to disseminate accurate information about the company and its products. And while he's right up to a point, the extent to which the public relations department insulates the corporation today — the extent to which PR guys insulate politicians and rock stars and just about anyone you might think of — can become instead a dangerous isolation. At the same time it can breed a vicious circle reaction on the outside that takes the form of righteous critics, hysterical complainers, and paranoid cranks (mea culpa), who prey on corporate PR departments, as well as thieves and vandals and even assassins, who prey on corporations in general, all in an effort, not always misguided, to regain the human touch or at least sever the antihuman vise grip. But even PR guys cover themselves. Accordingly, at Gillette, Doug Kenney is Manager, Corporate News Bureau.

As far as cubicles go, the office of the Manager, Corporate News Bureau, three or four cubicles down the row from reception, is rather sumptuous, if somewhat spartanly furnished, after a fifties industrial mode. Kenney rises and greets me from behind his desk, which is situated about the only place it could be situated, in front of the window. He motions me to one of the chairs that face the desk and the white winter sky behind. I tilt my head to block the glare and see. He's around thirty-five, trim, good-looking, and impeccably, even elegantly, dressed; formal-casual, you might call it, in conservative tie, tweedy brown sport jacket, and palest lavender shirt, to the left collar of which is affixed, like lieutenants' bars, a sort of tie pin made of his initials, DEK, stamped out in gold. The appealing flashy edge to this otherwise traditional look might be part youthfulness and part residual California,

114.

which, he now tells me, is where he grew up and earned his MBA degree from UCLA. He is articulate in that cautious, calculus manner of the corporate citizen, which he tempers with true warmth. Indeed, his voice goes on like steamed moisturizer. No doubt, he is a comer in the appearance industry. Young, flashy, and black, in a sense Doug Kenney is the archetype of a new kind of rock star: he is a businessman.

Kenney doesn't have a lot of specific information on hair dryers. Instead, he hands over an annual report and a corporate history booklet — following Gillette from founder King C. and his preposterous disposable razor blades up through Malibu Miracle Mask facial cleanser — put together for the company's seventy-fifth anniversary, and a sheaf of press releases, some with glossy photos attached, describing new products, most often the new Body and Curling Wand, which seems to be on the news bureau manager's mind. "You mentioned some appliances," he explains. "I didn't really get out the dryer line as I did the newer things, because the dryer industry pretty much has plateaued. It's not really perceived as a growth industry anymore. We're certainly into it and committed to it, but in terms of bringing out a lot of different hair drying products in the future, I don't see that. More into skin care, physical fitness, heat wrap/cold wrap, steam facial. There are some hair products such as Body and Curl Wand, which has done very well, which is really a more specialized kind of thing than a plain hair dryer." But when I press him on dryers, he dutifully consults a corporate "chronology" and reels off the rest from his impressive corporate memory.

"Okay," he says, looking up from the Xeroxed sheets of the chronology, "the product" — the portable hair dryer for men, that is — "was introduced in 1971. . . . They had gone from the simple toiletries line of hair grooming into appliances simply because there were other companies already on the market, namely Clairol, Norelco, GE, to a certain extent, and the market was seen to be available. We had established some hair-care products in that line for men as well as women, and it just seemed that — the Max for Men came out fairly closely after the regular Max line, so it was basically an extension of that. 'We've already introduced you to the Dry Look, folks. If you can use your hair spray, you can certainly use a dryer' — that's some of the logic involved with the message behind the product. But again, the research was there to substantiate that, or else it would not have eventually been undertaken."

I ask Kenney about the assumptions implicit in Max and suggest that they are similar for the makers of the "low calorie" beers — Lite beer, specifically — where dieting is supposed to be for women and sissies and beer is the macho drink.

"Yeah," he agrees, with qualifications, "but I think in both instances — and I think that's a good parallel — in both instances I think you were catching the male market in a period of transition, where they were beginning to accept different things. In the late sixties, early seventies, coming out of the sixties — the antiestablishment, the hippie period, whatever — going into a period where people were, say, looking more at appearances, the Dry Look was our first . . ."

"People were growing their hair long?" I interrupt.

"The hair was getting a little *shorter* then," he corrects, "and we said, 'Manage it better and do it this way.' The same thing with the beer aspects. The same thing with the heat wrap/cold wrap. We're getting people who are more concerned with their own physical fitness, and the cosmetics industry — or the *luxury* cosmetics industry — has certainly proved in the last five to ten years that there is a market for men's cosmetics as well as for females'. So there *is* ego gratification — macho notwithstanding — that can be fulfilled by the marketing of products that tell a man he can look good, feel good, and not be embarrassed by using X product or Y product. He can have his *own* basically."

We get to talking about product research and development — R and D, in business jargon — Kenney digressing to relate some of his experiences, prior to entering corporate news, as a product manager for Gillette's Lemon-Up cosmetics, and I inquire, regarding the Max dryers, about the development of product *lines*. Because if it seems that brand new products arrive on the glutted market every day, hourly even, it also seems that we are inundated with new configurations of the *old* products, all that "New! Improved!" stuff, things in new sizes and packages and with new formulas, what Kenney describes as "flankers." With the dryers, I note, there was first a Max, then a Super-Max, then a Pro-Max. "Is the whole development of the product set out from the start?" I ask.

"It depends on the technology you have available," he replies. "In the area of Max, or hair dryers in general, I think they started out with sort of low wattage, low voltage kinds of things, because this was really the first time people were doing this in their homes. Start off at eight-hundred watts, nine hundred watts — it might have even been lower, as a matter of fact — and you look at the acceptance of that and you look at consumer comments. You look at what marketing research says is the fallout. What do they want in the future? Want more power? They want more settings? They want hot and cold; they just want air? They want variable guns? They want it to sit on the counter so they can do it without handling that *plus* a brush or a comb? And that's how I think products develop."

When I follow up by asking Doug Kenney how the R and D department decides what products to invent or what discoveries to pursue, he is patient. My impression of research and development runs along the lines of Spencer Tracy in

Edison, the Man, i.e., the eccentric genius sitting around the lab dreaming. And though, as Kenney explains, R and D *does* do the scientific and technological research and then make the prototype of Gillette products, the real *inventing,* the dreaming, the new ideas, generally come from somewhere else.

"In terms of looking where markets are, where growth potential is," Kenney goes on to say, "our marketing research people are probably the ones who sniff out trends earlier and can alert both the marketing people and the R and D people as to what is happening with, say, hair styles — or lifestyles. So that they told, for example, the appliance division several years back that there's probably going to be a leveling off in hair dryers over the next couple of years: 'If we are going to continue our emphasis in terms of hair care, then some other things have to be accomplished . . .' They also look at what those trends are most likely to be: short hair, longer hair, curly styles, wavy, straight sixties, whatever, and then that information is fed into R and D, fed into marketing. Those two bodies within the division then start looking at product development, at what is going to fit into that — and out of which a product like Body and Curl comes."

One might say the invention — or, at least, the innovation — is not so much the new *product* most of the time as the new *market,* and the inventors are the market research department — with, Kenney relates, much significant data provided by outside consultants. He lists the major contributors: "Our advertising agencies are good resources for trend development. Our public relations people." By which he means to distinguish between those PR guys who work directly with the public and those, like himself, who work with the press. And lastly: "Yankelovich, White, and Skelly, whom we employ, is certainly something we rely on heavily in terms of long-term lifestyle development, and with all their sociological jargon that they throw in and all the research

118.

that they do, it has been very, very helpful to us over the years."

The house organ, *Galaxy,* in speaking of Yankelovich's "message" to Gillette, offers an insight into what we might construe as the message of its products: "One example of a major trend change reported through 1979 is one the *Monitor* calls 'The New Values Revolution.' In the past, according to the *Monitor,* most Americans led 'traditional lifestyles,' which included objectives of success, upward mobility and achievement. Those in the lifestyle also believed that the means to attain these goals was the 'work ethic.'" Then breaking down the information from Yankelovich's *Monitor* into byte-size bits, set off by typographer's bullets, and then into numbers, *Galaxy* continues:

> In the extreme, the traditional lifestyles included, among others, the following elements:
> - Don't be different. Buy what other people buy, what your parents bought, don't stand out.
> - The family comes first. One's own needs come second to those of the family.
> - One has to sacrifice in the present to assure having enough in the future.
> - In order to enjoy something, one has to work at it.
>
> The *Monitor* said that the traditional lifestyles, the majority view during the '50s and early '60s, began to change during the late '60s and early '70s. By 1979, the *Monitor* findings showed that only 20 percent of the U.S. population held completely with the traditional lifestyles, while 80 percent followed some form of the "new lifestyles."

And what would the new lifestyle be? *Galaxy* again: "The main thrust of this lifestyle in all its variations, the *Monitor* said, is an internal idea called self-fulfillment. In its extreme, self-fulfillment means that the most important personal goals are being able to answer 'yes' to the questions, 'Am I happy? Am I fulfilled? Am I interesting?'"

.119

More bullets:

> The means to these untraditional goals also are different:
> - Instead of conformity, people want to be different.
> - Instead of self-denial and living for tomorrow, live for today.
> - Instead of hard work, people want instant gratification.
> - Instead of thinking of others first, people think first of their own needs.

So welcome to rock 'n' roll.

Naturally Daniel Yankelovich, founder and front man for the firm, wouldn't know rock 'n' roll if it blew his face out (in the felicitous phrasing of the J. Geils Band), and has proved it by pulling together his *Monitor* survey results and some tidily representative "personal histories" into a comprehensive thesis on contemporary American life in the 1970s. The resulting book, published in the summer of 1981 and accorded the full royal sanction on the front cover of the *New York Times Book Review*, is about "Searching for Self-Fulfillment in a World Turned Upside Down," according to its subtitle and, with ominous overtones that were probably unintended, is called *New Rules*. While the master surveyor makes a lunge toward hip by picking up his epigraph from wimpy lit-rocker Tom Robbins's *Even Cowgirls Get the Blues*, he mostly ignores the hip origins of seventies culture — in favor of a more easily quantifiable economic explanation that blames OPEC. Indeed, rock 'n' roll goes unmentioned throughout.

In any event, Yankelovich's impression of what was going on is summed up by his client Gillette, again in *Galaxy*:

> These new values have changed society, and in doing so, have changed the nature of doing business. Companies can assume nothing about a customer. They must instead take into account myriad consumer attitudes, ways-of-life, needs

120.

and wants. They must also remember that the consumer's focus today is primarily on himself.

In broad terms, the Monitor findings indicate that products can now be placed in "we" or "me" use categories. "We" products are oriented to family use. Brand names in this category are less important and bargains are more important than they were in the past. For "me" products, however — those purchased for consumers' personal use — particular brands are important and price less so ... As a result, the market is becoming more and more fragmented, which will require even more attention to targeting products to consumers' individual demands ... However ... several of the Monitor's measured trends indicate that a positive selling environment exists for Gillette.

Adds Gillette's marketing liaison to Yankelovich:

"For example, people are interested more than ever in how they look ... and they are interested about products that will help them look better."

All of which surely does miss something of the profound disaffection underlying Americans' changing attitudes.

The *Galaxy* article concludes, not surprisingly, with a confident, steady-as-she-goes pronouncement from Gillette's vice president of corporate planning. "We look at the Monitor," he says, keeping one cool eye on "still more changes" expected in the eighties, "as a key part of the Company's efforts to scan the environment for early warning signals about what's emerging in the future." But what's interesting is that they didn't miss the disaffection at all. Indeed, Gillette — and perhaps American business in general — was aware enough of "warning signals" to call in the clipboard marines. And together, from a glass tower beachhead, they repulsed disaffection and captured the forces of sixties hip. Finally, of course, in a cultural Marshall Plan for Woodstock Nation — tacitly endorsed by such critics as Tom Wolfe and Christopher

Lasch — they divvied up what counterculture remained into carefully sized and attractively packaged individual lots, dispensed — at an affordable price — to eligible counterculturists interested in "self-fulfillment" for its own sake, in "narcissism," or just in the ever-selfish and silly "me." Now while Yankelovich, in *New Rules,* calls the business of self-fulfillment "sprawling, messy and unfinished," he nonetheless gives it — and, by implication, the counterculture out of which it was supposedly born — a conciliatory pat on the back as "a prime source of energy in American culture." In short: steady as she goes.

Surely I overdramatize. But perhaps Yankelovich understands. A few pages earlier in the book he writes: "Spontaneous transformations of life style are rare events, or so it would appear from history ... But every now and then a new way of conceiving life and its meaning arises spontaneously from the great mass of the population. When this occurs we had better pay attention, for this kind of unorganized social movement can transform America and the world." So saying, perhaps Yankelovich understands a certain sense of disappointment that what was to be no rules became new rules.

. . .

Doug Kenney is telling me in his soft, genial, even baritone about the marketing mix, the combination of advertising, promotion, and public relations by which they try to put across their products. "Does a company like Gillette have to do a lot more advertising than, say, a tire company?" I ask. "And especially for something as new and different as Max?"

"You have to qualify when you say lots of advertising or how much is a lot of advertising," he responds, with, again, a pedagogic patience. "It depends on brand. It depends on the category.

"I'm not going away from appliances, but it's easier for me

to relate to the stuff I was involved in. What do you have, a shampoo market? Each year it's getting closer to a billion dollars in retail sales . . . versus, say, a hair-spray market, which is, like, four or five hundred million. The makers — you've got, let's see, hair spray: Clairol, Alberto Culver, Helene Curtis — maybe four or five companies involved in the manufacture and sale of hair sprays in a market that's four hundred million dollars." The sales figures are staggering. One can only guess at the profits. Like most, if not all, corporations, Gillette refuses for reasons of competitive strategy to break down profits by category. In any event, watching out for cultural shifts is clearly no penny-ante game."

Kenney continues: "In order to reach their audience at a given time, either on television or in print, and where your user base" — that is, your primary customers — "is pretty selected at thirty-five to forty-nine" — that is, years of age — "although they're trying to expand it at the lower" — younger — "end with hair sprays called Soft Hold, that kind of thing, for people who don't like to use a lot of hair spray — but in order to reach *that* market you don't have to spend in as many places, or as much, as you do when you go up against the almost *billion*-dollar market with ten or fifteen companies competing in that category. In *that* case, you have to — in the jargon — make noise." But of course.

"You have to be seen in prime time; you have to advertise in newspapers and magazines, billboards — it just goes all over the lot. And your advertising expenditure in shampoo has to be at least triple what it is in hair spray — although you can make as much money over here." He makes a small, precise gesture to indicate shampoo. "On a unit basis," he adds, referring again to shampoo, "you just have to sell more than you do over here" — gesturing to hair spray — "in order to make the same kind of money."

Thinking of the possibility that a company might be something more than a distributor of cultural change, I ask Kenney about the importance of public relations to marketing at Gillette.

"We like to think that the public relations part is very important," he says, smiling professionally, "although we don't really get involved in product publicity out of this office. But the publicity or public relations aspect of products, we feel, is — I feel — is very important. Because as much as you are reaching your target audience by those other vehicles, you have people who either don't watch TV or regard commercials on TV as hype and really don't listen to the message; who may not be reading *Harper's* or *Mademoiselle* or whatever your magazine vehicle happens to be, but who *do*, for example, read their town weeklies and 'Dear Jane,' who writes that beauty column. If you can get a placement in something like that, there's that personal touch." He relishes a company with the personal touch. I am reminded of the episode of TV's *The Mary Tyler Moore Show* in which Mary, enraged by Louise Lasser as a bank officer who tells her she can't withdraw her time deposit before the time is due, protests: "It's my money!" Replies a smiling Lasser: "Don't be grumpy, Mary. *Banks* have to eat too." The corporate personal touch. But Kenney applies it here with a consummate finesse.

"The home permanent industry," he goes on, "is a good example of recent changes spurred by PR. Home permanents have been around for thirty or forty years — but always to a higher age bracket. Three or four years ago we took on a new public relations agency, and they had done research showing there was a new potential market for home perm: young people. They put together an exhibit, ran a contest, a sweepstakes kind of thing, at College Week in Florida. Part of the thing was you could go in and get a free perm. The place was mobbed the first day. And the amount of press they got out of that — the story came out of

124.

the Florida area and got play in just about every college town. And the company has dropped the user base, in terms of perm, to a younger skew."

"You can see that in the sales figures?"

"Yeah," he says, which surprises me. I had been under the impression that public relations, too, worked in more mysterious ways. But I do remember the office hippie in Detroit who went out to lunch one day with a scraggly mop to his waist and came back with a neat little curly corona. And then there was the tennis player Roscoe Tanner, whose temporary makeover into curls a few years back was, for some, almost as much a cause for comment as the fact that he made it to the Wimbledon finals. And then there was my brother-in-law, who topped his newly permed ringlets with a cowboy hat, which Dad, if he'd seen, might have called a mixed metaphor. Come to think of it, mostly I remember *men* with permanents. I mention this to Kenney.

"Sure," says Kenney. "The commercial was developed by the same people who did Silkience advertising for women — in *that* commercial, which was first released as a sixty [second] and cut down to a thirty, in *both* versions of that commercial they had one male model in there. He was there for maybe a second and a half or two seconds. Compared to the rest of a thirty-second commercial, or a sixty, he played a very, very little part of it. But there was identification enough in there that said, 'You're a man. If you want to get . . . more *body*, or whatever, in your hair, it's there for you to use.'"

Prolonged contemplation of the subtler techniques of mass marketing could probably induce an otherwise sound mind to some paranoiac tendencies. I wonder now about the connection between men's hair dryers and the 1975 Warren Beatty movie *Shampoo*, in which Beatty caroms off the stereotype to play a hairdresser as a hetero stud — who just happens to venture forth with a blower stuffed in his belt like a six-gun. And Warren Beatty a well-known real life stud. . . . What an image of a guy with a dryer! "Was that a Max in the movie?"

"I didn't see the movie," says Kenney flatly. "I don't know if it was." He continues: "We *are* approached, quite often as a matter of fact, to supply product to the filming of movies. *9 to 5* . . . The producers of *9 to 5* came and asked if they could get Liquid Paper for the movie, which was then supplied. The movie that came out last year, the thing with Kirk Douglas and the battleship . . . *Final Countdown* — they came to us. They called here directly, as a matter of fact, and asked if we could supply them with radio commercials from the thirties and forties era, specifically sports or boxing kind of things" — with which Gillette has been famously associated as a sponsor — "with a Gillette commercial attached to it, which we provided them. So there's some of that cooperation in there."

"Can you quantify any benefit from something like that?" I ask, by way of brushing up on my jargon.

"I think more than anything else," Kenney says, "it's a reinforcement of patterns that people already have. If a secretary seeing the movie sees the Liquid Paper on Dolly Parton's desk, or Jane's [Fonda] or Lily's [Tomlin], it may be a positive thing. It may be a negative thing. But it's there. But I think it would be very, very difficult to quantify. Because they don't identify this" — he holds up his bottle of Liquid Paper — "with Gillette."

As my allotted sixty-or-so minutes with the two of them draws to a close, I find that Doug Kenney and his company remain almost as opaque as Liquid Paper. I make one last effort to bear down.

"Your marketing people," I suggest, "will come up with the fact that people are growing their hair longer or taking care of it better, and then Gillette will *follow* that trend —

instead of *initiating* it, instead of saying, 'Why don't you grow your hair longer . . .' "

Kenney: "Oh, no. I don't think . . ."

"Or, say, when people are cutting it short," I interrupt, "would you ever try to work against that trend with your advertising and promotion to convince people that long hair should come back?"

". . . I don't think," he resumes placidly, "that companies have been that successful in establishing quote-unquote 'trends' in terms of appearance. When you first asked the question — we are, we *do* set trends in terms of product innovation. But not in terms of behavior or lifestyle development, because that comes from just so many different sources, as I think you'll learn a little bit from that [Yankelovich report]. There are lots of factors dealing with and hitting and bombarding people that affect the way they have their own lifestyle. I was just reading something this morning — I guess it was in the *Globe* — on Dorothy Hamill. You know, she's been the epitome of cuteness for so long now that she's sick of having her hair short and she's letting it grow. She wants away from the cute image. And I think if you look now at hair styles, you'd find you're almost going back to a longer style for women. That would have to be quantified by Yankelovich or our marketing research people, but that does happen."

I wonder whether Dorothy Hamill is Ice Capades or Miracle on Ice. And why "miracle" anyway? It occurs to me that these are oddly seasonal thoughts. I switch off the tape recorder and stow it and rise, as does Kenney. We exchange parting pleasantries of a seasonal nature and shake on it and then I leave. Outside on Boylston Street, the season is very much in the sting of the wind. I hustle past the Strawberries record shop, where the latest Talking Heads album is blowing its own kind of cold out of a sidewalk speaker. "This is not my beautiful house," David Byrne is lamenting over-anxiously, "This is not my beautiful wife." But perhaps another album cover in the window caught my eye, and I think now of another song . . .

Imagine that young American again, the defensive lineman. He has been graduated from college — but has failed to make good at the one thing college taught him good: tackle. The pros did not draft him, and when he tried out at training camps, they cut him every time. For a spell, there were too many mornings when he sat on the bed and looked into the abyss. Lately, however, things have been going very well indeed.

It was just a little over a year ago that a TV news director friend gave him a shot at doing the weekend sports on a local network affiliate, and it wasn't long after that when the other sports guy quit and they brought the lineman over to weekdays at eleven and then six and finally someone from the network picked him up to read scores between halves of the football games on Sunday: the *big* time. And now this: the president of the network announcing that the lineman had been signed as West Coast coanchor — with Tom Brokaw in New York and the actress and high school graduate Brooke Shields in Washington — of the network's prestigious evening news. Not just the big time, the *top*.

Surprising perhaps, but surveys commissioned by the network had found that the lineman was possessed of a surpassing charm: a great personality. But then he would almost have to be: he certainly hadn't gotten this far on looks. A big guy, hulking and intense beneath a heavy, protruding brow and with a beard which seemed to cover his entire face, neither did he have a keen sartorial sense. Suits were always short in the arms and legs and shabby around the cuffs, and his shirt collar invariably failed to make the vast circumference of his neck. The one aspect of his appearance that he did manage to get right with some consistency was his hair. He was proud of his hair, and he combed it and blew it and

128.

puffed it out every morning until it looked precisely as a successful TV newsman's should in the post–Alice Cooper era. And today, as he sits down with his pals from the newsroom at the front table in his favorite Polynesian lunch spot in Beverly Hills, he is most definitely a successful newsman. His colleagues propose a toast; he raises his mineral water and salutes back and then puts the glass to his lips. At which moment, a snide, LA singer-songwriter happens to stroll through the door. The singer-songwriter is mightily impressed.

"I saw a werewolf drinking a Perrier at Trader Vic's," Warren Zevon would later write and sing, "His hair was *perfect.*"

"**D**on't hit my hair!" yells Tony.

"Don't talk that way to your mother!" the old man yells back, taking another swipe.

With a cheeky street grace, Tony ducks again. Across the table, Mom is weeping silently. No hard feelings, though, it's just Saturday supper in Bensonhurst.

Tony pulls the napkin from the neck of his black satin shirt. "Can I go?" he asks politely, flashing irresistibly sad baby blues. The old man doesn't respond, taunting his son. Finally, drying her eyes, Mom says softly to go ahead. Tony grabs the white suit jacket and is off to the 2001.

The story of Tony's night out is, of course, *Saturday Night Fever.* One of the all-time great rock 'n' roll movies, nevertheless *Saturday Night Fever* arrived in 1977 bearing all the earmarks of commercial mediocrity: a faddish milieu; a journeyman hack for a director; a teen idol borrowed from a TV sitcom for a star; and a producer who had given over most of the all-important soundtrack to a washed-up Beatles sound-alike group whom he also happened to manage. But somehow the director turned out to be something more than service-able and the milieu turned out to be something more than faddish; and the teen idol star in his first movie role turned out to be John Travolta and magnificent; and most remark-ably, the soundtrack — by those Beatles sound-alikes the Bee Gees — turned out to be magnificent, too. What to many was a contradiction in terms is that it also turned out to be disco.

Twenty-two years earlier, in her introduction to *New Lives for Old*, warning us again about fear of change, Margaret Mead wrote: "Those who rear their children on the nostalgic memories of long-dead lilacs in the dooryard give their children's imagination thinner fare than tiny plastic jet-plane toys which crunch on the new scratch-proof floors with a sound out of which no one has yet written any music." Which may be as good a definition of disco as you'll find: artificial, antiseptic, attenuated, technological, the music of scratch-proof floors. If heavy metal was anaesthetic, disco was lobot-omy. And if not nostalgic, it was certainly invested heavily in the status quo. Disco was the ultimate commodity music, entirely formulaic and endlessly mass produceable. Disco could have been made by computer — and often was: the new generation of cheap and portable synthesizers was ex-tremely popular among disco producers, the genre's auteurs, who liked not only the range of sounds available, but the de-gree to which sound from a synthesizer can be precisely con-trolled; not to mention the money saved on musicians' fees. In a sense, disco was just a cipher of rock 'n' roll, a sign of it, a reductive abstraction that minimized, and sometimes even eliminated, melody and harmony and words in favor of the raw essence, the beat, which the disco bass drum pounded 1-2-3-4 relentlessly, in complete subservience to the needs of the disco dancer — the customer who, as in any well-managed retail business, is always right.

In a realm characterized by polarities of emotion, the reaction among some rock 'n' roll fans to disco still stood out as extreme. In Chicago a popular disk jockey organized as a pregame event at Comiskey Park a "Disco Sucks!" album-burning rally. Enthusiastically received, in an era of renewed book burnings it was perhaps not quite as funny as it was meant to be. But it was the punk movement that had raised the rallying cries of "Disco Sucks!" and "Death to Disco!" in the first place. Rock 'n' roll radio refused now to play disco, and the new disco stations refused to play anything but (and nobody played punk). If you hung out at discotheques like the actual 2001 in Brooklyn, you didn't go to CBGB's, or vice versa. In part, because most disco performers were black, the split was racial, representing a resurgence of an historic segregation in pop music, particularly on the radio, a not-so-latent racism that rock 'n' roll had always played off of and had once helped to break down. In part, it wasn't so much race as class that defined the split, with disco taken by would-be rockin' rebels as yet another garish accouterment of middle class strivers like Tony. And, in part, oddly enough, the split may even have been sexual, in that disco was first embraced outside of the black ghetto in the gay ghetto, where the popularity of dancing had not waned at the end of the sixties, and gays thus influenced the ironic humor and nonironic horniness of music and milieu. But beyond all that, there was in addition a simple, forthright hostility in rock 'n' roll, especially punk, to disco's machinelike, commoditized qualities, as well as its increasing hegemony.

But scratch-proof floors have a function and their own appeal, and besides, who or what in rock 'n' roll is *not* heavily dependent on the status quo? Moreover, for all its alienness, disco was still well connected to the rock 'n' roll tradition.

Long, monochromatic, dance-oriented rhythm pieces punctuated by the shouts and squeals and boasts and pleas of sex were James Brown's meat, so to speak, all through the sixties. But then smutty-mindedness goes back to Howlin' Wolf, the original Barry White, and beyond into the blues. The piss-elegant, upwardly mobile pose of disco goes back to Berry Gordy's original conception of Motown music in the early sixties. And the slutty pan-sexuality of guys like Sylvester and Prince is of course traceable again to Little Richard and the sick fucks — the Jaggers, the Bowies, the Dolls, and other glitter queens — who've enlivened rock 'n' roll from the beginning. The sing-along, clap-along aspects of disco were common throughout rock 'n' roll and came from gospel and, ultimately, Africa. The humor, common only throughout the best rock 'n' roll, was from blues. In fact, in a way disco was another new version of the old city blues, appropriate to the clean, white, climate-controlled, beeping and humming, post-industrial, high-tech workplace, as opposed to the nearly anachronistic Ford factory. And if it was hard to enjoy disco outside of the dance context, to just sit and *listen*, isn't the measure of good rock 'n' roll the other way around anyway: not whether you can listen, but whether you can dance? And who could complain about the beat in rock 'n' roll?

I could, for one. But then, like everyone else of my negative persuasion, I got turned around by *Saturday Night Fever*, by the Bee Gees' "Stayin' Alive" and "Night Fever," by the Trammps' "Disco Inferno" ("Burn, baby, burn"), and by John Travolta strutting the streets of Brooklyn. Like everyone else negative, I later fell for Donna Summer and "On the Radio" and "Bad Girls." And I gave in fairly easily to whoever it was that did Alvin Fields, Jr.'s, goofy, giddy "Let's All Chant." But for me, Disco Epiphany didn't really arrive until the utterly ridiculous group with the Indian and the cop and the construction worker in it, the one that had done a song about being all-American ultramasculine, followed

132.

it up with an ultramasculine, all-American song about being
. . . something else — and it went Number One from sea to
shining sea. "You can hang out with all the boys . . . It's fun
to stay at the Y-M-C-A." I mean, of course, producer Jacques
Morali's Village People, who not only got all America to sing
the body electric, but costarred on a Bob Hope TV special set
aboard an aircraft carrier. There was simply no denying the
Village People: they had the rock 'n' roll spirit the equal of
anyone. You could laugh to them, but you could dance, too.
There was something about the Village People experience
that made us all just a little more free.

If disco was just mindless escapism and commodity music
— indeed, another manifestation of our decadence — then
maybe there's something to be said for same. And maybe rock
'n' roll's search for authenticity didn't simply wind up grasping at air. Actually, the phenomenon of disco was amazing.
You couldn't have imagined it — not even, I suspect, if you
were Daniel Yankelovich for Gillette. And talk about Thomas
McGuane's "uneasy alliances": conceived in black America,
nurtured in gay America, and taken to heart by middle
America, in disco, discotheques, Donna Summer, *Saturday
Night Fever*, and the Village People was an impossible coming together of disparate Americans, an intermingling of
American subgroups and subcultures and individual idiosyn-
cracies that could have happened in no other place and time,
in no other moment. And if, say, rich didn't quite meet poor
(or did they?), it may be even more astonishing that punk
("Disco Sucks!") eventually met disco — in Blondie and their
breakthrough 1978 hit "Heart of Glass" — and got along famously, not to mention prosperously. And anyway, whaddya
want from pop culture?

Mary shoves back from the desk and swivels and hesitates. But then rises. She steps determinedly. But stops. She turns around and then turns back, raises a fist before the door and then freezes. She looks down; she looks up. She knocks. And hesitates. She turns the knob, opens the door, steels herself, and strides in. Finally, she's not a damn bit sure. "Mr. Grant," she says firmly, but her voice starts to tremble and the words trail away...

It's not that she's incapable of action. Depending on what's at stake and when, she can move more swiftly, more decisively than just about anyone. What's at stake is not often worth it. But even when swift and decisive, she's ambivalent. Beneath it all, there's always doubt. And if such an attitude conjures up invidious stereotypes of women, the "dizzy dames" and "dumb blondes" from the movies and television, that is unfortunate. There is much to be said for doubt. Under the right circumstances, doubt can be the wisest decision and most decisive action of all. At a time when human action can be so suddenly and universally and irrevocably decisive, a measure of doubt would be sacred balm. Anyway, Mary is a brunette and definitely no dizzy dame. Uncertain, scared, torn, full of stammered questions and stutter-steps, Mary Richards is a hero (and I don't just mean protagonist) for our time. Indeed, quiet, modest, kindly Mary Richards is a hero for our rock 'n' roll.

If only because the generation (or so) that has grown up with and on rock 'n' roll has also grown up with and on TV, there is a convergence — ignored in most rock culture tracts! — between the story of rock 'n' roll and that of television. It's not surprising that television has influenced rock 'n' roll, nor, for that matter, that rock 'n' roll has influenced television back. What is surprising — considering the technical (i.e., audio) and the social and political (i.e., censorship) constraints on the medium — is how *much* effect TV has had on rock 'n' roll music and culture. Lately, of course, it has been cable's MTV that has broken the music business wide open for new wave. But at critical junctures in the development of rock 'n' roll, of the whole rock 'n' roll culture, it was actually regular old *network* TV, particularly as opposed to radio, that made the difference (and pointed up, incidentally, that rock 'n' roll is almost as much visual as aural). Specifically, of course, I mean those historic moments that changed not only the music and culture but the world, those mythic Sunday evenings when TV-variety-show impresario Ed Sullivan introduced all America to Elvis Presley (albeit, from the waist up) and then, just eight years later, in 1964, the Beatles.

For the most part, however, TV's influence on rock 'n' roll was probably less explicit — which is not to say less substantial. In fact, Margaret Mead was just one of many observers over the years who has blamed — and credited — television for stirring up the young people of the sixties and seventies against the "hypocrisy" of the older generation. "People born after World War II," she told *Psychology Today's* interviewer in 1971, "were not brought up in a single culture defined by their parents or neighbors. They were brought up in a TV world where the people in power — who could in the past edit truth and set it up for kids — no longer edit anything, not even violence or sexuality. When Jack Ruby shot Lee

Harvey Oswald on TV, Mother could not explain that it did not happen." In other words, TV — like rock 'n' roll and with it — is inextricably a part of the American Noise. And Mary Richards is inextricably a part of TV.

Mary Richards is a hero — but of course she was *also* the protagonist of Newton Minow's "favorite" TV program, *The Mary Tyler Moore Show.* "When it went off the air," said Minow, the former Federal Communications Commission chief who gained a brief notoriety back in the early sixties by calling television a "vast wasteland," "I cried." But Newton wasn't alone. Indeed, though it never quite achieved the through-the-roof ratings of the *most* popular shows, whatever little it lacked in audience size was more than made up for in audience devotion. Surely — outside of soap operadom — there was never a more involved group of TV viewers. Nor a more diverse one.

When *Esquire* magazine proposed to do a tribute to the show and its star (whom they headlined, not inaccurately, as "America's Sweetheart") on the occasion of the show's demise (only one of many publications to do so), a veritable parade of the nation's literati — the kind of people who ordinarily might not admit to *owning* a "boob tube" let alone watching it — double-timed forth, eager to gush along. More recently, in the course of an otherwise high-flown literary seminar on Dick Cavett's program, the former chief book reviewer of the *New York Times,* John Leonard, favorably compared *MTM's* celebrated "Death of Chuckles the Clown" episode with most (or did he say "all"?) of contemporary fiction (which he *likes*). At the same time, the TV syndication company, Viacom, has bet big money — the most, in fact, ever paid for TV rerun rights — that vast numbers of the masses love *MTM* too and will love it enough to watch again and again and again. And thus far, if New York is any indication, Viacom would seem to have won its wager: the decision by a local station to temporarily shelve the postmidnight half of its twice-a-day, seven-days-a-week *MTM* rerun schedule to give the show a rest was met by a telephonic outcry the likes of which had been surpassed only once in the station's long experience, according to a spokesperson, when a crucial football contest got yanked off the air inside the last minute of a tie. Neither mistake has recurred. And once again, all down the canyons of Manhattan, three o'clock in the morning of the soul only means that Mary's on.

What could possibly engage such bleary devotion? Well, for starters, *The Mary Tyler Moore Show* was all at once the best-produced, best-written, best-acted, funniest, warmest, and most truthful series in the history of American television, at least. And about that of course, there can be no doubt.

On paper, however, you might never suspect it. On paper, in fact, *The Mary Tyler Moore Show* looks a lot like the same old TV shit. But then, compared to all the ostentatiously "relevant" and "issues-oriented" and "controversial" comedies that came up with it as part of television's belated response to the sixties, compared especially to Norman Lear's *All in the Family*, which immediately preceded *MTM* in CBS's Saturday night lineup, compared even to the comparatively mild *MASH*, TV's serialized antiwar protest, which immediately preceded *All in the Family* in the schedule, perhaps *MTM* was a bit old-fashioned and mainstream. Certainly it was less obviously different — starting with the hero herself.

With her deep-dish brown eyes and dueling Steinways smile, her face wide and legs long and lean, Mary Tyler Moore looked every yard the former Roseburg, Minnesota, cheerleader that her character, Mary Richards, was said to be. Cute and clean; perky and neat; lily white, Anglo-Saxon, and Protestant; full of doubts, yes, but to such charming effect; also, said boss Lou Grant, full of "spunk;" Mary Richards, in turn, was the embodiment of just about everything in television that is corny or saccharine or bland. A Dorothy Hamill of nonskid terra firma. "Miss Perfect," teases a coworker —

but even her very best friend takes refuge from Mary's perfection in the occasional jibe.

Her very best friend, by the way, is Rhoda Morgenstern (Valerie Harper), the wise-cracking, New York–bred husband hunting girl who lives upstairs — a contemporized Eve Arden perhaps, in any event strictly from formula. And which of these characters isn't on paper? At Minneapolis's WJM-TV, where Mary works as associate producer of the news, there's her not-so-secret admirer, the newswriter Murray Slaughter (Gavin MacLeod), a middle-aged sad sack who vents his frustrations in cutting one-liners aimed at WJM's anchorman; there's Ted Baxter (Ted Knight), that same anchorman, an outrageously vain, insufferably pompous, silver-haired numbskull who has enough difficulty just pronouncing the news, as Murray might say, never mind comprehending it; there's Sue Ann Nivens (Betty White), hostess of WJM's own *Happy Homemaker*, whose prim exterior never quite conceals the rapacious maneater underneath; there's a breathy-voiced, dumb blonde, Georgette (Georgia Engel), who later weds the dumb anchorman; and lastly, there's The Boss, Lou Grant (Ed Asner), a hard-drinking news veteran whose own gruff exterior never quite conceals — you guessed it — a heart of gold. On paper not much more than a collection of clichés, *MTM* on screen gives those clichés a magical twist.

As the series opens, the ex-cheerleader has recently turned thirty and arrives in Minneapolis on the lam from a live-in love affair recently gone bad — and the first twist is that in TV-land, in 1970, things didn't often go bad, and, secondly, love affairs of the live-in variety did not go at all. Another is that a single woman on TV looked for a husband — constantly, desperately, hilariously — not a job, and an attractive single woman protagonist over thirty years old simply did not exist. Still another: that after Lou Grant tells Mary she has "spunk," he adds, "I *hate* spunk!" and slumps back into his hangover, muttering. Furthermore, in 1970, on TV, it was a twist that Rhoda Morgenstern was not just "New York-bred," but openly, *really* Jewish; that Murray, the sad sack, was *really* sad; that Grant, the drinking man, was *really* drinking and, gold heart or no, his gruffness was sometimes *really* mean; that Ted Baxter was just enough of a buffoon to be almost *real*, an accurate reflection of TV-newsdom; that the dumb blonde, while not as dumb as she seemed, had to be a little thick to have married him; and that, down deep, *really*, the Happy Homemaker was not so much horny as lonely — but, deeper still, had nothing against getting her rocks off. Everywhere the real was made to seep back in as conventions were set up and then subtly breached: Betty White, as Sue Ann Nivens, playing off her own long-established image as a chirpy, prissy Happy Homemaker–type TV spokeswoman; Mary Richards living in a studio apartment, instead of the palazzos usually assigned people of modest means on TV, and sleeping on a convertible couch; her working in a TV newsroom and the parodistic show (Ted Baxter's *Six O'Clock News*) within a show that results; and so on — all of it amounting to the transformation of a group of standard TV characters into some recognizably twisted human beings.

But the big twist, what set off *MTM* from all the competition, was its transformation of those tens of millions of human beings in the television audience into a community. Which brings us back to Mary Richards as hero.

The greatest heroes of postwar American culture are probably not, in the long run, the Alice Coopers or even John Lennons. The greatest heroes of postwar culture are probably the heroines, that is, postwar women and the women's movement.

Certainly the rock 'n' roll movement owes to them. Friends, we of the mainly middle-class rock 'n' roll generation were mainly raised by women, who in the conventional, middle-class manner of the 1950s, pursued their life's work at home, serving as Dad's "housewife" and our mother. And when

142.

Richard Nixon and Spiro Agnew and other so-called conservative social critics blame the rebellious youth of the sixties and seventies on "permissive child-rearing," what they really mean is "mothers" — in much the same way that Dad himself used to say that Mom was spoiling us rotten in his absence. In fact, Nixon and his cohorts weren't far wrong.

Indeed, it shouldn't have been so surprising that with those women as our primary image of adulthood, amid the comforts of the new affluence and household technology, we should grow up to demonstrate suspicion, even contempt, for the conventional "work ethic" — not to mention the "real" world in which it operated — that we should become introspective and spiritual-minded, involved with psychology and religions and drugs, and latch on to ideals of "peace" and "love" and, for all our grandiose, world-shaking politics, tend in actual fact toward the most intimate microcosmic view, and thus that we should become disillusioned; that we should manifest an exceptional interest as well in the arts — a preserve, according to the stereotype, of (eccentric) male practitioners but female appreciators — and in crafts, in things "*home*made"; that the boys among us should let their hair grow long and buy hair dryers and put on platform shoes and even makeup and dresses; and that the girls among us, after they had gotten out of the house and into college or a job, should never want to go back. It shouldn't have been so surprising, the way our mama's raised us, that we should become the generation of boys that would lie down for the generation of girls that wouldn't stay down; that this generation of boys, in other words, should grow up to be a generation of men, *real* real men, man enough, human enough, afraid and uncertain enough, to live and work alongside a generation of women who are woman enough — like Mom, in one sense — to live and work alone.

And after all, it was a postwar mama's boy from Memphis who started rock 'n' roll and became its very first king.

.143

But while those homebound women of yesterday helped pave the way for rock 'n' roll, you could argue that rock 'n' roll did eventually return the favor to the outbound women of today. Which is not to claim feminism and the accomplishments thereof for rock 'n' roll. In fact, the relationship of women and the women's movement to rock 'n' roll has long been problematic and frequently diseased. Basically, the attitude of the counterculture toward women — whether "old ladies," "earth mothers," "groupies," or simply "chicks" — wasn't counter to the prevailing norm at all. And in the music business itself, in fact, the advent of the hippie turned things from bad to worse. At least the early sixties had their "girl groups" — Ronnie Spector and the Ronettes, the Shirelles, the Crystals, the Dixiecups — ghettoized and subject to male svengalis though they might have been. But by the late sixties heyday of the counterculture, with a few exceptions (Janis Joplin and Grace Slick) and not counting Motown (the Supremes, who were banished to another category, i.e., soul), the boys were taking all the bows as rock 'n' roll stars, too. Thus did the notion — based only in part on the male-dominated tradition of the electric blues — take firm root that, de facto, "girls can't rock." And while there would always be anomalies, a Carole King (who had earlier written many of the girl-group hits) with *Tapestry* or a Joni Mitchell, clearly it was going to take a fundamental change, a change in context, to establish women as regular guys in rock 'n' roll.

That change began in 1975 with the release of an album called *Horses* by a performer named Patti Smith. If the Dictators were actually first, it was Patti Smith who with *Horses* made punk's first big splash and who with the Ramones and Television (her boyfriend's group) would be one of its most influential exponents. And it was not coincidental that one of the pioneers of punk was a woman. Punk knocked down barriers partly because Patti Smith — a poet, a musical amateur, and most especially a woman — had a lot of barriers to knock down in order to gain admittance to rock 'n' roll. "This is the era in which *everybody* creates!" she would later declaim, by way of exhortation. And of course she meant women, too. Indeed, if she was not a coincidental punk, nor was she an incidental woman. Smith makes that clear from the very first cut of *Horses,* a three-chord ready-made of a song called "Kimberly," in which she seizes an overwrought, Ronnie Spector–style vocal from its old puppy-love context to invoke a blood love forged in the apocalypse of childbirth; in which she inarguably rocks from the soul and in which the soul is inarguably that of a woman.

The punk rock that followed Patti Smith, however, did not necessarily have anything to do with women. In fact, in some of its earliest and punkiest manifestations, it had a decidedly misogynistic cast — even if that misogyny, more often than not, was just another outrageous, ironic pose. Then again, punk did have to do with liberty. Reacting against the increasing corporatization of rock 'n' roll, the artistic conservatism and technical slickness, the oligarchic tendency toward "superstar" bands, the cynicism and greed, the mechanical efficiency of arena rock in live performance and so-called "MOR" (middle-of-the-road) pap on the radio, the punks sought to strip the music down, technologically, economically, musically, and lyrically, to where anybody could do it — and nobody could own it — and so perhaps everybody could feel it again. Implicitly as much a social and political movement as a musical style, punk aspired to reclaim rock 'n' roll's cultural resonance and reinstate the opposition on its foundations in the music itself and return rock 'n' roll to its roots as the truly popular, truly *democratic* art form. While its reactionary excesses sometimes led it down the same old dead ends — primitivist punks playing to a new lumpen and artsy punks playing to a new artsy elite, for example — punk fulfilled its mission more than one could have ever expected, revitalizing the music, as well as the opposition, and breaking open the music business with an endless proliferation of local bands playing small, local venues and recording for small, local record labels gotten up by their fans and local entrepreneurs. The anybody-can-rock ethos of punk and the do-it-yourself nature of the punk music business was finally the break that women needed. And by the late seventies there were more women in rock 'n' roll than ever before. There was Chrissie Hynde fronting the all-male Pretenders and Debbie Harry fronting the all-male Blondie and Joan Jett fronting the all-male Blackhearts. There were all-female bands, most notably the Go-Go's, whose *Beauty and the Beat* (1981) was the first all-female (that is, written, played, *and* sung) Number One LP. There were bands that were more evenly mixed, like the B-52's and the Waitresses. There were solo singers like Marianne Faithfull, redeemed by punk from the sixties, and Laurie Anderson; as well as groups like the Talking Heads, whose bass player just happened to be a woman, no big deal. And although — except for incursions by the Wilson sisters of Heart and Pat Benatar — heavy metal's macho maidenhead remained fundamentally unbreached, for women the music was at least beginning to live up to its best promise.

Which is still not to claim feminism for rock 'n' roll.

Rooting around for that point of convergence between rock 'n' roll and feminism, it finally occurred to me to consult Ellen Willis. A noted feminist writer, Willis is probably unique in that she's also a noted rock critic and thus a shining example of the rock-feminism connection all by herself. And while in the title essay to her 1981 collection *Beginning to See the Light* (also the title of her favorite Velvet Underground song) she readily admits to difficulties in reconciling her twin devotions to rock 'n' roll and the women's movement, at the same time she reaffirms her preference for the Sex Pistols — even their putative anti-abortion diatribe "Bodies" — over most "women's-culture music," explaining: "music that boldly and aggressively laid out what the singer wanted, loved, hated — as good rock 'n' roll did — challenged me to do the same, and so, even when the content was antiwoman, antisexual, in a sense antihuman, the form encouraged my struggle for liberation. Similarly, timid music made me feel timid, whatever its ostensible politics." Which sounds like a rationalization — except to those of us, male and female, who've tried to account for the enormous power of this idiot music in our lives, who've tried to understand how some dumb Rolling Stones song made us want to shake the world and how some dumber AC/DC hit on the radio this morning made us want to get up and do it again. Rock 'n' roll taps into some vital essence and helps us feel alive in an increasingly dehumanized, increasingly dead world — in other words, it pushes us to be free (even if that freedom must sometimes be delusion, the momentary freedom of drugs, perhaps, and so the simulation — but surely not the reality — of death). And in that way, rock 'n' roll has helped to fuel feminism just as it has helped to fuel all the important social, political, and cultural movements of the last fifteen or twenty years.

Feminism cannot belong to rock 'n' roll, of course — nor can no-nukism or the gay rights movement. Feminism belongs to its own heroes and its own hard-won history — which happens to go back more than half-a-century before rock 'n' roll plunked note one. And yet without rock 'n' roll — the freedom it suggests and the atmosphere of change and freedom it has fostered — it's possible that the feminist transformation of today would not be. In the concluding essay of her collection, Ellen Willis, for one, finally seems to say as much, kicking off a description of her own reverse exodus out of the Holy Land back to modern America with this epigraph, again from the Velvet Underground: "You know her life was saved by rock 'n' roll."

·   ·   ·

.147

Mary Richards is a hero — up there with the great ones, no gender qualifications implied — because she transcends her culture and time. But she was also a heroine. A young, independent, working woman at the time of the emergence of the young, independent, working woman, Mary Richards was an example, a beacon, even a standard-bearer — TV's answer to Patti Smith. And *The Mary Tyler Moore Show* was thus not only about a change in our culture and time, it was party to it. But, more than just being TV's answer to Patti Smith, Mary Richards was demonstrably a rock 'n' roll hero, too.

It's hard to pin down exactly why, but the feeling is undeniable. In part, it's because *MTM* shared certain values of sincerity and authenticity with the rock 'n' roll culture, at the same time sharing some of its ironic attitudes toward — and fascination with — the mass media. In part, in other words, it's because *MTM* despite its surface squareness, was hip. And in part it's because, despite its hipness, *MTM* was square. Indeed, it was *squareness* that lent Mary Richards, above all pop culture heroes, balance. Mary didn't react, but then she didn't quite revolt either — she simply . . . hesitated. That is, she considered. And in the end, when she changed, the change was more meaningful — ultimately for all of us. In a way, *MTM*'s Mary Richards functioned as a media superego to a wired-up generation following its media libido right down the tubes. Now there were *two* Richards to go by — on the one hand, Mary; on the other, Keith.

In any event, when I left a rock 'n' roll club the other night saying aloud that I had to get home to Mary, more than one person looked up as if to ask "Is it three yet?" — while Handsome Dick Manitoba turned animatedly to his little coterie and explained: "He's got a whole *chapter* on *Mary* in his book." Which is true. Which is also, in part, why.

Time magazine hated it. *"Blasted* it," says Allan Burns, which is why *Time's* adoring farewell to the series, an essay headlined "Goodbye to 'Our Mary,'" is framed on the mementos shelf in his office. But Allan Burns, who appears to have none of that tightly wrapped madness characteristic of the electronic show-biz veteran, is not really being vindictive.

. . .

Allan Burns is an authentic California beatific, and beneath the stylishly long and graying and gently neatened hair and in pleasing counterpoint to the drooping line of his pastel-tinted aviator glasses, he is smiling the broad, shadowless smile of one who communicates with the dolphins. Or is he the cat that swallowed the canary? Allan Burns does have reasons to smile. He has had a hit TV series that presumably made him wealthy but has certainly made him respected, which is almost a contradiction in terms. Allan Burns has achieved a California dream. He is golden — literally, too: of robust complexion, long, trim, unobtrusively handsome, forever floating, it would seem, in some idyllic fortyish prime of life, he belongs in his pristine white shirt, opened two buttons down, and is instantly and simultaneously an invitation to East Coast snobbery and its irresistibly sunny West Coast rebuke. Which is not to say he's flashy. Call him the mensch that glows. And though Allan Burns may not be the representative voice of the television industry in our time, he is just the kind of ventriloquist one would hope to find behind Mary Richards.

In college, before he flunked out, Allan Burns had wanted to be an architect. He was lured away from architecture and from college by television after a summer job at NBC as a page, the traditional apprentice slot there, from where he progressed to a position with the network's story department assessing new scripts, and then onward and upward, or just about. Because, in a sense, it was a round trip, and Burns wound up as an architect after all. Actually, his own well-balanced self is some kind of feat of architecture, but more to the point, so was his famous hit series. In fact, in the multi-tiered plots erected to accommodate the disparate concerns of its characters on a half-hour site, in the dangerously suspended jokes that soared out of sight in the opening minutes only to return at the close in one or another impossibly canti-levered punchline, in the quake-proofed solidity beneath its supple, fleshy facade, and literally, in its stage sets, *MTM* was an ingenious structure, elegant yet fully functional, with its depths of complexity — perhaps like those of its architectural cocreator — well concealed.

And just as the whole was meticulously designed, so was each of its parts. Even the heroic character of character Mary Richards — not to mention her landmark flesh — was imbued with an architectural quality. Indeed, one *MTM* episode suggested that Mary's heroism (if not her flesh) was shaped along the most venerable classical lines. In that episode, Mary is compelled to pick up the gauntlet when, under pressure from the station manager, WJM News hires a glib, pompous, talk-show-circuit author named Carl Heller to serve as an on-the-air culture critic, and he promptly takes off for a sat-uration bombing of "benighted" Minneapolis culture, eventu-ally doubling back to level WJM itself, including its news team: anchorman, writer, and producers alike. Mary is en-raged because the criticism hurts (and especially because, as she admits, it's not necessarily untrue), but she enters the fray because it's such overkill. And so, pressing past boss Grant, who is winding up to fisticuffs, she confronts Heller as he emerges from the studio, and, on behalf of the entire station, with trembling voice, she delivers a heroic coup de grace. "Have you no sense of *proportion?*" she rails. And in that climactic moment — presently to be leavened with literal pie-in-the-face slapstick as a forgotten setup returns for its punchline — the architecture of her heroism came clear. In fact, her architecture and her heroism were one and the same. Squareness, in a way: Mary Richards was a hero precisely because Allan Burns (or someone like him) gave her an architecture — that is, her own sense of proportion. And thus, we might infer, the golden rule is nothing but the golden mean.

Allan Burns did not go directly from the NBC story department into neoclassic video architecture. But while one might like to imagine, out of envy or perhaps out of a sense of dramatic proportion, that between the job in the story department and fame and fortune Allan Burns paid some heavy dues, that doesn't appear to have been the case. There were some setbacks — he was dispatched from the story job during a spasm of mass layoffs at NBC — but, at least in his professional life, they were momentary events: after leaving NBC, Burns took his budding talent for drawing and writing funny and, with a friend, formed a greeting card company to do "contemporary humor greeting cards," but within a few years the business had become so successful that the pair found themselves confronting a buy-out bid that young men with bigger plans don't refuse. Burns is charming, but he's also charmed.

"So I found myself out of work again," he recalls cheerfully, "and really wanting to get back into television. I sort of went in the back door by doing animated commercials and working for Jay Ward, who did Bullwinkle and Dudley Do-right and all those. This is all the time during which Jim" — Brooks, his *MTM* partner — "is doing fruitful work at CBS News, documentaries and all that. I was off frittering away my time doing stuff we're all a little embarrassed about. When you're a grown man writing for mooses and squirrels . . . I once said that to Bill Scott, who in addition to being one of the writers was also the *voice* of Bullwinkle. He would say to me" — and here Burns shifts into the characteristic goofy tones of Bullwinkle the Moose — " '*You* feel thilly??? I have to do *thith* for a living!' " The imitation is perfect. Burns eyes me sidelong, cagey. I don't laugh easy, but finally can't help it. Perfect. Burns's genial facade breaks into a broad, satisfied, mischievous grin and laughing crinkles around the aviators. And I had had him figured for the straight man.

Studio City, the modern quasi town where Burns's office is located, lies just inland over the mountain from Hollywood. Winding upward from the bleached, adult-bookstore realm of Sunset Boulevard through the residential tropic zone of Laurel Canyon, one crests the summit to behold this developer's spanking new parking-lot metropolis that has replaced the studio lots of old, its asphalt acres all freshly marked off with a veritable football chalk-talk of white lines and arrows that are the basic form of government in this place where cars can vote. Old Los Angeles has its out-in-the-sun-too-long charms, but this new Los Angeles is El Dorado only in the strictest General Motors sense. Past a supermarket the size of an airplane hangar and a couple of prefab drive-in banks, the rental car is seized by a big white arrow and slants left to deliver me slightly behind schedule to the guardhouse of a stubby, sunglassed office tower. The guardhouse, with paramilitary guard, is a vanity, one suspects, something the new studio moguls — the bankers and insurance execs — saw in a movie about the old studio moguls. There are no movie stars here, no lights, cameras, or action, no Hollywood glitz whatsoever. It would be hard to imagine anyone wandering in uninvited, let alone some latter-day bobby-soxers — armed with Soviet-made AK-47s — storming the place for an accountant's autograph. But the guardhouse does reinforce the feeling that this is temporary barracks America and that late modern living is akin to being in the army or maybe prison.

Checkpoint Charlie validates my visa and crisply directs

152.

me to the wrong office, where I am courteously redirected to another wrong office, where I am promptly misdirected again. At the last stop, I don't even bother to enter, halfheartedly shouting to a receptionist from out in the hallway. She looks up and, with genuine concern, says, "We wondered what happened to you. We called the hotel." She gestures behind her as I approach cautiously. "Go right in," she says, "Allan's waiting."

We are seated in what Mary Richards would stammer and call the "living . . . ah . . . area" of Allan Burns's moderately capacious office. I sit in the corner of the couch, Burns in a chair half facing me, with the toes of his loafers perched on the edge of a coffee table. Rocking slightly backward, relaxed, but not ostentatiously so, the cocreator of *The Mary Tyler Moore Show* is actually enjoying the not entirely extemporaneous monologue he weaves here on the subject of his own career. So am I. But then Burns and his partner are a couple of heroes of mine — literary division, that is, but *almost* up there with Mary and the rock stars. And if you want to believe that John Leonard is right about that "Death of Chuckles" episode being as fine as any new novel, maybe they're not such bad heroes for a young writer to have. In a postliterate age, maybe they're even perfect. And I mean *that* as a compliment.

The first series Allan Burns created, he tells me, was *The Munsters,* a determinedly lowest-common-denominator copy of *The Addams Family,* the popular and surprisingly bright TV comedy, loosely derived from Charles Addams's *New Yorker* cartoons. In TV parlance, creating a show, he explains, means developing the characters and the format and writing the initial scripts. In the case of *MTM,* however, Burns and Brooks continued to guide the series, supervising all aspects of the production as well as contributing story ideas and sometimes rewriting scripts, in their additional capacities as executive producers.

Because of some not atypical Hollywood fast deal, Burns resumes, he and another partner never received credit for *The Munsters* — which in the long run, he admits, may be a blessing. Subsequently he and the partner created the Smothers Brothers' first series — "not their good show," he adds, "but the bad show they did where Tommy played an angel" — and after that a series with Richard Benjamin and Paula Prentiss called *He and She*. Something of an update on the old Tracy-Hepburn vehicles, *He and She* was a short-lived critical success in the late sixties, and Burns says, "probably the first good writing I did. It was the first time my old partner and I were writing comedy that wasn't broad sitcom. It was believable people. It still had a nod toward sitcom in that they would get in fairly ridiculous spots. But even the old Dick Van Dyke show, as real as that seemed at times, would always have one where Laura got her toe caught in the bathtub spigot in the hotel and couldn't get it out. But doing that sort of thing whets your appetite to say, 'Comedy does *not* have to be sitcom.' There's a way of doing character comedy and reality comedy that's probably more satisfying than the Lucy [Ball] type thing — not that I put that down, but just for me."

With *I Love Lucy*, which just about invented the form, and to a lesser extent with the later and infinitely inferior *Here's Lucy*, Lucille Ball was queen of the sitcom. Her name crops up often in conversation with both Burns and Brooks, but then sitcom is their bête noire. Burns runs down some more history:

"I did take one minor step back in one way, after *He and She* went off, in doing *Get Smart*" — the spy spoof starring Don Adams, to which Mel Brooks also contributed, and one of TV's funniest slapsticks — "which, although it was an admired show and fun to do, was a step back toward cartoon and unreality. I did *Get Smart* for a year. And then went off to write a couple of movies that didn't get made. At about

154.

that time Jim and I met. He was working for David Wolper, I believe, doing documentary work, and we liked each other. He had a very comedic turn of mind, and I always wondered what he was doing serious documentaries for, and he always kept pumping me about comedy and loving my ideas and, 'Jeez, why aren't I doing that?' and all that sort of stuff. Then while I was off doing screenplays, Jim, along with Gene Reynolds [later producer of *MASH*], created *Room 222* and asked me to come see the pilot. And I said, 'No, I don't want to see the pilot because if I do, I'll like it and I'll start to write for television again and I don't want to write for television again' — this is, mind you, twelve years ago or something — thinking I was finished with television. But he still kept working on me, so I went and saw the pilot and said, 'Okay, where do I sign up?' The first year was terrific stuff. The show later degenerated quite a bit, and became what ABC wanted it to be, which was considerably less worthwhile."

A comedy-melodrama set in an urban high school, *Room 222* was the first serious effort on TV to depict the intricacies of contemporary race relations. Sometimes Polyannaish — but sometimes, in that first year, warming, too — nevertheless it was a breakthrough. Sadly, it was *still* a breakthrough nearly a decade later, in the late seventies, when MTM Enterprises essayed a similar series called *The White Shadow*, which, as Burns notes, also met a similar fate — and then cancellation.

"As a matter of fact," he says, "I saw something in the paper this morning about *The White Shadow*, an article somebody had written about 'Isn't it too bad what's happened to *The White Shadow*?' Because it started out as a sort of hard-hitting, gritty — if not totally accurate — portrait of blacks in high schools, minorities and all that, and it has lightened up to the point where it's almost frivolous. And somebody said, 'It's almost like *Room 222*.' And I almost took umbrage. And yet I remember that this guy's recollection of

Room 222 was probably not the first year or second year, but the fourth and fifth years, in which it did become sort of lightweight." Burns explains the process.

"The networks begin to meddle in a show that is not working completely to their satisfaction. It may be getting marginal ratings and they think it should be getting huge ratings. Or it may not be getting very good ratings and they may just want to try and save it. And they don't know how. Literally, they do not know what the fuck they're doing. I seldom have met *anybody* in the networks who does — and this may sound arrogant, but it's true — because they're not creative people, for the most part. They're guys out of sales and they're lawyers and they sort of end up with these jobs by default — generally because nobody in the creative community wants them. Which maybe people in the creative community should share the blame for." Burns doesn't, it turns out, smile all the time. "This is a digression," he apologizes, not smiling, "but we'll get back to that because I have some really strong feelings about the people who run television."

"Writing *Room 222*," Burns now tells me, "was the first chance I had to work with Jim head-to-head." It was also, he adds, where he and Brooks got to know Grant Tinker, who was the production company executive overseeing the show's development ("a job for which he was clearly overqualified"), and where Tinker first made the pitch for *MTM*. I ask Burns what the original idea was for that creation.

"What we wanted to do," he replies readily, "was divorce, that Mary was a divorced person. We wanted to say she's a person who is over thirty years old. We wanted to be real about that and not do Doris Day — where Doris at forty-five was still playing an ingenue. And Mary — as attractive and pretty as she is — *looks* thirty. Let's *say* she's thirty, we thought. But what's she doing single? Lucy was single [on *Here's Lucy*] . . . that's what they used to say at CBS: 'Lucy's single and nobody ever asks why.' And we said: 'But that's

156.

Lucy and that's sitcom and we don't want to do that kind of thing.' They'd say: 'And Doris is single and nobody ever asks why.' And we'd answer the same thing — we also weren't great admirers of *that* show, which was then on CBS. We said we wanted to know why a girl at thirty is single. Chances are, at *that* time, it was because she was divorced.

"Now this is really pre–women's lib by about three and a half minutes. That whole women's movement began literally as we were developing the show. All the Germaine Greer, Kate Millett, Gloria Steinem stuff hadn't happened yet; it was almost ready to happen. So we were pretty limited in our thinking saying that a woman who was thirty had to be divorced to be single. That she might *never* have been married — we couldn't imagine that."

Why did they want her to be divorced?

"It just seemed that nobody had ever done that," answers Burns. "That was the one thing that had never been done. It was a new idea for television. At one time or another every comedy writer we knew had pitched the idea and been turned down. But we thought that with Mary we could get away with it because Mary . . ." Burns falters momentarily. The pause seems to sigh: you just have to understand about TV. But with a deep-breath effort he tries to make it clear: "There were all those negatives whenever you went in with that idea. You'd say, 'I want to do this show about divorce' and see the network executives' eyes glaze over because they'd heard it six million times before. And they always had stock answers — which were all from research: 'People hate people who are divorced. If they're divorced they've failed and people don't want to watch failed people. They want to have heroes.'

"So anyway, we went back East and had a meeting with Mike Dann" — then head of CBS programming and the penultimate authority regarding what shows would air and where in the schedule — "and there they were: the research guys

... I'll never forget. We were in this sort of womb of a room. It was an executive screening room that in the bright of day was *enormously* dark and everybody was sort of in shadow, and there was a light that came down and hit a table, but everyone was off it and you had to look at people through the shaft of light and they were . . . just shapes.

"It was an awful feeling," he goes on, "such a downbeat atmosphere. Bob Wood" — the innovative former CBS president and ultimate programming authority — "was there, but he wasn't saying much. And Dann sat there and listened. And the programming guys were, in the main — this will sound wrong when I say it — were, in the main, New York-bred, divorced, Jewish guys who were sitting in this room and telling us" — based on the research guys' data — "that what America hated most of all were people from New York, people who were divorced, and people who were Jewish. The only thing we had suggested that nobody hated was that she [Mary] was a woman. Oh, and people with mustaches, America hates people with mustaches. And Mary clearly did not have a mustache, but those were the only two things going for her."

Burns's point, which may not be new but nevertheless remains crucial, is that the contempt network television radiates at its audience is the self-contempt in which network television is grounded. The point may not be new because the self-contempt of the networks is very much the self-contempt of the old Hollywood moguls tarted up with pseudoscience. But the flattening that results, so much more severe, so much more evident in TV than it was in movies, is also very much in line with the general flattening perpetrated by technology. And so perhaps if the TV execs didn't flatten ethnicity — and diversity and humanness in general — the technology would; and does, no doubt. But listening to Burns, what surprises me most is not the programmer's timidity, but their bad business sense. No wonder the audi-

158.

ence is turning to cable or video games, or simply turning off, as they are in mounting, unprecedented numbers: what the TV programmers and research guys, for all their blinking, beeping quantitative computer analysis, fail to see *at the bottom line* of which they're so enamored is that while Hollywood (or Studio City) is spooning out Velveeta, the nation is binging on ethnic food.

But it's the same all over: at the record companies today, no less than at the TV companies, no less than at Chrysler or eventually, no doubt, at Gillette — for all the white-smocked, research-guy minions of Yankelovich. Corporate America is more and more out of touch with the American people, who since the sixties and the counterculture, since Vietnam and Watergate, since rock 'n' roll, have become altogether too skeptical on the one hand and too open on the other, too big and unflattened and *free*, basically, to be captured by any quantifying machine. So corporate America resorts more and more to the tactics of takeover and merger, to monopoly, to a kind of capitalistic totalitarianism in order to get us all back in the checkout line. Finally, the personal touch must clench.

Allan Burns resumes: "We had a long flight back to LA from New York. We were massively depressed. We felt we had something good but we were on the verge of saying, 'Just forget it.' But Grant Tinker had been so decent with us, and we liked Mary so much that we felt we owed them and thought, let's give it a week. And in that interim time, that was when we came up with the newsroom idea and all those characters, which excited us a little.

"But we still had that nagging thing about divorce, which we wanted" — but which they obviously did not get. Burns continues, perhaps a little resigned: "So we simply gave on that, quite a bit." Now perhaps a little defensive, he adds: "But we did insist that she have a past history, that — and we did this in the pilot and CBS again tried to get us to take

.159

it out — that she had been having this long-term affair with a medical student, and since his graduation and hanging up his shingle he still didn't want to get married. And she said, 'Screw you, buddy,' and left the town they were in — which was something like Rochester, Minnesota, where the Mayo Clinic is — and there was all this kind of feeling that she came to Minneapolis to start up a new life. We wanted that feeling and CBS thought it was tacky, that she had had an affair with somebody and all that business and 'Why must you insist on this.'" Burns brightens. "But it was the one thing we insisted on holding on to, and I'm glad we did. Because it established singleness, and I think singlehood was the one thing we had to sell. It was always an important part of our series.

"With the women's movement breaking about that time, we were able to latch onto that and really use it in the story. And we had a lot of women writing for us who were into that." At a time, I might add, when there weren't a lot of women writers in television — not that there are now. "So it gave us a lot of perspective the show would not have had if we had just ignored it, her past, her singleness, and stuck her out there and said she's a secretary, or whatever. But the girl was really attempting to succeed in a male-oriented world, and she was scared about it, which most girls were at the time. Even the women writers who were working for us were tentative about it, trying something new, and it really gave us an undertone to the whole show which I always felt was important. Even if it wasn't always obvious, it was implicit."

Predictably, CBS remained unhappy with the prospective series even after the fine first few shows were already in the can. Burns enumerates some of the reasons why. "We still had this Jewish girl, Rhoda Morgenstern. 'Stick a pin in that one,'" he says, in imitation of the programmers. "Cloris Leachman, the character she played [Phyllis Lindstrom, Mary's downstairs neighbor], was a 'very unpleasant character' — this was all their research after we did the first show; they tested it, and this all came back to us. 'Mary's a loser, even in this part, because of the boyfriend, the lost boyfriend; she's a loser.' And a very pedantic vice president at CBS, who's now a very pedantic vice president at NBC, had us to lunch over there, a long, boring lunch, where he told us one by one what the problems were with our series. And he's a guy who's never produced anything successful in his life — he's tried, but never has. And one of the points was, he's saying about Edward Asner: 'Edward Asner is one of the really fine dramatic actors in television; I'm underlining the word *dramatic* . . .' That's the way he talked, boring as shit: '*Dramatic* actor, *dramatic* — are you hearing me? — *dramatic* actor; why don't you think more about that . . .' Needless to say, there's some satisfaction that Ed won four, five comedy Emmys for what he did, as did the Jewish girl, you know, as did all of them. Those were nice victories."

In its first run, though consistently drawing thirty and more million viewers each week (an awesome number anywhere but TV), "the show was never a smash hit," according to Burns. "We would languish in the bottom of the top ten or the next twenty, so we seldom got up *very* high. I think we hit second once, and that was a fluke. It was a long-term show that was well respected, got good healthy numbers, but it was never a runaway smash hit." So, in a very rough sense, perhaps CBS and the research guys were right after all. Then again, perhaps ratings lie.

Ratings, of course, are a completely gross evaluation of reality, as even the networks themselves realize, which is part of why they have research guys. Some of the things that ratings can't measure are heart and soul and brains — how much a show has, as well as how much it elicits in return. And by such criteria *MTM* would have to be counted a runaway smash indeed. I ask Burns to describe the show's fundamental appeal.

"I think what people liked about the show," he says quietly, "was its underdog quality. That *everybody,* even the biggest winner in the show, was identifiably an underdog. *Mary* was — *despite* her prettiness and her good legs and her popularity with all the people around. She was somebody who was always fighting an uphill battle. I think people could identify with that. I have talked to so many women who said, 'I worshiped that show because it was my *life,* it accurately portrayed what it was like to be a single working woman in the seventies.'" If in his enthusiasm Burns becomes a bit self-serving momentarily, that's not to say he isn't accurate. He chuckles now describing their mangy underdog.

"The station that Mary worked for was a struggling station, and Lou Grant was a not altogether successful news director who had a drinking problem and a wife who left him and a pain-in-the-ass anchorman who was none too bright and who he had to deal with *every day;* and there were people who fantasized that there was something going on between Mary and Lou — all of which was implicit. And I think that was its major quality that people liked, that indefatigable underdog, never quite beaten. Certainly Rhoda was part of that: the girl fighting her weight all the time and fighting it with" — here he makes a special stress — "*wit* and finally triumphing to a degree and getting her act together" — he stresses again — "*almost,* never totally, just getting it together enough, but never triumphing. And the triumphs in the show were small triumphs and believable ones. I don't think we ever did much that was out of the realm of believability. We never wrapped anything up and tied a ribbon around it. That was Jim's *grail,* that we would never solve major problems in a half hour. If you can make that one step toward a solution or an understanding, that's a lot."

"We were writing *people*," says Jim Brooks in his office overlooking Central Park, across the country from his erstwhile partner. "We used to get mad at everybody who said *sitcom* to us. We were *paranoid* about it. We just didn't want to hear that phrase. People would say *sitcom* and we felt reduced and demeaned by the phrase and felt it didn't . . . but we were *crazy*. We would *strangle* people who said it. We just didn't want to hear it. We knew we were doing people. We weren't writing situations."

Brooks is New York to Burns's California, Lennon to Burns's McCartney, Rhoda even to Burns's Mary. Edgy where his old partner is bemused, slightly disheveled where his partner is smoothed down, dark-haired even where he is light, Brooks nevertheless shares with Burns an almost naive openness and a genuine generosity of spirit. There is little about either man that suggests the jiving, high-powered TV pro — which may have something to do with the relative low power of the writer in the TV hierarchy. There's a genuineness in general about both of them. In fact, I enter Brooks's office to find him dumbly staring down the nearly blank sheet rolled into his old manual, complaining, like the lowliest among us, about some diabolically unyielding material. That extra measure of welcome in his manner I instantly recognize as relief that distraction has come at last.

Softening, but not slowing, Brooks continues to lay out some of the difficulties with creating character comedy in a sitcom world. "The tradition in television comedy up till that time was that everything would end up to a great block scene, a great block comedy scene at the end where all the miscues came together. And we moved that scene. We did the fun scene the second scene into the show and then went someplace else. As we were trying to find ourselves, people kept trying to pull us back and say, 'Well, what you're trying is this . . .' NO! No, *please*, we're *not* doing that. . . . So that was a struggle until we got our feet."

When I ask him about TV shows he has admired, Brooks rattles off a list, remarkable for its nonbrevity, that includes the old Dick Van Dyke show, Burns's *He and She*, *Get Smart*, the Sgt. Bilko series starring Phil Silvers, *Car 54, Where Are You?*, and finally *All in the Family*. "*All in the Family*, as a show that came along with us," he says, "knocked me out. I just think *All in the Family* has real greatness in it."

Premiering on CBS just half a season after *MTM*, and later joining it as part of CBS's invincible Saturday night lineup, *All in the Family* was the most watched comedy series of the last decade, as well as, not coincidentally, the most controversial. And while today the Smithsonian counts Archie Bunker's armchair in its collection of contemporary Americana, it began its nine-year run by continuously stirring up hornets' nests, agitating guardians of decency from coast to coast by repeatedly testing the limits of both permissible language and subject matter on television. Let-it-all-hang-out, do-your-own-thing, terribly righteous and terribly hip, *AITF* was Lenny Bruce as sitcom, the definitive post-Woodstock TV show. It certainly changed the face — if not the nature — of broadcast TV, specifically by opening it up to a never-ending parade of maudlin, message-laden, so-called "issue-oriented" television productions offering soft-core sensationalism in the guise of public service. But after numerous declarations of admiration for the show, Allan Burns sums up the *All in the Family* success formula in much the same way: "It said things that were taboo, and that got people's attention." One of the things it said that was taboo on TV was "nigger." Some critics credit the show for the resurgence of that epithet over the last ten years, much as its BBC forebear

164.

'Til Death Do Us Part was said to have rekindled racist embers in the UK in the late sixties.

MTM took a somewhat different approach, Jim Brooks is explaining.

"But sometimes," I prod, "you dealt in the same things . . ."

"Never with an ax to grind," he responds, "and never with a point to make."

"But sometimes a point did come across."

"Because they were consistent with the characters we were writing. Not *our* point," Brooks insists. "*All in the Family* — which I just think could be one of the great achievements in popular culture; I can't praise it enough — but there was never any question that Norman Lear's ideas, thoughts, and values were being projected every week. We didn't want that. . . . I loved that we coexisted that way at the same time. But it wasn't what we wanted to do."

"Still, when it did come across," I continue, "say, a reference to Nixon . . ."

"Jokes, though, jokes. Our point would be — the consistent thing that I think we tried to do was not to take easy shots. Basically, the things that we tried to do were good writing. Not to have one-dimensional things, not to have easy marks. We had our biggest argument because, under the pressure of deadline, I was unable to stop a show about anti-Semitism. And it was the only message show we ever did. And I just hated doing it. I hated doing it."

"I don't remember it," I tell him.

"It's not a memorable show. Somebody didn't like Rhoda 'cause she's Jewish. And if you saw it, you wouldn't get upset about it; you'd just say, 'Oh, that's a nice show,' I guess. But it wasn't what *Mary Tyler Moore* should have been doing."

Allan Burns has described the *MTM* approach to current events quite succinctly: "Instead of dealing with issues, we dealt with getting through the day." Which of course is the only place the "issues" of our day — the politics, the economics, the sociology, and the research guys' statistics — have any meaning. Which is also why *The Mary Tyler Moore Show* finally has more meaning than *All in the Family*. For all its moments, particularly for all the brilliance of Carroll O'Connor's Archie, *AITF* is just yesterday's papers. While *The Mary Tyler Moore Show* remains fresh by being very much like its hero, in whom the ideological is never less than personal.

MTM pulled off one of its funniest bits of "issue-oriented" comedy — not much more actually than an aside — in the episode in which news director Grant, much like real-life news directors across the country at the time, finally succumbs to the pressures to hire a woman for an on-the-air position — typically, as an editorialist presenting "a woman's point of view" rather than as a reporter. The woman picked for the job, after the requisite audition alongside anchorman Baxter, also happens conveniently to be black, i.e., two tokens for the price of one. In any event, at the end, on her way to the personnel department, she again encounters Baxter, who is drifting across the newsroom in a vast empty thunderhead of self-importance. "Oh hi, Mr. Baxter!" says the new editorialist. "Remember me?" Arching an eyebrow in imitation of intelligence and flashing a dazzling smile of self-recognition, Baxter shoots back cheerily, without pausing, "Sure! You're the black one!" And then off he purposefully drifts. And in that throwaway is contained more about race in America, more about the bland, self-congratulatory racism of the liberal, post-sixties, post-Woodstock era, than was contained in a dozen strenuously didactic "message" shows.

I cite this show to Brooks. He cites back: "And Gordy being the weatherman, and always for the first group of shows — because he was John Amos and black — everybody always assumed he was the sports guy. Why does everybody as-

166.

sume..." Brooks laughs. "We *do* that," he says. "And you
know we did an issue that was very much within our province when Mary went to jail for not revealing her source on
a story. But even that — it was somebody who didn't *want*
to go to jail..." Though finally she does, modestly stoic and
stoically modest to the end. "But it wasn't *heroic*," says
Brooks, laughing again.

Returning later to the subject of message shows, I ask
Brooks about the dangers inherent in writing for TV's audi-
ences of millions. "When you realize who you're reaching each
week with your ideas," I continue, "is there..." But Brooks
interrupts. The mass media, propaganda, and power are subjects he has already put some thought into.

"We were real good at policing ourselves on that," he says.
"Feminists would complain about something and we wouldn't
care. When we did *Room 222* and black groups would say
things, we'd say that you can't tell us that these people —
these are *my* people, you can't tell me that you know what
this black person would say 'cause you're a black. I know
what he'd say 'cause I *wrote* him. If he sounds like he's full
of shit, it's my fault — but, God, it's my character; it's not a
representation of blacks in America. Mary was influenced by
the women's movement; she was not a representation of that
movement. We didn't want her to be."

Brooks admonishes would-be TV writers, "Keep it *yours*.
When you sit down at the typewriter and you start saying,
'Will they allow this? Will they like that?' it's not writing
anymore. You have to come up with a different name for it.
It's serving. It's waiting on tables." As for promoting one's
own ideology, he says, "I think there's a seductive thing in
that that hurts the work."

But no matter what, I suggest, some of your own beliefs
must come through the TV, and just the possibility is raw
power. "But you can't deal with the power," Brooks insists,
even as he frets. "All my life people have been saying what

you're saying to me. The answer is you can't deal with that, 'cause to deal with that is to be consumed by it. There's no way to deal with it. It's too big — just what you're saying: 'How do you deal with that? How do you deal with forty million people are seeing you?' You don't. How do you deal with the fact that your body is going to rot and decay someday? You don't deal with that. It's too enormous to deal with. We're not equipped to deal with it."

If there was, however, any remotely systematic ideology that came through on *MTM*, it was that of the modern women's movement, of feminism. But on the one hand, that was perhaps an unconscious expression of the writers' bias; and on the other, it was a quite conscious effort, not to propagandize, but to evoke the contemporary setting. "I've been married for a second time," says Brooks with some uncomfortable hesitation. "But I was married to . . . my first wife was somebody who was a very early feminist. We used to have big arguments about the way I was doing the show, real *arguments*, and after I'd argued with her, I couldn't help but be influenced by what she was saying. Early on, I mean *early* on — this was seventy, seventy-one. And that did influence the show.

"So one of the most significant things about *Mary* is that it could draw on the culture enormously. I mean, single women were suddenly a focal point as they never had been before, who we saw in a perspective that we'd never held before, and it helped make the series vital. We drew on that so often — not so much for shows, but for moment, for character.

"Mary, as a character, inhabited the world of the seventies and went through what other women were going through. The thing where it's okay to be alone, the thing where she's not hustling for a husband, the thing of camaraderie with a woman friend, where it's the key relationship in her life. A working *professional* woman — who you saw *start* from incompetent, *bumbling* woman; who had a dull job — the

168.

first show we just saw her sharpening pencils at her desk, not knowing quite what to do that first day on the job. And that evolution — where she was getting promoted (she got, like, two promotions), challenging her boss for more money, becoming a real part of it. It evolved. Which is the great thing a series can do. Nothing else can do that."

If television — like most contemporary corporate entities — never innovates directions in a culture, it can validate — as we've seen with Gillette. And whether intended or not, Mary Richards was a persuasive image of the new feminism. Thus, while shunning ideology and propaganda, the creators of *MTM* nonetheless may have done as much as anyone to pave the way for what was perhaps the most significant change of this era of change, the emergence, in irrefutable numbers, of the independent, single, self-aware working woman. "If week after week America is shown a single working woman," I say to Jim Brooks, "then America may well start to *accept* single working women."

"Yes," he agrees, but that wasn't the point. He explains something of his own ideology. "Yes, in popular culture if you do a thing well, millions of people are feeling less alone. And that's proper. That's what you're after. That completes the communication. It's the best thing you can hope for, that you've touched them, that people somewhere are saying, '*Yes,* that's accurate.' Or, 'I wish I could be like that.' Or, 'It's *okay* to stay home on a Saturday night alone.' I used to go nuts the other way. When I watched *Father Knows Best,* it tormented me that people were having that kind of life. It was so much better than mine. It was so much happier. I felt alienated and lost. I would have loved to have seen a show about somebody like me.

"We did a show about Gavin MacLeod [as Murray] realizing he'd never amount to anything special, and then we wrote ourselves into a corner because in the last scene Mary has to say something to make this guy feel better. And he was a man of small talent who had just reached forty, had three kids and a mortgage and a job that — he wasn't going to write the great novel, it was so clear. And what do you say to him? And she finally said, 'Ah, your life's not that bad. Gee . . .' And there was something in the show that said the kind of contact we make with other people is a very significant part of our lives, as opposed to achieving and stuff like that."

• • •

Reading *MTM* solely as a story about the women's movement is as much a mistake as reading the women's movement as having only to do with women. And the women's rights movement — like the civil rights movement, like the gay rights movement — is part of a human rights movement in which everyone, everywhere, has a stake, as Jimmy Carter, to his eternal credit, insisted on pointing out. Feminism is a facet — albeit pretty fucking fundamental — of humanism. That was the *real* ideology of *MTM*. In a way, the show's feminist trappings were a front. The show wasn't about women and gender, nor was it about sex. It was about love. And the drama of the series, the serious subtext underlying all the comedy, was that Mary Richards, like any good rock 'n' roll protagonist, was looking for love. What was surprising was where she managed to find it.

"I know what Mary needs," says Sue Ann Nivens, WJM's perennially horny Happy Homemaker: "a *man*." But as her friends gather, in this episode from late in the series, to figure out a cure for Mary's uncharacteristic depression, it becomes obvious that *any* man is not the problem. In fact, just about every other guy who walks in the door makes a play for her. But even a list of serious boyfriends is extensive. Jim Brooks recites: "There was a schoolteacher she was involved with for a while, a journalism professor. There was sort of a sad comic. There was a guy who worked in industry who she

170.

really had an affair with, who was sort of an attractive guy."
Still, as Brooks explains, "they were just attractive, bland
men who walked through and didn't say much. Which I
think is true of a dating life — bland, attractive, dull, okay
men." As Mary Richards herself explains to her friend
Georgette (Georgia Engel): "After twenty *years* of dating"
— she winces — "let's see, two dates a week, that's" — she
winces again — "two *thousand* dates . . . jeez! And maybe ten
percent — maybe there've been two hundred good ones . . ."
Mary thinks about that for a moment. "Georgette," she says
finally, from the heart, "you know how you go along hoping
you'll meet the right person? Well, for the first time I don't
think that's going to happen." Then Georgette suggests she
try Lou Grant.

Lou Grant is a short, fat, bald, middle-aged slob, the very
definition of unattractive in our culture, the all-American
grotesque to Mary's all-American girl. Nevertheless, almost
from the start there has been a special bond between them.
Indeed, early on in the series, Lou refers to Mary as being
"like a daughter." Later, he proclaims protectively that she's
"like a sister." Toward the end of the run, the relationship
undergoes an unstated change. "Did you conceive of Lou as
an eventual love interest for Mary?" I ask Brooks.

"I had always felt it," he tells me. "Some other people connected with the show felt it was preposterous. I felt it."

"Right off when you saw them together?"

"No, no. *Began* to see it. Because as they were intimate
over a period of time — and very often they turned to each
other — they were sort of spiritual lovers."

"But then the level changed," I venture.

"Yeah, yeah. . . . And he got divorced. Remember, that
changed everything. He was an available man. And he was a
real, good *rock* of a . . . a bedrock husband. He was a terrific
husband whose life was blown apart by the women's movement." Grant's wife, Edie, leaves the marriage to find herself

now that the children are moved out and her role as the traditional "housewife-mother" has been emptied of much of its meaning, along with its chores. While the split is, as the wishful expression goes, "amicable," after twenty years of being married Grant is damaged, if not devastated. During the marriage, Brooks continues, "He didn't look at another woman. He didn't think that way. He was a good, decent, loyal husband. Now when he was divorced, then it was there. Suddenly there was time to fill. He turned to Mary during that period.

"And then more and more women started to tell me that they'd love to meet Ed Asner, who is married. And every one thought she was the only one who found him attractive. But they all did. So we started to get this feedback. Part of a series works as communication with your audience. And then the other people on the show began to hear the same thing. We were all hearing it."

"Is that why you got him divorced?"

"No. We did it to keep things moving, to take advantage of what series TV is, to evolve. We separated them maybe with the idea of getting them back together. We didn't know which we'd do. We didn't know what was going to happen. We had *two* separations, by the way. We had one, and it worked. And we did it again. But the first one" — in which Lou stomps out in protest of his wife's return to college — "ended, 'Hey, Edie, I'm comin' home.' And it was wonderful. But it happened again." And finally, the second time, after the divorce, and after many a stutter-step and stammer, Lou receives an invitation to dinner, chez Richards. "I want to," Mary clarifies, "go on a date with you . . ."

Mr. Grant, as Mary always calls him, arrives in his slob's Sunday best, armed as well with a bottle of wine, a box of candy, and not one but three bouquets. Mary dims the lights and, avoiding his eyes, struggles to call him Lou. Now, a little rushed, they sit down to eat. Avoiding *her* eyes — and

172.

a little forced — Lou summons up his slob's best dating manners and struggles to compliment Mary on the salad. Grant, gurgling appreciation: "How do you make this?" Mary: ". . . I pour oil and vinegar on lettuce." "Oil and, ah, vinegar," Grant ruminates, desperately filling up the awkward spaces, "Hmm . . . I'll have to remember that . . ." But these old friends know each other far too well for this. At last, Grant lays down his fork and summons up his courage. "Mary," he says, turning to face her, "we're both wondering what's going to happen here . . . *after* . . ." She looks back at him nervously and intently. "I don't know about you," Grant goes on, "but the suspense is killing *me* . . ." After a moment, Mary agrees. "All right," she says with some relief, whereupon the two promptly and seriously adjourn to the sofa.

As graceful as teenagers on a first date, they pucker earnestly and lean slowly toward each other. Lips touch, but just barely, and first one and then the other opens an eye and, in turn, starts to giggle. In a moment, they fall apart in hysterics. "That's the silliest thing . . ." says Lou, catching his breath between laughs, "kissing *you*. . . ." "I know, I know," says Mary, "*stupid* . . ." Finally they regain their composure, and smiling, Lou pronounces their experiment over. "I think we both just found out something," he tells her, "in record time." They stand and shake hands. "Good night, Mary," he says. "Good night, Lou," she replies. A wisp of melancholy hangs in the air, and then Mary turns the lights back up, and they head back to the dinner table. "Let me tell you what Ted did in the office today," we hear a jolly Grant say as the scene fades. "What was that, Mr. Grant?" comes Mary's reply.

When it was announced that the 1976–77 season would be *MTM*'s last, a lot of fans were hoping it would end with a wedding, that Lou and Mary might live happily ever after. After all, everybody *knew* they were in love. "We never thought it would end with the two of them . . ." says Brooks.

"We joked a lot — you know, ending the series with, 'Why, Mr. *Grant!*' in the darkness. But it was romantic, that show, and the romance in it finally won out. Because there was something very romantic about them kissing and laughing at the notion that they would take off their clothes and stick things at each other. It was romantic. It was more pure, chaste, from afar. You know," he adds, "there are some times when you're better than life."

If the architecture of the show owes to the personality of Allan Burns, much of the stuffing, the guts, the heart — and the heartache too — comes straight from James L. Brooks. At times, Brooks eerily echoes Murray; at other times, Rhoda; at still other times, Lou or Mary herself. The connection here between cocreator and created is almost palpable, almost real. For instance, trying to describe Mary Richards's appeal, I mention to Brooks my sense of her heroic insecurity. He looks out the window and summons her, now offering his own admiring description: "She had humanity, but the character had humanity. She was very comfortable ... she had values, and yet she was not a judgmental woman. But she had class and style and taste and something *American* to her. There was something at her core that was good and decent. And she was fair." In other words, Mary was a hero to Jim Brooks too, a kind of Miss Liberty made flesh. But she was also something more.

Indeed, listening to him speak of his relationship with Mary Richards, I almost get the feeling that he held her back from Lou, from marriage, from a sustained love affair, for selfish reasons. "I had affection for her," he says, staring askance. "I had real affection for her, real affection for the character. In other words, a girl ... if I were to date Mary Richards, I would've had a lot of fun teasing her about herself. That would've been the way we related. I could appreciate what she was, but I couldn't resist teasing her. She could tease herself; she could laugh at herself. And my way of making contact with her would be to engage her that way. Somebody else could just . . ." He trails off, finally concluding: "So I felt a relationship with the character. And I think I understood her, 'cause I had affection for her."

In Jim Brooks's metaphysics, loneliness is original sin, the fundamental condition from which there is only temporary respite in the impermanent state of grace called love. He doesn't spell this out, but the references in his conversation are repeated and clear. So are the references in his show. During the last season in particular, there is a general aloneness that threatens to engulf Mary and in any case tugs at the show's laughs like a sad undertow. Mary remains as charming and physically attractive as ever — indeed, *more* so, the crow's feet at the eyes and the lines by the mouth helping to transform a fresh, bubbly, all-American TV cutie into a woman of substance, of mystery, of *true* beauty — but it is becoming evident to her, no less than to us, especially after the anticlimactic date with Grant, that she is not likely to find that "right person," that there is not going to be a marriage, kids, probably not even a "cohabitant," that Mary Richards will make her passage to the inevitable with dignity and grace, but that she will do it, alas, all by herself.

Her cocreators, I might add, didn't intend such a melancholy light. "I think it just probably happened," Allan Burns tells me, "as a result of her being seven years older than when we started, and you suddenly realized that when you do something like that, unlike Lucy, you're not in a time warp, and she did get older. Lucy never got older, and Mary did. And she went off and saw Rhoda get married . . . things changed. But I never thought of it in those terms, of it being sadder." Jim Brooks now ventures a similar rationale. "What's terrific in a thirty-year-old," he says, "is not in a thirty-seven-year-old, necessarily, which is the age span of the character." But when I ask if he feels Mary Richards became somehow tragic, he demurs, reconsidering perhaps before he adds:

"Certainly not *tragic*." "Then she was fulfilled?" I continue. "No. She was fulfilled," he replies, "and then she needed *new* fulfillment. Life isn't a final fulfillment."

In the final episode of *The Mary Tyler Moore Show* the melancholy approaches critical mass and hopelessness looms, the situation all the more poignant because it's also very funny — as things *are*, as *we* are, when all appears lost. And it is up to our hero, Mary Richards, whose situation may be most lost and poignant of all, to save the day. And sure enough she does, rescuing hope by achieving some kind of final fulfillment in spite of life, and proving, finally, that she is not all by herself.

To understand what happens in that last episode is to understand that, in a way, Mary's life was as "blown apart" by the women's movement as Lou's. Jim Brooks recalls her "background story": "Went with a medical student; good American girl who was going to get married. This was in late nineteen sixty-nine, we thought. Good American girl goes with a medical student for four years, lives with him, and then they break up; he drops her. And she missed that rung where her life would have been down a predictable slot: doctor's wife; kids; Midwest; everything fine; what she was prepared for. And suddenly there she is. That's where we begin our first show."

In the first show Mary moves to Minneapolis into the apartment her friend Phyllis has found her, gets off to a rocky start with her upstairs neighbor, Rhoda Morgenstern, and within a miraculous day or so has landed the job at WJM. But at WJM her boss is often drunk and mean and the work at first is mostly shit, answering the boss's phone, making his coffee, doing his shopping, and always humoring him. Eventually, however, with new friends behind her and whole new movements for equality growing around her, Mary Richards is able to see the job as something more than a holding action until marriage, to see *herself* as some-

176.

thing more; and then in a changing world Mary Richards is able, not without a struggle, to *be* that something more. So if the women's movement didn't exactly blow her life apart in the first place, it helped make certain that when she put it back together it would never be the same.

Freedom, independence, and a serious career, the chance to make a mark in the world. Still sometimes it seems like a loveless life — particularly when your station is sold and you lose your job and that serious career starts to fizzle, as does Mary's in the final episode. In fact, it seems like a loveless life to Mary, at least for a moment. "Sometimes I get concerned," she tells her chums, all of whom, with the exception of the one *true* incompetent, Baxter, have also met the ax in the new station owner's purge, "about being a career woman, that my job's too important to me . . ." Her voice trembles — but with resolve. Teary eyes seek her out. ". . . But the people you work with," she continues deliberately, "are just people who make you feel less alone." A beat. "And loved." Stifling a sob, Mary inhales the last word. Her friends float toward her: Lou, Murray, Happy Homemaker Nivens, Georgette, and Ted, too, all of them transformed for the moment in their notions of community, of family, of love. They fall into a sloppy mass embrace, a damp, whimpering huddle, around Mary. For the moment they see, with Mary, that community is everyone, and family is just where you happen to find it, that love is in the most fleeting exchange, and that in a dark world, through a lonely passage, even the dimmest love is a guiding star. Hopelessness lifts; lovelessness vanishes. Here is a love beyond lubed-up parts. Here indeed is a fine marriage.

Mary's marriage stands in the middle of the newsroom weeping. It decides, between sobs, that it needs some Kleenex. "There's a box on my desk," says Mary. And in the climactic comic scene of the last show, spontaneously, without once breaking ranks, the huddled marriage shuffles over to

.177

Mary's desk. But then all good marriages are naturally cooperative and naturally awkward affairs. But then all good marriages are deadly serious comedies. Ted extracts a hand from the embrace and distributes tissues. The marriage dabs at its face and blows its nose and hangs together for as long as it can. But finally it is time to leave. "How're we gonna get out of here?" Murray wonders. And, in fact, they aren't, not like this, not together. Marriage is only for the moment. And in the next moment, this one breaks up.

Grabbing their coats, and one last look back, the marriage partners pass through the newsroom exit in strict single file. As we watch the closing doors, a spate of credits rushes by. A sad silence. Then suddenly the doors crack apart again. Mary Richards peeks back in, alone. She surveys the scene with a tender expression, now thrilling us with a brave and hopeful smile. She remembers this time to douse the lights, and she turns around in the dark, and she leaves. This time for good.

But life goes on. New marriages do form. And Mary, of course, she endures.

. . .

Of all the risky things we did in the sixties and seventies, in rock 'n' roll and out of it, screwing around with men and women was surely the riskiest. Screwing around with men and women is screwing around with screwing, and while Margaret Mead may have said that with change we had to go all the way, screwing around with screwing is quite literally risking our entire future. And for what?

At the end of *Beginning to See the Light*, reentering the reverse promised land of New York City, her home, after a flight, both literal and figurative, from Israel and the bondage of her patriarchal religious heritage, Ellen Willis, for one, comes to wonder, too. And as tears arrive, a new rock 'n' roll song replaces Reed's in the jukebox of her mind. But this one

178.

has nothing to do with salvation. "How does it feel," taunts Bob Dylan, "To be on your own/ With no direction home/ Like a complete unknown?" Indeed, what Lou Reed neglected to mention was that saving her life was only the beginning. Thus, much like our friends the Manus, as we shed old values and institutions on passing through the gates of the 1960s into the post-Woodstock promised land, a lot of us were beset by sadness and doubt. "Eighteen," sang Alice Cooper, "I get confused everyday." But some of us were well past thirty.

Mary Richards hesitates. On the face of it, she has it made: smart, attractive, set up with good friends and a job that is glamorous and responsible, if not extremely lucrative, that she likes to do and does well. In fact, as the final season of *The Mary Tyler Moore Show* opens, she is moving up again — literally this time: out of her Victorian-era studio into sumptuous digs in a brand new high-rise with a view. No more leaky old pipes and broken-down boilers, no more cramped kitchenettes, no more dressing in the closet and sleeping on the sofa — "My own *bedroom!*" Mary exults to her friends — no more living like a kid. With Rhoda and Phyllis long gone, and so nothing more to hold her at the old North Wetherly place, Mary's going to live like the respected and successful and grown-up executive that she is...

• • •

On the face of it, the present we gambled the future on is unquestionably a better world for women. Freed from the conventions of motherhood and housewifery, women are pursuing their economic, social, and political interests as never before, competing and contributing and thus fulfilling themselves to an unimagined degree. It's an oft-repeated litany, but no less amazing to those of us who knew different: women are becoming truck drivers and construction workers, coal miners and cops on the beat; they're going on to higher education in huge, unprecedented numbers — indeed, they now represent more than half the college population — and becoming tenured professors, scientists, doctors, lawyers, and, having gained entrance to the military academies for the first time, even regular army, navy, and air force officers; women are writing and painting and rocking and being taken very seriously at it, for a change; there are women mayors, district attorneys, Cabinet officers, governors, and a justice of the Supreme Court; there are corporate vice-presidents who are women, as well as architects, astronauts, TV news anchors and TV news producers.

Oppression — as best symbolized by the defeat, for now, of the Equal Rights Amendment — persists, sometimes surging to heave women back a step or two, to reinstate suffering (as in recent sanctimonious assaults — by true believers and hypocrites and mostly by the merely misguided — on the rights of women to their own wombs). Women who work — now fifty-one percent of all women — are often ghettoized in lower-paying positions with fewer opportunities for advancement, still. But the monolith of women's oppression has in fact been smashed, and no desperate rear-guard actions will be able to stem the rising historical tide for very long. In short, if there is going to be a future (and surely there is), a girl growing up is going to have a much greater future in it. And in the end, the liberty of women must mean the liberty of men.

.   .   .

180.

... But Mary hesitates, standing in the center of her bare new living room clutching the letter *M*. The *M*, familiar from her old apartment, stands about eighteen inches high, is carved of wood and painted gold. An elegant piece of old-fashioned, serif type that might have been plucked from the middle of the proprietor's name on a proper English store-front, more likely it was plucked from the middle of an alphabetized rack in the local five-and-dime, where it was recommended for household deployment as a "decorative accent" à-la-mode late-sixties. In the relatively close quarters of Mary's old studio, however, the big gold capital *M* on the wall was something more than an accent. And hovering there in the background of *MTM*'s domestic interludes, it was also something more than just Mary's monogram (though *MTM*'s cocreators will deny it). Certainly Mary seemed to freight it with additional, cryptic significance. So when friends show up to spirit her off to a surprise housewarming dinner on that first day in the new apartment, Mary feels impelled to send them on ahead. "I just have something to do first," she explains, but with such solemnity that Lou Grant takes her aside to ask if she's all right. Which she is — or will be. But first of all on this first day she must hang her mark on these cold, empty rooms and once more claim the void as home ...

· · ·

On the face of it, in the gamble for women's rights, everybody wins. So why is the feminist writer crying? And how come the female news producer doubts?

· · ·

... Mary aligns the golden letter on the wall and decides it's right — and then pivots to answer the door. A trim, jaunty man of early middle age, an ersatz Donald O'Connor in jaunty patterned pants and a pullover and a jaunty tweed hat, slouches with a jaunty, flirtatious air against the door jamb. "Hi ..." he says, jauntily stretching the one syllable into two, introducing himself as Jim so-and-so, but adding, as he executes a smart sidestep inside the apartment, "Call me Jimbo." He is, of course, Mary's compulsively single and effervescently swinging new neighbor. "Come in ..." Mary mumbles with some dismay after he does. "Hey!" he exclaims, spotting the *M* and pointing to Mary. "Let me guess ... Michelle!" No reply. "Marilyn!" Silence. "Melissa! Maisie! Mona...?" Mary tries to interrupt. "Listen, Jimbo," she says, exasperated, "when I took this apartment I *specifically* asked if this was a singles building and the manager told me no." But Jimbo rattles on, pointing and exclaiming, bouncing up and down in a jaunty dance of desperation, until Mary can ease him back out the door, which with a loud sigh she finally closes. Returning to the chore at hand, she realigns the *M* on the wall and, pleased again, reaches for hammer and nail. Suddenly the door pops open. "Mandy!" Jimbo cries, leaping in and pointing in triumph. "No!" Mary shouts back, pointing to indicate the exit. As she marches toward him, Jimbo reluctantly backpeddles out, his babbling rising to an abjectly frantic pitch: "Myra, Melody, Maureen, Monica, Mommy ..." The door shuts. Mary turns ...

• • •

Everybody wins — but somehow still there are losers. Somehow still that air of defeat. Summing up her compelling vision more than a dozen years ago in what was to become a basic text of the new feminism, Kate Millett wrote in *Sexual Politics*:

> The enormous social change involved in a sexual revolution is basically a matter of altered consciousness, the exposure of social and psychological realities underlining political and cultural structures. We are speaking, then, of a cultural revolution, which, while it must necessarily involve the political and economic reorganization traditionally implied by

the term revolution, must go far beyond this as well....
[T]he most profound changes implied are ones accomplished
by human growth and true re-education ...

In other words, Kate Millett was arguing — as Jimmy Carter
would later on, as Ellen Willis does — that the gamble for
women's rights is and must be a gamble for human rights.
Freeing women — and so freeing men — within a society —
rooted in patriarchal traditions — that is enslaved to its technology — and so antihuman — is an empty achievement, at
best a rehearsal for the real liberation that must follow. I am
most saddened when, as I did just yesterday, I find myself
standing on the line for the Boston shuttle plane watching the
women with the little briefcases leading the men with the
little briefcases up the ramp. This is when I begin to think,
some revolution. ... Indeed, are we any better off if a woman
pushes the nuclear button? And such, of course, is the much
greater danger to our future. As things are presently consti-
tuted, then, saving one's life may mean losing one's soul; that
is, saving one's individuality may mean joining the mass, and
asserting the freedom of one's will may just mean learning
anew to submit. And maybe winning is losing — certainly it
is when winning is taken as vindication, when by winning we
come to partake of the fudamental flaw of postwar America,
when we embrace the hubris.

The only gamble we've won so far is that we gambled at all.
And until we've assumed our complete humanity, we must
continue to slide our chips — that is, our selves — to the line.
We must continue to doubt; we must continue in doubt. We
must know that we don't know. So Ellen Willis on her way
"with no direction home" is headed in the right direction. And
Mary Richards wondering — doubting herself, but even
more, perhaps, giving others the benefit of the doubt — is
doing the best she can. They have that which we most lack,
simple humility.

.183

A realization dawns that Mary Richards is not unlike that first liberated woman of American fiction, Nathaniel Hawthorne's hero Hester Prynne. "And, as Hester Prynne had no selfish ends, nor lived in any measure for her own profit and enjoyment," Hawthorne wrote,

> people brought all their sorrows and perplexities and besought her counsel, as one who had herself gone through a might trouble.... Hester comforted and counselled them. ... She assured them, too, of her firm belief, that, at some brighter period ... a new truth would be revealed, in order to establish the whole relation between man and woman on a surer ground of mutual happiness. Earlier in life, Hester had vainly imagined that she herself might be the destined prophetess, but had long since recognized the impossibility that any mission of divine and mysterious truth should be confided to a woman stained with sin, bowed down with shame, or even burdened with a lifelong sorrow. The angel and apostle of the coming revelation must be a woman, indeed, but lofty, pure, and beautiful; and wise, moreover, not through dusky grief, but the ethereal medium of joy; and showing how sacred love should make us happy, by the truest test of a life successful to such an end!

. . .

... Mary hesitates and turns back and turns back again: a double-take. *"Mommy? ...."* she says aloud to herself, and shakes her head and smiles ...

. . .

Hawthorne: "So said Hester Prynne, and glanced her sad eyes down at the scarlet letter."

. . .

... Mary picks up the hammer and nails an *M* to the wall for democracy.

184.

*L*iz Holtzman has recently lost, and she is not pleased. A popular and well-respected congresswoman who had quite reasonably expected to serve as the next junior senator from New York, she finds herself after the 1980 election serving instead as a visiting professor at New York University, where, in what is surely an aspect of the agony of defeat, I have been able to get her on the phone. "Why do you want to talk to *me?*" she says, picking like a prosecutor at apparent inconsistencies in my statement of purpose and hastily recited curriculum vitae, "*I* don't know anything about music." Like a perjurer, I fumble around in the intimidating silence that follows trying to explain she doesn't have to.

• • •

Elizabeth Holtzman was part of it whether she likes it or (just my guess) not, part of the whole thing that spread out from the music and mass media and bubbled up from blacks and women and trickled down from the affluence of the fifties and sixties, part of the freedom riders and women's libbers, of Woodstock Nation and the hippies and the era of rock 'n' roll. One of a group of populist, nonregular, left-liberal electoral activists catalyzed by the presidential campaigns of Gene McCarthy and Robert Kennedy in 1968 and George Mc-

.187

Govern in 1972 and by the reduction of the voting age in 1971, Elizabeth Holtzman was part of the change that Margaret Mead said must take place and party to it as well — indeed it was visionary leaders like Liz Holtzman who, according to Mead, were all that ultimately stood between a rapidly changing society and the nihilism of the cargo cults. In short, Elizabeth Holtzman, no less than Mary Richards in fiction or John Lennon or Alice Cooper in semifictional fact, was part of the American Noise.

She was also part of something else, however. The newsweeklies liked to call it the New Politics. But the Who said: "Meet the new boss . . ."

Elizabeth Holtzman: Born 1941, Brooklyn, New York; student body president, Brooklyn's Abraham Lincoln High School (twin brother, now a doctor, was vice president); magna cum laude, Radcliffe, 1962; Harvard Law, 1965; enters politics, 1972, seeking nomination for Congressional seat of Brooklyn Democratic boss, Emanuel Celler; following upset primary victory over Celler, bucks Republican "landslide" of November 1972 to win in general election. A contender.

Handily re-elected to House in 1974, 1976, 1978; serves district, country with courage, compassion, imagination; eyed by some local left-libs as future presidential timber; comes to national attention for initiating class-action suit against US to halt bombing of Cambodia and as highly active member of House Judiciary Committee which in 1974, for only second time in US history, votes Bill of Impeachment against president.

Liz Holtzman — New Politician by conscience, by definition. One of group of New Pols who, drawn from the ranks of the disenfranchised — the young, the idealistic, the black, and the female — were to be political occupying army of an American cultural revolution that would return us to the principles of the revolution that went before.

• • •

"Disenfranchised?" says Liz Holtzman flatly. "I don't think of women as disenfranchised. There have been women in Congress for a long time. The *interesting* thing is that the percentage of women in Congress now is not greater than it was." She is not being sarcastic. "But I don't necessarily think of myself as part of a group of people. When I ran for Congress, I was against the war, for women's rights, and for greater integrity in government."

Critics have described Liz Holtzman as "cool" and "aloof." In part, I suspect, that's just the kind of personal adjustment a woman must make on entering the men's club of American politics; in part, I suspect further, it's an insult, just the kind men apply to any woman of will and accomplishment. Anyway, to be cool and aloof in that all-too-cozy milieu must surely be counted a virtue, moral if not political. Which is not to say the critics are all wrong. Youthful, lean, impeccably pressed and coiffed, sharp-featured yet handsome, Liz Holtzman surveys me coolly from behind tortoise-framed lenses. The erstwhile Goliath-slayer, now part-time college prof, has granted me a thirty-minute audience and means it, so I plunge ahead. I suggest that the power to change things proved illusory to the generation of change when it came to power. In other words, *thud* . . .

Or, in still other words: "Same as the old boss . . . ?"

"Well, I don't know," says Liz Holtzman, in a manner that implies she does. "The war was ended in my first year in government. We legislated the War Powers Act [of 1973]" — the law, inspired by Nixon's secret invasion of Cambodia, requiring the president to win congressional approval in order to deploy combat troops for more than sixty days, a law whose wisdom again becomes apparent in light of Reagan administration bellicosity. "I brought a lawsuit to stop the bombing" — of Cambodia, stepped up *after* the war was officially "ended" for America. "We changed the seniority rules, and we changed the caucus rules [in Congress], so that there has to be a vote of the majority of a committee in support of the chairman. We enacted the campaign financing and disclosure laws to promote and ensure greater integrity in government. We enacted the Freedom of Information Act and opened up government to the press and to the public. I think that in the Ninety-third and Ninety-fourth Congresses we accomplished a lot."

But aren't those accomplishments now proving to have been flimsy, transient, and, in some instances, even counterproductive? I ask, citing specifically the case of political action committees which, having formed in a loophole of the new campaign financing laws, threaten to make justice strictly cash-and-carry.

"Extreme right-wing groups have organized — the Moral Majority and such — to promote their views," Holtzman replies, "but I think people like Jerry Falwell and Phyllis Schlafly want to return to another time, take a step into the past to a time that accorded with their religious views, and that's just not going to work." And that's not arrogance. What sometimes sounds like arrogance in Liz Holtzman is revealed on closer inspection as a flaming optimism, an optimism — quite in line with sixties utopianism — fueled by an essential faith in the people she has served so faithfully. And it is this optimism — which lies just beneath her rational, well-modulated surface and which is probably, at least in part, a rational thing of itself — that is Liz Holtzman's strength and appeal as a leader and her weakness as a contemporary political operator. It's the thoughtful nature of her optimism which now leads her to qualify that last profession of faith with some pithy and resonant apprehension. "I think Jerry Falwell is an American Ayatollah," she warns, long before it would become easy to do so. Connecting the dots between that day's disparate headlines to make clear the bigger picture that others — especially those extreme right-wing others who rally to the notion of theocracy in America even as they rail against

190.

it in revolutionary Iran — refuse to see, Holtzman repeats, "there are a lot of similarities between Falwell and the Ayatollah."

Richard Nixon was never much of an optimist — twenty years ago, on the occasion of his gubernatorial loss in California and his "last" news conference, he was already pronouncing himself through as the national scapegoat. Certainly Nixon never had much faith in the people of this country — who, through their representatives in the press, have nevertheless maintained him in a goathood unrivaled to this day. And it is commonly understood that this lack of faith, this flaming pessimism which the faithless subterfuge of the "plumbers" was meant to douse, was the source of Nixon's undoing. However, as we all know, such lack of faith was not unique to Nixon. And his undoing, advanced as yet another triumph for American justice and as proof positive of American constitutional safeguards, may have proved only that if you run with donkeys, don't be a goat. "Would Nixon have been forced from office if he had been a Democrat?" I ask Liz Holtzman, who was there.

"Johnson," she says, backing up to the Democrat without whose duplicity Nixon's duplicity would not have been, "was immune to reaction to his war policy. I think it would have been a lot more difficult with a Democratic President because the Congress was controlled by Democrats. I don't think a Democratic President would have been impeached" — which, in effect, or at least in committee, Nixon was. "But Mr. Nixon," Holtzman continues, anger rippling her surface, "committed a crime: he obstructed justice. And those were the grounds on which the committee voted to impeach. The Judiciary Committee rejected the articles relating to the war and the bombing" — articles boldly and famously put forth by Congresswoman Holtzman — "and voted for impeachment on the grounds that President Nixon committed a crime and had engaged in gross abuse of power."

What about that third layer of travesty, the pardon? If Nixon had wanted to ensure his continued role as national scapegoat, he surely could have done no better than to accept the dubious blanket pardon granted him by his dubious successor, Gerald Ford, the man he appointed to the vice-presidency when his first vice-president, Spiro Agnew, resigned in disgrace. Indeed, the pardon would appear to have been Nixon's ultimate obstruction of justice.

"The pardon was a mistake," Holtzman agrees, again restraining anger.

Why?

"Because it indicates we have a dual system of justice. And I think it's responsible for some of the cynicism about politics in this country today. It probably cost Ford the election too, and I think he recognizes that now. The idea that impeachment — and we [the Congress] hadn't even voted impeachment — the idea that this is enough punishment is wrong and promotes the idea that this is a dual system of justice. Impeachment should not be a bar to criminal prosecution," she reiterates, icily, "and, in fact, the Constitution specifically states that it is *not*. The Constitution says that impeachment shall not substitute for, or stand in the way of, prosecution for any crimes."

But there is no revenge on Nixon. After Nixon, there is only his revenge on us. I am thinking of a born-again Georgia peach speaking the tongues of hippie rock 'n' roll. "How was an unknown named Jimmy Carter elected president?" I inquire of Holtzman.

"I think Carter was elected because people wanted a new face and were angry about Watergate and at Washington at the same time," she opines. "I think the same is somewhat true of Reagan."

And why was Carter turned out?

"Because we have a campaign process that does not inform

192.

people properly," says Holtzman. "People are encouraged to get their hopes very high and then are naturally disappointed. And because we don't have a critical press. And because the number of people who think a president really matters is growing smaller and smaller. Look how many people voted — less than half the eligible population. There is a great deal of cynicism among people who have been promised so much and then disappointed. The candidates are campaigning on glib slogans, and we just don't have a critical press in this country. I read a *New York Times* editorial about Reagan's economic program, and they seemed to be saying that anyone with a plan deserves a chance. But you can't have a tax cut and a forty-five-billion-dollar deficit [as then projected] and greatly increased military spending and expect to stop inflation. It won't work. But the whole political establishment has fallen on its face for this. I think," she concludes quite rationally, "that the plan is a formula for social unrest."

In the title song of his *The River* album, Bruce Springsteen, the eighties' Woody Guthrie, portrays a newlywed blue-collar kid who with his pregnant wife has run away from hard times in the city only to find that hard times have followed. "Lately there ain't been much work," he is explaining to a stranger, adding with a knowingness that belies his bewilderment and desperation, "on account of the economy." But of course that's what the guys on TV said: "It's the economy." And isn't it odd how they say it about good times no less than bad — in the sixties it was affluence, a fat economy, that was to blame for those white punks on dope run riot in the streets. And of course it's no less a dodge than blaming the dope itself. Presented to us as a deus ex machina (not to mention a fait accompli) before which we must go limp, in fact the economy is increasingly a reflection of an ideology that is increasingly a reflection of unmitigated greed, a more or less coherent series of decisions by those with money, including

.193

the government, about where that money will go, which is mostly, I find myself ranting to Liz Holtzman, back into *their* pockets. The rich get richer. An old story. But with a diabolical new twist in the seventies and eighties with the advent of those geographic and financial behemoth's, the multinationals — talk about a formula for social unrest ...

"I don't think you can blame everything on the multi-nationals," says Liz Holtzman evenly, and of course she's right. "There has been an unwillingness on the part of many of these corporations to invest in basic research and development," she goes on by way of some constructive, if disappointingly mild, criticism, "and that is a problem. We create the technology here in America and then license it overseas" — instead of retaining the technological processes and selling its *products* overseas for a profit in the long term — "and because of this and because there is less basic scientific research, we are losing our edge, our competitive and technological edge, to Japan and other countries."

"What about the multinational oil companies?" I press Holtzman. "Do you believe the oil crises of the seventies were real?"

"Yes, it's true that we have a long-term shortage," she replies, "that we are running out of natural resources. But in terms of the short-term crises, I don't think there is a shortage of supply. At least in the case of natural gas, it has been fairly well demonstrated that they were holding back on supply, waiting for decontrol."

"How could we prevent such manipulation? Should such national resources be entirely held in private hands?"

"Well, most of the current reserves are on public lands, but we do practically give them away. We should at least get a fair return. And yes, perhaps we should have a government-run oil company that can put pressure on the price offered by private companies and can also get a more accurate

194.

assessment of potential and supply. The problem is we rely on oil companies themselves for the analyses and assessments of reserves. There aren't adequate procedures for auditing."

The issue of our time, as we seem to have only recently realized, the issue that sets our time apart in time, the issue, indeed, for all time from now on, is nuclear Armageddon. It's an issue linked to the multinationals insofar as so many of them, from Lockheed to GM to Proctor & Gamble, derive such a significant portion of their revenues from Defense Department contracts and thus have a vested interest in the maintenance of the "military-industrial complex," through which most wealth in America flows. It's an issue linked to the baby boomsters because they were the first to grow up entirely within its shadow, and perhaps it is only within that shadow that some of what they (we) do and are makes sense.

"Has nuclear war been a presence in your life, something you've carried in the back of your mind?" I ask Holtzman.

"It is now," she says, characteristically veering away from subjective testimony before continuing. "It's a false issue that the Soviet Union is militarily stronger than us. It's totally untrue. The fact is we have nine thousand nuclear warheads, and they have six thousand. We have a third more than they do. So it's just not true that they're stronger. But since World War II we have lost every war we've been in — we've been in two wars: we lost in Korea, in essence, and we lost in Vietnam — to a barefoot army. We lost our moral position; we lost militarily and in prestige. And I think people have a sense that they can make up for that. We just have not learned."

"Are you suggesting that we would go into, say, Poland if the Soviets went in?" I ask, thinking she is referring to one particular hot spot in the news when, actually, she is referring to another.

"El Salvador," she corrects. "We have not learned. It's entirely possible that we might send troops in there — and then we'd be right back where we were in Vietnam. Before we got into Vietnam, it was a fight between the north and the south, and then we came in and *we* became the enemy. We were the enemy there."

"Do you then think we should stop propping up the government in El Salvador?"

"Propping up?" says Holtzman, pointing to the absurdity of such an idea in such a place. "Oh sure, we can prop them up militarily for a time, but in countries like El Salvador it's not a military problem. It's a problem of severe, crushing poverty. A government cannot survive there that does not ameliorate those conditions. Since we are responsible for putting a number of those [Latin American] governments in power — most recently in Chile — we have a responsibility to try and ameliorate those conditions. We must apply pressure. We have, and we should *continue* to try and pressure them with aid to change."

Liz Holtzman checks her watch: a cool two-minute warning. Briefly I return to the question of nuclear war. "Is it conceivable that we would start throwing around nuclear weapons sometime in the near future?"

She does not equivocate: "Yes, I think it's conceivable. There are people who say a nuclear war is survivable. That's what the neutron bomb is all about. With such an attitude and so many weapons around, it is conceivable."

Liz Holtzman is not a dilatory conversationalist. Shunning political demagoguery, she likes to speak to the point, but mostly, like the well-prepared attorney she is, she likes to let the evidence speak for itself. In an effort to coax her into a parting overview of the American scene, however, I ask if she concurs in Jimmy Carter's onetime diagnosis of a "malaise" among his fellow citizens. I get a little rise, if not much

196.

of an overview — but then to Liz Holtzman the evidence in this case is all too clear.

"There's no malaise among the people. That's nonsense. There is a certain amount of cynicism, and perhaps we aren't willing to wait as long for things as we should be willing to do — there are cultural values, perhaps, such as instant gratification, that make us too impatient. But talk of the people sacrificing puts the onus on the wrong people. What we have," says Elizabeth Holtzman, "is a government, as well as a press, that operates on slogans." And then she gets up and sees me to the door.

. . .

Youthful, intelligent, idealistic, honest, right-thinking (to my mind), and true, Elizabeth Holtzman is all that the sixties and seventies would have been and all that they weren't. It's not so much that she lost the 1980 Senate race — forced into a three-way contest against (1) an ancient and venerable liberal incumbent who ran independently after losing his party's primary, thus siphoning off key liberal (and ethnic) votes and (2) a rat-like conservative demagogue with Republican cash and Republican presidential coattails, a zest for the low-road, nay for the *trench,* and an incessant media campaign starring his sainted, ratlike mother, Holtzman *still* managed to come within a fraction of a percent — *a thousand votes* — of winning, *almost* bucking Reagan's "landslide" as she had once done Nixon's. It's not that 1980 was her political end — following a semester in exile she returned to the political fray and in a move that may have been as understandably vengeful as it was forgivably opportunistic, threw her considerable nationwide political weight against the wheezing remnants of the late Emanuel Celler's Brooklyn Democratic machine and in 1981 won overwhelming election as Brooklyn District Attorney. And it's not that being Brooklyn D.A. is a comedown — it *is*, of course, but not so far down that a halfway decent politician couldn't come back (and didn't Richard Nixon prove long ago that, politically, there's no place too far down?). No, that's not the problem either. In fact, it may well be that the problem — the failure of the New Politics of the sixties and seventies, the failure of the American Noise yet to find effective political form — is not with the positions or the performance or even the popularity of this or any other semi-hip politician. It may be that the problem is politics itself.

Maybe Americans are too cynical — though a most cursory review of recent political history might suggest a few reasons why. But the fact is that the mainstream, two-party politics of this country, ever a thoroughly cynical business of itself, is getting worse. Indeed, somewhere it seemed to have crossed a line where it ceased to mean a whole lot to a whole lot of the people. And why should it? We can recognize fewer and fewer of our founding ideals in our elections; we recognize nothing of ourselves in the pumped up and propped up and vacuous and venal candidates; and we realize that the big money — inevitably corporate and likely tainted — takes all. Same as the old boss, indeed.

The problem may be that to be in politics today is to come too late and, by definition, be too little. Too bad.

Tin soldiers and Nixon's coming,
We're finally on our own.
— *Neil Young, "Ohio," 1970*

Or is it that everything and everyone political shrinks beside the godhead of postwar American politics, the godhead bowed yet unbowed, slain yet risen, again and again and again, the goathead godhead from which all else —including his negations, Jimmy Carter, for instance, and the assassin Elizabeth Holtzman — sprang, the goathead godhead who is Father (as Mary Richards is "Mommy"?), the irrepressible Richard Milhous Nixon? Yes, let's look at these politics from the other angle . . .

I was born the day they first elected him vice-president. *I* certainly think of him as a kind of second Dad. But then so does Neil Young: the exhilaration mixed in with the outrage and fear of Young's Kent State call-to-arms is unmistakable, and unmistakably adolescent, too, aware that being "finally on our own" also means breaking away — and breaking away, of course, that sense of teetering on the brink of liberation and the abyss, the exhilaration of hot-wiring the American promise, just happens to be the essential feeling of good ole rock 'n' roll. Indeed, if rock 'n' roll is the sound of perpetual adolescence, making of adolescence a model for the whole of life, then Nixon was surely the father figure who filled out the metaphor and finished the equation for an entire generation of rock 'n' roll adolescents, mama's boys and girls. And it was Nixon in particular, not just any president — Ike, bald and forever golfing, was too much the distant, retired grandfather; Kennedy too much the big brother; Johnson, with his basset face and archaic political ways, a grandfather of another sort, and, in any case, far too indulgent for the rowdy, rebellious offspring we sought to be. Nixon fit the part — and then, with his tirades against "permissive child-rearing" and the like, played it to a T. And so it can hardly be counted as coincidence that under his properly resistant, totally graceless and thick-headed patriarchy our American rock 'n' roll movement grew and cohered as never before or since.

In other words: "Meet the old boss . . ."

• • •

If the relationship was mostly shaped in conflict — and conflict *is* mostly what we remember — I should emphasize that it wasn't entirely adversarial. There were accommodations by both sides. For his part, like any father, like mine, Nixon made *some* effort to comprehend the children (and women) running amok in his house and on numerous occasions even made some effort to change. Like any father, he could never be positive they were dead wrong in their complaints and, like any father, sometimes he just wanted to avoid a ruckus. And they could raise *some* ruckus: that scene they made outside the 1968 Democratic Convention in Chicago, an ugly, violent scene which cast doubt on the leadership abilities — if not the probity — of his opponent and rent, perhaps irreparably, the unity of his opponent's party, may well have swung the margin in Nixon's marginal presidential victory that year. Accommodation, as the "New Nixon" of 1968 had come to realize, is often the shrewdest gambit of all — in fact, the whole "New Nixon" front itself (which the old Nixon would maintain steadfastly through his presidency) was largely an effort to head off, by means of accommodation, the "New Politics" of his kids. Thus, not only did he sometimes *act* like a peace creep, letting his hair and sideburns grow and appearing on TV's *Laugh-In* to say "Sock it to me," he actually ended the draft and eventually the war. Thus did he travel to China and make it no longer "red" and implement

200.

busing to integrate public schools and advocate and finally sign into law the bill lowering the voting age to eighteen. Thus did his Justice Department initiate the largest antitrust actions in history, against some of the nation's largest and wickedest corporations, while his Supreme Court —or at least the Supreme Court he had *tried* to make his own, appointing four justices in all— decriminalized abortion. Thus did he make dozens of moves to the left, to the hip, many of them, ironically enough, certain to be judged by the history he so desperately courted as among the wisest of his rule. Thus: "Same as the new boss . . . ?"

Well, now. Richard Nixon, of course, made many other moves that weren't so cool, at least not to the kids, who rose up to counter them in the great domestic conflicts for which the era and its president are indeed best remembered. One of those conflicts took place at Kent State University in Kent, Ohio, on May 4, 1970.

The events of that day, in which a National Guard unit fired into an unarmed crowd of student protesters, killing four and wounding three, have been documented thoroughly, if not very well, and endlessly discussed elsewhere, if not very perceptively. The most striking documentation of the events is the emblematic photo of a Kent student wailing on her knees over the bent, lifeless body of a fellow student. The most enlightening discussion may in fact be Neil Young's "Ohio," performed by him with Crosby, Stills, and Nash, in which the banjo-style rhythm guitar, strung with razor-wire and strung out tautly over a funeral march beat, explains just about all you might need to know. The 1980 TV movie, which is doubtless all that some younger people know of the Kent massacre, was enlightening only as an example of effective trivialization. A smug, shiny factoid of a "docudrama" called *Kent State*, a nostalgia piece, really, in the form of a soap opera, it climaxes with a ludicrous tableau vivant of the famous news photo and tries to glom additional historical import by overlaying Young's song on the soundtrack. But my point is that while Richard Nixon didn't actually pull the trigger at Kent State — the itchy trigger fingers of angry, poorly trained, overarmed, and understandably frightened National Guardsmen were most immediately to blame for that — with his demagogic, reactionary jingoism about "law and order," a phrase he hammered at constantly as a candidate and as president, Nixon did a lot to create the atmosphere in which the trigger was pulled. And of course, he invaded Cambodia, which was the move that the kids at Kent State — the kids on campuses everywhere — were protesting. Nixon was enough to blame then that even he felt pretty bad about it — much like any father might who has his adolescent son beaten to a pulp.

It was in the wee hours of May 9, the Saturday after the events at Kent State, that Richard Nixon made his most touching, perhaps most pathetic, certainly his most paternal effort, to get hip to the trip. An advance guard of Saturday afternoon's mass demonstration against Kent State and the Cambodian invasion had begun to assemble around four in the morning on the ellipse in Washington across from the White House when Nixon, awake early and listening to Rachmaninoff while he watched the gathering from a Lincoln Sitting Room window, "impulsively" grabbed his valet, Manolo, and, alerting neither staff nor press, went out among the children. Manolo Sanchez had volunteered that he had never seen the Lincoln Memorial at night — "the most beautiful sight in Washington," according to Nixon — and this was the ostensible reason for the odd jaunt. But the real reason, for the president, seemed to have more to do with penance.

"Those few days after Kent State were among the darkest of my presidency," Nixon writes in his memoirs, *RN*. He felt especially bad that some offhand comments of his might have helped precipitate the tragedy. The comments, made on the run to a friendly crowd at the Pentagon, had concerned the increasing violence of campus antiwar protests. Contrasting the protesters to the "proud," dutiful GIs in Vietnam, Nixon had said: "You see these bums, you know, blowing up the campuses. Listen, the boys that are on the college campuses today are the luckiest people in the world, going to the greatest universities, and here they are burning up the books, storming around about this issue . . ." Nixon says now he meant only "the arsonists at Berkeley and Yale and the Stanford firebombers and others like them" and insinuates that the news media, led by the *New York Times*, fostered "the widespread impression that I had referred to all student protesters as 'bums.'" In the dark days after Kent State — where, incidentally, two of the victims were just bystanders — his comments, it seems, had come back to haunt him. "I felt utterly dejected," he continues in the memoirs, "when I read that the father of one of the dead girls had told a reporter, 'My child was not a bum.'"

His predawn penance among the "bums" at the Lincoln Memorial, however, proved unsuccessful as expiation, particularly as measured by the PR. And it stung Nixon, he records again in *RN*, when the next day the newspapers got hold of the incident and reported that "I had been unable to communicate with the young people I met, and that I had shown my insensitivity to their concerns by talking about inconsequential subjects like sports and surfing." Which is in fact how that night is generally remembered: Nixon, the out-of-it oldster, trying to rap on surfing to the kids. It stung Nixon badly enough that he includes two versions of the incident, covering a full eight pages in the memoirs.

The first version is a memo responding to criticism of the incident by his own domestic affairs adviser, John Ehrlichman, a memo sent not to Ehrlichman himself, of course, but to chief of staff Bob Haldeman. In it Nixon defends the impromptu excursion as entirely in keeping with the mission of his democratic regime, which, as opposed to the regimes of "the socialists, the totalitarians who talk idealism but rule ruthlessly without any regard to the individual considerations," has "respect for personality." Taking a pro forma swipe at college professors and radical theorists, he further defends his actions as an effort to "lift [the student demonstrators] out of the miserable intellectual wasteland in which they now wander aimlessly around." The second version, another memo to Haldeman but in the form of a diary entry, is more human. A detailed exposition rather than a pat political defense, it illuminates Nixon's yearning to be understood and, in his obtuse, fatherly way, to be accommodating not only on Cambodia and Vietnam, but on a variety of issues with which the kids were identified as the anti-Nixon opposition. Obviously, Nixon had a vested interest in — as the countercult pols used to say — "co-opting" this opposition. But as this second, somewhat maudlin account suggests, while he may have been suffering delusions of his charisma, it's hard to believe he was being simply shrewd and disingenuous. The account suggests just how much these rock 'n' roll children, by dominating the national dialogue, had become father to their own semiclassical Pop.

"Manolo and I got out of the car at approximately 4:40 and walked up the steps to the Lincoln statue," Nixon writes. "By this time a few small groups of students had begun to congregate in the rotunda of the Memorial. I walked over to a group of them . . . and shook hands. They were not unfriendly. As a matter of fact, they seemed somewhat overawed, and, of course, quite surprised." One can imagine. "To get the conversation going I asked them how old they were, what they were studying, the usual questions . . .

"Two or three of them volunteered that they had not been able to hear [Friday's] press conference" — a particularly acrimonious encounter focused on Kent State and Cambodia — "because they had been driving all night in order to get here. I said I was sorry they had missed it because I had tried

204.

to explain in the press conference that my goals in Vietnam were the same as theirs — to stop the killing and end the war — to bring peace. Our goal was not to get into Cambodia by what we were doing, but to get out of Vietnam."

Acknowledging to the assembly, which eventually numbers about thirty, that "probably most of you think I'm an SOB," Nixon proceeds through an anecdote about the heroes and villains of his own political education and, by way of an unrelated anecdote, comes to exhort the kids to "travel when you are young." His efforts to "draw them out," predictably, produce little or no response. Discovering that a newcomer to the group lives in California, Nixon directs his efforts at her:

> In trying to draw her out, I told the rest of the group that when they went to California that they would see there what massive strides we could take to deal with the environment which I knew they were all interested in. I said that right below where I live in California there was the greatest surfing beach in the world, that it was completely denied to the public due to the fact that it was Marine Corps property, and that I had taken steps to release some of this property for a public beach so that the terribly overcrowded beaches further north could be unburdened, and so that the people could have a chance to enjoy the natural beauty which was there. I said that one of the thrusts of our whole "quality of life" environmental programs was to take our government property and put it to better uses...

Which is not much about surfing at all.

Nixon next returns to the travel theme in order to emphasize, he says in hindsight, "my thrust... that what really mattered in the world was people" and speaks of all the noble peoples he has come across, even in Russia. He then stresses to his audience "the importance of their not becoming alienated from the people of this country, its great variety" and relates his "distress that on the college campuses the blacks and whites, while they now go to school together, have less contact with each other than they had when they weren't." He goes on to reiterate "the point I had made in the press conference, that while we had great differences with the Russians we had to find a way to limit nuclear arms" — a point we might now see as an advance lobbying effort on behalf of the first SALT treaty, another of Nixon's worthwhile accomplishments — and he closes his talk by reaffirming his fundamental solidarity with the kids, while admonishing them that

> Cleaning up the air and the water and the streets is not going to solve the deepest problems that concern us all. Those are material problems. They must be solved. They are terribly important. . . . But you must remember that something that is completely clean can also be completely sterile and without spirit.
>
> What we all must think about is why we are here — what are those elements of the spirit which really matter.

To the reader, he adds:

> I just wanted to be sure that all of them realized that ending the war, and cleaning up the streets and the air and the water, was not going to solve the spiritual hunger which all of us have and which, of course, has been the great mystery of life from the beginning of time . . .

Which is all very Zen. Trying to accommodate even in conflict, certainly Nixon had changed — perhaps he really was "New," perhaps even "New Age."

Perhaps not. Following this lengthy quotation from the second memo to Haldeman, Nixon briefly sums up the general public opinion of the time on Cambodia and Kent State, finding it to have been fairly solidly behind him and against the student demonstrators. By way of proof, he cites a Gallup

206.

poll of mid-May — in which fifty percent approved of the Cambodian invasion and fifty-eight percent "blamed 'demonstrating students'" for Kent State — and offers the example of the construction workers. "On May 20 the New York Building and Construction Trades Council sponsored a parade to City Hall in support of the President," Nixon tells us. "There had already been scattered incidents of scuffling between the hardhats and various groups of antiwar demonstrators, especially after Mayor John Lindsay had ordered the flag on City Hall to be flown at half-staff as part of a 'Day of Reflection' about the Kent State tragedy. The hardhats decided to show their support for our war aims, and more than 100,000 people came out to march with them." Whereupon, says Nixon, "I invited the leaders of the construction workers' unions to come to the White House." While the former president is careful to soft-peddle the hardhats' demonstration — a loud, angry display marked by sporadic violence and calls to "Impeach the Red Mayor" — as a "parade" and to soft-peddle hardhat violence — some vicious hippie-headbashing — as "scuffling," he might be guilty of nothing more than partisan reporting were it not for information we have received subsequent to the publication of RN. Only recently, in fact, has it emerged on a newly transcribed White House tape that those hardhats — who came to be, for both sides, the embodiment of Nixon's "silent majority" — were frequently under the general direction, if not in the direct employ, of none other than Richard Nixon's White House — and specifically in the case of that New York "parade." And not only did the Nixon administration condone the hardhats' hippie-bashing, but considered having them do it again, with more selectivity. For instance, to Abbie Hoffman. "He's a Jew, right?" remarks Nixon on the tape in an even more ominous note.

Which is not very Zen at all — though it's not clear at all that Richard Nixon, like any desperate but well-meaning

.207

father, could have dug the diff. His personal — but far from unique — bigotry aside, Richard Nixon probably convinced himself into believing the convenient peace-love-and-ecology platitudes he spouted at the Lincoln Memorial — thus helping to make peace-love-and-ecology the apple pie and motherhood of the seventies. Problems arose, however ,when he set about building our utopia by the principles of Machiavelli.

Similar problems beset the Weather Underground, which, still as the Weathermen, embarked on its most explosive year in 1970 on behalf of the "revolution," issuing an outright "Declaration of War" following Kent State. With less drama, but perhaps more significance to the rest of us, such problems undermined Nixon's nemesis, Abbie Hoffman, too. And such problems must certainly plague anyone, even Liz Holtzman, who tries to play ball with the hardballers of the two-party monopoly. Problems with means. They have beset all our political endeavors. But then no matter how much he might act like a buddy to him, the father will always be father to the child, too. And, for all our kicking and screaming, we were still growing up to be Richard Nixon's kids.

· · ·

For *our* part, the accommodations were more convoluted. Which brings us back to Neil Young. The electric guitar that is made to sound like a lethal banjo in order to tell the story of "Ohio" tells much more than that — which is why "Ohio" remains undulled at such a distance from the event and the politics which inspired it and which it commemorates and why it still leaves us raw. That guitar, unmistakably Young's, tells us several versions of America, in fact the several versions that *are* America. While its voice is that of the contemporary electric guitar, dialed to the electronic max, the voice of "the kids today," the words and syntax that issue from it, the notes of the guitar and the way they are picked, are that of the Appalachian front-porch four-string, the hard, precise, intricate, and ultimately spare language of the banjos of those kids' grand- and great-grandfolks. The voice is new, but its bitter, somewhat mournful modal inflections are as old as the hills in America. Beyond that, the "new" voice of the guitar harks back to the saloons of black Chicago and on to the road-houses of the Mississippi Delta, while the old syntax has even older echoes in the folk songs of the British Isles on back to the Celts. But of course that drum-headed banjo came originally from Africa and passed into the hands and folkways of Anglos in America only after Afro-Americans had invented it. In Young's guitar there is city and country America, black and white, young and old, rich and poor, and the various combinations and permutations thereof, some of them merely implied, but many as explicit as a fiddler and a flat-picker in a Tennessee hollow or the garage band down the block. There is history and breaking news in that guitar as it slices through the layers of time and myth and peoples in search of an impossible nation. Though Nixon may invoke his silent majority of Americans, Young can call forth their deafeningly diverse noise. Though Nixon may claim for his silent majority the "old values" and "tradition," Young's noise swells with that tradition's very breathing. And though Nixon may stand finally on his authority as the knows-best father ("executive privilege"), his overgrown teenager, Neil, can step from the tumult holding hands with gramps. Young connects his outrage with the outrage of a previous revolution. In the tragic conflict of Ohio, he finds the synthesis of "Ohio." Neither denying nor compromising, he accommodates Nixon's America by gulping it down.

That Neil Young is so successful, here and throughout his singular career, at accommodating many apparently antithetical notions of America within his vision of it is a testament to the sharpness of that vision, to its veracity, and to

.209

Young's incisive talent, not to mention his American-scale ambition. But his success in seeing might also have something to do with the fact that he is Canadian born and raised and so has a good place to stand off and look from, a special psychic vantage point. Which is not to say that he is any less American — such would not be in keeping with the fact of our immigrant heritage, or, for that matter, with what Young has taught us about ourselves. Obsessed with this country (and to some extent with Nixon, too), a willful immigrant, perhaps he's even more American than those of us deposited here by birth (American that he is, Young would surely reject such an idea as undemocratic). But I mention his Canadian origins because the rockers who most obsessively plumbed the old myths of this country, in their words as well as their music, and with similarly singular success were the Band, all but one of whom also came from Canada. And I mention the Band because they too were exemplars of a new yearning in rock 'n' roll, as the sixties ran out, to meet the silent majority, or something like it, halfway.

Their number one fan and most devoted chronicler, Greil Marcus, best describes in *Mystery Train* what the Band was up to. Setting the scene for the release in 1968 of their unique and ominous first album, *Music from Big Pink,* with its unique and ominously ugly packaging, Marcus also keys in on Nixon: "In 1968 rock 'n' roll was coming out of its San Francisco period ... a fabulous euphoria in the middle of a war, innocence and optimism running straight into the election of Richard Nixon. It had been a fine time, with many chances taken and many chances blown, but it was over, it was soft underneath the flash and it had exhausted itself. ... *Sgt. Pepper* ... now seemed very hollow, a triumph of effects. The Yippies showed up to take over the politics of the decade, and defrauded them. ... We had gone too far, really, without getting anywhere." Turning to the album itself, Marcus writes:

210.

The pictures inside *Big Pink* — of the Band, their friends and relatives, and their ugly but much-loved big pink house — caught some of what they had to say. Against a cult of youth they felt for a continuity of generations; against the instant America of the sixties they looked for the traditions that made new things not only possible, but valuable; against a flight from roots they set a sense of place. Against the pop scene, all flux and novelty, they set themselves: a band with years behind it, and meant to last.

Many young Americans had spent the best part of the decade teaching themselves to feel like exiles in their own country; the Band . . . understood this, and were sure it was a mistake. . . .

. . . Their music was fashioned as a way back into America, and it worked.

Indeed, the sound of *Music from Big Pink* was so much the sound of an older America — pre-sixties, pre-rock 'n' roll, premodern — that in 1968 it was completely alien, surely from another country. But it was only another America: a patriotic, God-fearing America, a place where the Fourth of July is taken seriously, almost as seriously as the wily temptations of Satan, an America that is mostly the American South, and mostly its grit, not its gentility, an America of the land, wide open and suffocating all at once. And the voices that testify to it are voices we'd never heard, voices in fact from before Edison: the voices of Matthew Brady's soldierboys from the War Between the States; the black-lung voices of a coal shaft in Kentucky; the lonesome, strangled voice of a hopeless suitor in his too-tight collar and Sunday coat; the voices of whittlers in unmatching harmonies. The instruments are likewise ghostly and American: the ragtag horns and homely bass drum of a small-town marching band, a mountain mandolin, a cigar-box guitar playing rubber-band funk, a church organ with the Vengeful Lord stop all the way out. So old it was new, *Big Pink* was a "way back into America" that never left us behind. Says Marcus: "[Y]ou could recognize yourself in that sound." In other words, it rocked, too. *Big Pink* enfolded all of America, past and present, in its resonances. Rock 'n' roll was thereby changed, and so perhaps were we Americans.

It wasn't just Papa Nixon leading the charge backward — the Band, veterans from back near the start of rock 'n' roll, had been working up to this for a long time, and Neil Young's countryisms could probably be traced to some distant hootenanny night of his folkie beginnings. The patriotic, God-fearing, old American, old South, and sometimes redneck strains were always there, as the Band well knew, at the bottom of rock 'n' roll, which of course came from country & western music — then called hillbilly — and gospel, as well as from the dirty blues. The music, as some, including Nixon, might not realize or might like to deny, has a righteous pedigree of its own — which is how come it knows so well about sin; which is how come Elvis knew to repent every other record with a gospel disk and always closed his latter-day concert extravaganzas with "Dixie" and "The Battle Hymn of the Republic" and "America"; which is how come Little Richard always scurries back to preaching. In part, the reemergence in the late sixties of this deep current within the music had to do with the essentially pastoral character of the hippie fantasy of utopia — a place to walk barefoot among the flowers, living off the unprocessed fruit of the land — a pastoral fantasy that was intensified as its original urban settings, in Haight-Ashbury and the East Village, became increasingly crowded and dirty and dangerous. In part, rock 'n' roll's revived interests in its roots, particularly in country & western, had to do with other fantasies carried forward from the movies and TV shows of our childhoods, fantasies of mythic American forebears, the cowboys and -girls and the pioneers, of Davy Crockett, Wild Bill Hickok, Annie Oakley and Buffalo Bill, Jesse James. In part, this new "traditionalism" was

212.

a camp thing, a "goof" at first, another road down from the acid heights — beer here instead of Quaaludes, dumb country instead of dumb heavy metal — a reaction, like heavy metal, to the gentle, "feminine" dogma of the counterculture. But all these tendencies were finally galvanized into a cultural trend, as well as what would become several rock 'n' roll subgenres, by the apparent rebuke to the counterculture — to its proud "relevance," to its patriotism, even to its "manhood" — of the election of 1968, in which Richard Nixon, self-appointed pater familias and protector of the true American way, gained the presidency — and credence.

Inimitable in its specific musical approach, the Band wasn't necessarily the first rock 'n' roll group to restake its claim to America. With the release of their *Notorious Byrd Brothers* album, also in '68, the Los Angeles group the Byrds, who would later give up David Crosby to Crosby, Stills, Nash, and Young, veered from the folk-rock sound they had coined when they electrified Dylan's folk songs toward the sound to be known as country-rock. Not so inimitable, it was in fact the Byrds, rather than the Band, who most literally coined country-rock as a sound. On *Notorious* and its follow-ups, *Sweetheart of the Rodeo,* their country masterpiece, and *Dr. Byrds and Mr. Hyde,* their valiant, intermittently successful attempt to link the old frontier with the new, high frontier of space (and drugs?), the cover of which juxtaposed cowboys and astronauts, the sweet, pop-gospel harmonies laid down by the Byrds over tastefully restrained guitars and banjos and a lightened backbeat fairly well defined the most commercial, and eventually most popular, aspect of country-rock — most lucratively exploited not by the Byrds in the sixties, but by the Eagles in the seventies. And it's the title of one of the Eagles' many catchy, if sometimes anemic, hits that probably best describes generic country-rock and suggests something of its appeal to a frazzled, post-sixties world: "Peaceful, Easy Feeling." Indeed, much of the seventies country-rock which took off from the Byrds' model was strictly escapist fare, pleasant and — Mr. Nixon must have been pleased — thoroughly conservative, perfectly suited to the conservative tastes of the new radio businessmen serving up "soft rock" and "MOR."

But before our accommodation got the best of us, there were many exciting experiments in this new/old hybrid form, some of which seem destined to be classic. The most arresting departure of the time and the experiment most significant to the development of country-rock was that of the man who was the vehicle for the Byrds' initial success and who first brought the Band, then called the Hawks, to renown in the mid-sixties by hiring them as his backup group. Bob Dylan was always departing — from protest music to love songs, from love songs to rock 'n' roll, and then in 1966, after breaking his neck in a motorcycle accident, from rock 'n' roll to a mysterious two-year silence. Dylan departed from this silence, much to the relief of his great and anxious public, with *John Wesley Harding*, an elegiac album of outlaws and gamblers, of Ellis Island immigrants and East Side landlords, which evinced a certain amount of cross-pollination with his old backup group (and new neighbors) and in which Dylan reached to his roots in America and in an American folk music tradition predating his hero Woody Guthrie. Dropping his frantic run-on rhymes — and his whiny voice to a lower register — and mixing some country — a pedal steel guitar and Charlie McCoy's harmonica — into the basic folkie texture in songs like the title cut and "All Along the Watchtower" (superbly reworked into its most famous version by Jimi Hendrix — talk about cross-pollination) and the bouncy, almost hokey "I'll Be Your Baby Tonight," Dylan showed himself a master of American myth making and the American troubadour tradition. But *John Wesley Harding* did not prepare us for the next departure, which was the one that connected popularly, putting Dylan back on top of the charts, and country with him.

In 1969 Bob Dylan headed to Nashville, Tennessee, storied home of the country & western music business, and there, in essence, made his peace with the silent majority. As far as late sixties rock 'n' roll was concerned, it was almost as if U. S. Grant had gone to Appomattox to surrender to Robert E. Lee. Today, when country stars like the Nashville "outlaws" Willie Nelson and Waylon Jennings are also embraced as rock stars and, to a much lesser extent, rock stars, most recently former punker Elvis Costello, are permitted to "cross over" to country, it might not seem so strange. But when Dylan made that trip south in order to make a real Nashville country record in a real Nashville studio with a real Nashville producer and all the famously real Nashville studio players backing him up, the twain were not supposed to meet. And not only did they meet on the resulting album, but on its opening cut, an old Dylan folk tune called "Girl from the North Country," they actually sang a duet: Bob Dylan, the rough-voiced rock 'n' roll prophet, in ragged, aching harmony across a chasm of culture, politics, and even pop history, with Johnny Cash, the rough-voiced former rockabilly star, Presley contemporary, and Nixonian patriot, then the reigning king of Nashville, riding high on his own network TV variety show hit. Always an appealing song, this new performance of "Girl from the North Country" had magic about it.

The rest of the *Nashville Skyline* LP was not so inspired, at least not as music. In fact, it was inspiration that was singularly absent from the new music — and probably on purpose. Dylan, it seems, was so determined to be the dutiful pupil — actually inviting producer Pete Drake's singing lessons — so determined to make a country album that was really real — actually inviting producer Pete Drake to *produce* (arranging, recording, the works) and at great, costly length, the antithesis, in other words, of a Dylan session — so determined to sound like the new, grinning shitkicker Dylan of the album's cover, that he actually wrote up a bunch of corny, formulaic country songs and the whole thing came out sounding almost authentic Nashville and almost completely overcooked. Dylan's peace with Nashville was so peaceful and easy, however, and such a novelty to boot, that it just about floated out of the record stores. While the single "Lay Lady Lay" has become a soft rock radio perennial. But, as with a lot of things in rock 'n' roll, the greater significance of *Nashville Skyline* was not in the grooves. It was in the idea of Bob Dylan holding hands with Johnny Cash and Pete Drake amid the swell of a pedal steel in the shadow of the Grand Ole Opry, that country & western Carnegie Hall cum silent majority mecca where Elvis Presley begged for his first big break and a beleaguered President Nixon, doing a yo-yo trick for the clamorous crowd, begged for one of his last.

After *Nashville Skyline*, after Dylan did it, country once again had to be reckoned with in rock 'n' roll. And with the public now properly prepared, country-rock boomed. Thus, in an even more radical departure from form than Dylan's — but one that was still less of a shock — those founding fathers of San Francisco psychedelia, the Grateful Dead, turned away from the cosmos and endless electric jamming in 1970 and back toward wooden instruments and four-part harmonies, rooting around in our mythic common heritage to offer up a pair of homespun folk- and country-rock albums, *Workingman's Dead* and *American Beauty*, that were so warm and thoughtful and so full of the grimly optimistic native faith as to sound almost religious and to be most beautifully American. That same year, across town from the Dead, acid rock cofounders the Jefferson Airplane threw off a splinter group called Hot Tuna, composed of guitarist Jorma Kaukonen and bassist Jack Casady and chartered for the dissemination of

216.

country blues. And down the coast in LA, already well on its way to becoming country-rock's Nashville, Linda Ronstadt, whose roots and clear, emphatic, slightly overwrought singing were pure country but whose first hit single, "Different Drum," with the Stone Poneys in 1968, had pandered to the audience for "English"-sounding rock 'n' roll, was parting with the Stone Poneys and moving gradually toward a more authentic rock 'n' roll sound, as well as a more progressive record company, Asylum, on her way to becoming, by the mid-seventies, the queen of country-rock and, indeed, the dominant female voice in all of rock 'n' roll in the last decade. Meanwhile, one of her favorite songwriters, Jackson Browne, would in 1972 release the first of his increasingly popular, country-inflected, folk-rock albums on Asylum, on its way to becoming country-rock's Motown, and also on Asylum, also in 1972, Ronstadt's latter-day backup musicians would release their first album as the Eagles, on their way to becoming the kings of country-rock.

Neil Young's much lamented first group, the Buffalo Springfield — pioneers, along with the Byrds and perhaps Ronstadt, of LA country-rock — went down the drain in 1969 with *Last Time Around,* the most countrified of their three fine, country-tinged albums, but Buffalo Stephen Stills surfaced almost immediately with the first ready-made "supergroup" in (loosely speaking) country-rock, Crosby, Stills, and Nash (Graham Nash came from the Hollies), which was officially joined by Young in 1970 just in time for the rush-released single of the group's greatest hit, "Ohio." Other alumni of the Buffalo Springfield also went on to spread the country-rock faith in the seventies by founding Poco (Richie Furay), Souther-Hillman-Furay (again), and Loggins & Messina (Jim Messina himself).

Other alumni of the Byrds, however, went on in 1969 to found the Flying Burrito Brothers, whose definitive, surely classic debut LP, *Gilded Palace of Sin,* may be the definitive

.217

country-rock LP as well. Indeed, with Dixie's rock 'n' roll prodigal Gram Parsons in the lead, it effortlessly out-countries Dylan to capture the Nashville authenticity prize — which is no doubt why it never captured any more than a fanatical cult for an audience — while at the same time speaking to our present predicament rather than to history or the singer's redneck reveries. Aptly titled, *Gilded Palace of Sin* presents a conscious dichotomy, in fact, between its tradition-bound country music and the brave-new-world ideas of its lyrics. And it manages this dichotomy by sometimes ignoring it — a statement, of course, in itself — by sometimes mocking it, by judicious irony, and by never compromising either half and never condescending. It's Parsons, really, who manages it; and when he departed to make a couple of haunted solo albums, the group sank — because the dichotomy was him: the Waycross, Georgia, boy with the eastern education and the rock star ways, the God-fearer with Keith Richards for a best friend. On the first Burritos album cover, he is proud in his swank new suit, custom-made by Nudie, the legendary tailor to the legendary Nashville stars, but he is sniggering too: close inspection reveals that the embroidered doodads depict a dizzying array of pills. Hank Williams had that dichotomy too in his time, but he didn't dare throw it up in our faces or even to believe it could really work. Gram Parsons, citizen of rock 'n' roll America, isn't looking for his stake in Nashville America on *Gilded Palace;* he is dealing with the stake which, for better and for worse, he already has. In his characteristically reedy, shaken tenor, all approach and avoidance (country-rock's Mary Richards, in a sense), on a song called "Sin City," Gram says he understands that "On the thirty-first floor/A gold-plated door/Can't keep out the Lord's burning rain."

In 1973, after two Burrito albums and two solo sets, the rain that he may have understood but could certainly never control snuffed out Gram Parsons's life at the age of twenty-six. And the inescapable footnote to his death is that, en route to the family burial plot, his corpse was hijacked from the Los Angeles airport by a friend with a borrowed hearse and, apparently in keeping with the singer's wishes, spirited off to the California wilderness at Joshua Tree National Monument, set afire atop a makeshift pyre, and returned to the American dust.

. . .

A corollary to the rise of country-rock was the rise of what became known as southern rock, in which southerners unironically plumbed their roots themselves. Southern rock was also young people restaking claims to America — but as southerners, not as young people. These young people were primarily responding not to their alienation from their elders — that was simply a given at the time in rock 'n' roll — but to their alienation from the rest of the counterculture. To the rest of the counterculture, a *hippie* southerner was suspect and a hippie southerner with pride of place was deemed not much better than a redneck. And if some of those musicians gearing up for country-rock out in LA remembered that the South had given us Elvis Presley, many of the younger fans didn't think that was such a bargain anyway — the only Elvis they knew was a greasy relic and a shlockmeister. And where other stereotypes would get all of them, fans and musicians alike, up in arms, for the most part they heartily acquiesced in this one of the South as a monolith of racism and reaction and all that the counterculture opposed, a South embodied by Alabama's Governor George Wallace. Country-rocker Neil Young, in an unfortunate lapse of acuity, in 1970, even wrote a song based on the stereotype, detailing the white southerner's brutality to his black brethren and righteously crying out in the refrain: "How long, how long/ Southern Man?" Southern rock was not only a matter of pride, then, but a matter of honor. So a few years later, southern rockers Lynyrd Skynyrd finally replied to Young, as only southern rockers could, in their first and biggest hit, "Sweet Home Alabama." "In Birmingham they love the gov'nor," the lead singer explained, while a backup chorus gave out with an emphatic "Boo, boo, boo!" "Well, we all do what we can do," the singer continued, adding pointedly:

> Now Neil Young does not bother me,
> Does your conscience bother you?

Not coincidentally, the rise of southern rock paralleled the rise of what has been called the New South. In fact, the two movements reflected much the same basic impulse and achieved much the same results. Both sought to refute the stereotype, to restore southern honor and pride, and so southern will and vitality, by realigning southern institutions, necessarily undermined by the turmoil of the sixties, along more equitable, representative, democratic lines. Southern rock was a refutation of that stereotype as it was specifically applied to the culturally paramount music of the South; at the same time, the New South was its refutation in general. The New South — the *New* New South to those who would differentiate it from the dispirited *old* New South of the post-Civil War Reconstruction era — proved, most notably with the election in 1973 of Maynard Jackson as the first black mayor of the southern capital city of Atlanta, that racial progress, if not yet complete equality or integration, had come to the South (indeed, while it was — and is — still to come to many northern capitals — New Politics or no — whose consciences may or may not be bothered). And southern rock proved that *cultural* progress in the South had resumed at last — again, in a way, one and the same thing.

If the rise of the New South is best told as the story of Atlanta, the rise of southern rock is best told as the story of another town down the road apiece and the six-man band that put it and southern rock on the contemporary map. I mean, of course, "the Allman Brothers Band from Macon, Georgia," as they so proudly bill themselves, and in fact their story is not simply the best, but the only story to tell of this music. The rest of southern rock — Marshall Tucker Band, Wet Willie, Charlie Daniels Band, and Lynyrd Skynyrd included — followed not just in the Allmans' footsteps, but in their long shadow.

"People would come up and ask me how could white people play that way," recalled the Allmans' manager Phil Walden (who also directed the late Otis Redding throughout his career) in *White Boy Singin' the Blues,* critic and southerner Michael Bane's obsessive examination of rock 'n' roll's black and white and southern roots. "Well, that's the only damn way they can play! They can't play Bach and 'Sentimental Journey,' that's not a reflection of their culture. . . . Gregg sings like a black guy — well, that's the only damn way he knows how to sing." Gregg Allman, the band's main vocalist and keyboard player, is white, as was, of course, his late brother Duane, lead guitarist and leader of the band through its first and most fruitful years. With the exception of the black drummer, Jaimoe Johanson, the original Allman Brothers Band which created southern rock, the classic Allman Brothers Band with which we are concerned here, was all white. But they were all trained black. Walden to Michael Bane again: "Somebody asked Duane why, when he was growing up in Daytona Beach, he and Gregg were always playing in black bands. Duane said, 'White kids surf; black kids play music.' They never thought anything about it, being in black bands." While the studied diffidence of Duane's reply suggests he may have thought about it a lot way back when — white boys singin' (or playin') the blues, as Bane details in his book, have never been in it strictly for the music, especially not at that time, in that place — Duane Allman did get good enough at the music part that he was hired on as a guitarist at the now-legendary Muscle Shoals Studio in Alabama, where Atlantic Records was recording, among others, Aretha Franklin and Wilson Pickett. In any case, when he and Gregg, after an abortive fling with pop as the Hourglass, went back to scratch — and to Macon and Phil Walden's brand new Capricorn Records — to put together the music of the Allman Brothers Band in 1969, it was no surprise that, like the first great rockers, they began with the blues.

There were lots of white blues bands in the mid- to late sixties — many of which mutated into lots of heavy metal bands in the seventies — but none of them did the blues like the Allmans did, starting right with their eponymous first album in '69 on through the breakthrough third release in 1971, the two-disk concert recording that apotheosized Duane and the original group, *Allman Brothers Band Live at the Fillmore East*. Beyond the extraordinary musicianship of Duane, both as a soloist and leader, the distinctions begin with the band's highly formal, densely arranged approach to the blues. It's a dangerous approach because basically it's at odds with the very nature of the music: formally, the blues is supposed to be simple, an almost mythic musical structure of a certain standard duration and beat and a few standard chords, a common musical ground on which soloists, including vocalists, can hold forth uncommonly with unobstructed improvisations. But the Allmans didn't mean just to play standard blues — though a number like "Statesboro Blues" on the live album demonstrated they could play standards (and Duane the slide guitar) with the best. They meant to rock the blues, to make of it rock 'n' roll. Toward this end, they assembled the steadiest, most forceful rhythm section in rock 'n' roll — bassist Berry Oakley (sadly, a motorcycle casualty in 1972, like Duane the year before) and not one, but two drummers, Jaimoe and Butch Trucks — a combine up to driving even the *most* heavied-out blues.

To complicate matters, however, for such extended show-pieces as the extremely weighty, all-instrumental "In Memory of Elizabeth Reed" and the show-stopping "Whipping Post," they would prescribe various polyrhythms, numerous tempo shifts, and even difficult time signatures culled from modern jazz (no less) — but still never lose it. In fact, due to the unstinting rhythmic drive of their long-haul concerts, the Allmans, and subsequently their southern rock progeny, gained another more descriptive moniker — and some especially hard-rocking and hard-partying aficionados (e.g., the unnamed maniac of legend shouting for "Whipping Post!" on *Fillmore East*) — as the "southern boogie bands."

Complicating matters again, into this jazzed-up, rocking-blues amalgam co-lead guitarist Dicky Betts deposited country licks too, and later his own country songs ("Blue Sky" and the hit single "Ramblin' Man"). Finally, if the Allman's music was all brought into focus by Gregg's big, macho, slow-burn blues growl (the boogie brigade growls back in approval), it was indisputably distinguished as original to the Allman Brothers Band by the dual guitar leads that became the group's signature and its most durable contribution to the rock 'n' roll lexicon. As conceived and executed by Duane and Betts — sometimes as short fills, sometimes as long, thematic melody lines — the harmonizing leads, like so much else in the Allmans' rock 'n' roll blend, seem to have been inspired by diverse, unexpected sources, evoking jazz guitar duets and certain jazz and soul horn arrangements. After the Allmans, of course, harmonizing guitars would characterize the whole southern rock genre, but would also turn up as far afield as the music of the Eagles and Todd Rundgren and, perhaps most surprisingly but to great lyrical effect, on an album called *Rock 'n' Rock Animal* by that old New York demimondain Lou Reed. After the Allmans, there were busted categories all around and all around the glint of possibilities.

One possibility was perhaps not as obvious as the rest. The commercial success of the Allmans, his very first Capricorn group, had afforded Phil Walden the wherewithal for expansion, which meant signing up a bunch more of the southern rockers, and soon enough Phil Walden was enough of a power in Georgia that he had gotten to know the governor. By 1974, when the governor undertook a quixotic and protracted run for the presidency, Walden, as head of what had become a forty-million-dollar business and the biggest independent record company in the country, was in a position to help out his fast friend and fellow Georgian in a big way. Which he did, gathering the southern rockers for a round of benefit concerts that generated coast-to-coast publicity — one widely reprinted photo of the governor and Gregg Allman backstage together sticks in the mind — and dropped nearly half a million dollars directly into the candidate's kitty, with another half million in matching funds deposited by the federal government, in accordance with the new campaign financing law. "Insiders say the Capricorn money arrived just as the fledgling campaign was beginning to feel the financial pinch," writes Michael Bane; "some even credit the money with saving the campaign." And, Bane continues, when the governor "reportedly asked Walden what he wanted in return, Walden replied, 'A southerner in the White House.'" Alas, in what would be the crowning triumph of the New South — *and* its new musical culture — on election day in 1976 Phil Walden got his wish. The governor, of course, was Jimmy Carter, thirty-ninth president of the United States.

Early on in his then unannounced campaign, as part of a Law Day observance at the University of Georgia Law School (coincidentally, it was four years after Kent State to the day), Governor Carter made a speech that would gain national attention later, when the memory of it prompted *Rolling Stone*'s "gonzo" politics reporter Hunter Thompson to scramble out onto the thin limbs and, with some underwhelm-

224.

ing reservations, offer up to newly declared candidate Carter his first national endorsement. It's not easy to see now what got Thompson so hard — it wasn't all that easy to see then — but in the context of deepest Watergate, as well as the context of a big deal occasion at a law school (where Thompson was to have covered Ted Kennedy, another speaker), Carter's populist address on the failures of American justice and his specific, if moderate, criticism of lawyers might well have felt fresh and exciting. Anyway, in his introductory remarks that afternoon the governor made striking reference to the two main men of his philosophy. One was the German philosopher Reinhold Niebuhr. "The other source of my understanding about what's right and wrong in this society," Carter went on to say, "is from a friend of mine, a poet named Bob Dylan" — whom in fact Carter had hosted at the governor's mansion earlier in his term. "After listening to his records about 'The Lonesome Death of Hattie Carroll' and 'Like a Rolling Stone' and 'The Times They are a-Changin',' I've learned to appreciate the dynamism of change in a modern society." Whatever that is. Concluding the introduction, he explained:

> I grew up as a landowner's son. But I don't think I ever realized the proper interrelationship between the landowner and those who worked on a farm until I heard Dylan's record, 'I Ain't Gonna Work on Maggie's Farm No More.' So I come here speaking to you today about your subject with a base for my information founded on Reinhold Niebuhr and Bob Dylan.

You could say that he was merely grandstanding. But, as Thompson suggests, to whom? The establishment lawyers in his audience were unlikely to be favorably impressed, and a governor of Georgia's Law Day speech at the university is hardly news even in Georgia. The rising "anger in his voice" that Thompson noted that day might be further evidence of

.225

his sincerity. But Carter's sincerity, even after four years of his presidency, was never the big question. It's also somewhat beside the point here. I excerpt his remarks not for their truth, but their symbolism. And isn't that what modern politics is all about?

Traditionalist and revisionist, shitkicker and technocrat, friend to Gregg Allman and Bob Dylan alike, Jimmy Carter was reaching for the same kind of big, bold synthesis as rock 'n' roll. And he was going to bridge those great divides of the sixties and seventies, of Vietnam and Nixon and Watergate, not so much by building bridges, but by being one. His basic campaign promise, proffered in explicit contrast to the duplicities of Richard Nixon, was not in fact political, but personal, a pledge to honesty and humility and charity and downhome American piety. If he was still an accommodation of an accommodation, not the candidate of everyone's dreams — and I, for one, exercised my right *not* to vote in 1976 — in that contest of the blind, he was at least the one-eyed. And if some of us in the younger generation initially resisted making him king, watching him walk down Pennsylvania Avenue on Inauguration Day I, for one, took heart in his accession, suddenly stricken with a sneaking hope, like Hunter Thompson on Law Day, in spite of myself. It seemed then that maybe he was one of us after all, that maybe Jimmy Carter would be the triumph of the sons and daughters and not just the New Boss come again.

• • •

Back at the beginning of the last decade, as dawn's early light broke over the Lincoln Memorial to end a strange night in May, the thirty-seventh president, accompanied by a trusty manservant and attended by Secret Service guards and a physician (the quorum, evidently, when our leaders wander off — he said it — "alone"), was dutifully headed for his limo and home when one last spasm of paternal penitence

226.

seized him in his tracks. Wrapping up the second memo to Haldeman, Nixon described it like this:

> A bearded fellow from Detroit was taking a picture as I began to get in the car. I asked him if he wouldn't like to get in the picture. He stepped over with me and I said, Look, I'll have the President's doctor take the picture, and Tkach took the picture. He seemed to be quite delighted — it was, in fact, the broadest smile that I saw on the entire visit. As I left him I said . . . that I knew he had come a long way for this event and I knew, too, that he and his colleagues were terribly frustrated and angry about our policy and opposed to it. I said, I just hope your opposition doesn't turn into a blind hatred of the country, but remember this is a great country, with all of its faults . . .

And remember we did, devotedly. And what we eventually remembered by remembering this great country was that the America we hated was Nixon's, not ours.

When we offed the bastard, as kids must do to dads (and politicians to one another), we congratulated ourselves in the belief that we'd got this great country back. But as it turned out, it wasn't Nixon's America we hated: it was Ford's. And Carter's. And Reagan's. And I suppose Liz Holtzman's too — if she hasn't exactly sold us out yet, that's not to say she probably won't. And if indeed she *won't*, then she also won't last long — and her successor *will*. And now perhaps we will roll up our sleeves, remembering that in America the Boss works for us. Or, as some earlier colonials once declared, in America we are finally on our own.

KINDERNACHT

Rock and roll adolescent hoodlums storm the streets of all nations. They rush into the Louvre and throw acid in the Mona Lisa's face. They open zoos, insane asylums, prisons, burst water mains with air hammers, chop the floor out of passenger plane lavatories, shoot out lighthouses, file elevator cables to one thin wire, turn sewers into the water supply, throw sharks and sting rays, electric eels and candiru into swimming pools . . . play chicken with passenger planes and busses, rush into hospitals in white coats carrying saws and axes and scalpels three feet long; throw paralytics out of iron lungs (mimic their suffocations flopping about the floor and rolling their eyes up), administer injections with bicycle pumps, disconnect artificial kidneys, saw a woman in half with a two-man surgical saw, they drive herds of squealing pigs into the curb, they shit on the floor of the United Nations and wiped their ass with treaties, pacts, alliances.

Been down in the subway lately? Indeed, our "Old Uncle Bill Burroughs," as he once called himself, literary uncle to our aliterary rock 'n' roll generation and Patti Smith's favorite novelist, could see it all coming twenty-five years ago. And in *Naked Lunch* (whence the passage above), twenty-five years ago, he plainly laid it all out: the night of the sons and daughters.

It was a night of exultation at the untimely demise of Richard Nixon. It was a night of frustration at his ultimate deliverance. It was a night of fear: Nixon's was the first of our modern assassinations that could not be dismissed as the work of our deranged loners — our Oswalds and Sirhans, our Meredith Hunters maybe; there was no question this time, we were the deranged loners (we the people, we the children, we the Senate, we Liz Holtzman and the House Judiciary Committee) and the assassination of Nixon was a conspiracy theory made flesh. It was a night of anticipation: if we could do it to Big Daddy, who could we do it to next? It was a night of fear: if we could do it to America, could America do it to us? It was a night of confusion. For the sixties, it was a night of vindication — and a night of vanquishment for being too little and too late. It was the night of the subway train graffiti painters and the streetcorner rappers with their giant radios, of the college kids in wimpy drag and the Rastas in dreadlocks and the spiky-haired, ripped-up, black-leather punks. It was the night of antisex and heroin, amphetamine and blind hatred like you never saw. It was the night of the ugly. It was the night of the Noise.

> I can definitely tell you there's no *one* I'm afraid of. Except in the sense that we're all afraid, let's say, of a madman, of which we seem to have a surplus at the moment.
> — Roy Cohn, famous attorney, in
> Andy Warhol's *Interview* magazine,
> September 1981

It was a night of madmen and madwomen, and the last incorruptibles. And it started, more or less, as a joke, as these dangerous things so often do (e.g., "I didn't know it was loaded . . .")

"The boy looked at Johnny," she recites hoarsely over the building, percussive sound of a guitar chord not fully fingered. "Johnny want to run . . ." Finally the guitar finds its

232.

notes, drums arrive, a band, and, hiccupping into gear, the
singer takes off —

> Do you know how to pony?
> Like Bony Maroney?

— tearing into Wilson Pickett's sixties soul smash "Land of a
Thousand Dances."

Or:

A slow, sad piano vamp: "Jesus died for somebody's sins,"
the singer sneers in counterpoint, "But not mine . . ." The
band lopes in with some slinky, muted r 'n' b; the voice looks
at her fingernails: "I went to this here party/And I just got
bored . . ." She looks up — "And then I look out the window
see her humpin' on the parking meter" — getting interested
— "Leanin' on the parking meter" — getting hot — "And,
ooh, she look so good . . . that I'm gonna . . ." BAM! BAM!
the band hits twice — "Unh-unh! make her mine" — and
they all roar away toward a chorus of Van Morrison's classic
paean to teenage sexual frustration: "And her name is G . . .
L . . . O . . . R . . . I-I-I-I . . . G-L-O-R-I-A!" But it's not just
about sex here. "And the tower bells chime," the singer wails
remorsefully at the end as the band decelerates, arriving full
circle: "Sayin' Jesus died for somebody's sins . . ." Full stop.
Silence. Yes? " . . . But not mine." Then suddenly, full tilt:
"G-L-O-R-I-A!" Here it's about *holy* sex — "Gloria!" — holy
perverted sex — "G-L-O-R-I-A" — indeed, sin *as* salvation
— "Gloria! . . ."

Or:

Breathlessly, in a whirlwind of cymbals and piano and
moaning guitar:

> Mothers standin' in a doorway lettin' their sons be,
> not presidents —
> They're all dreamin' they're gonna be prophets . . .

And so is the singer, as she helps to invent punk.

After all, it was only a joke up to a point. And beyond that, everyone knows that dangerous crazies laugh at odd things, at odd moments — it's practically their definition — and that sometimes at the same time they cry and curse the sky. On *Horses* then, her first and most affecting album, released in the summer of 1975, Patti Smith — not the first crazy to call herself a prophet (and not the last punk either) — pretty much encompassed the limits of that laughter.

Bony and long necked and bug eyed beneath a feathery, hacked-off, jet black mop of hair, certainly no woman in rock 'n' roll had ever looked so much the psychopath. Certainly no woman had acted it so well — or was she acting? On her records and her record covers, too, no less than onstage or in person, Patti Smith seemed incapable of the predictable or normal reaction, even when she tried. Like Lou Reed, one of her heroes, she was always giving herself away. When she was magnanimous and giving toward her audience, she was a little too magnanimous. When she got soulful and passionate, she was a little too soulful. When she got tough — her basic pose (see the cover photo on *Horses*) — she was not unlike the squirrelly little kid in the movies who isn't deemed tough enough to join the local tough gang and finally goes out and kills a cop to prove she is — much to the gang's disbelief and then revulsion. Patti Smith *always* laughed in the wrong places too. Like a lot of us in this generation, in this culture, Smith lived in a world of her own. Like a lot of the punks who came after her, she just about succeeded — with our help — in wishing that world into being. Which is much the way it used to be before rock 'n' roll turned pro.

Patti Smith imagined herself a rock 'n' roll star. She imagined herself Jim Morrison, whose shamanistic performing style she imitated, and Keith Richards, whose sartorial style she imitated, and Jimi Hendrix, in whose Electric Lady Studio she recorded *Horses* — during which time she claimed to have been in contact with his ghost — and she imagined her group to be Lou Reed's old group, the Velvet Underground, whose copilot, John Cale, produced *Horses*. Patti Smith had already imagined herself a poet — primarily the nineteenth-century French symbolist Arthur Rimbaud — and had a book of her verse published in the early seventies under the title of *Whitt* (and another, called *Babel*, after she became a rock star). And in fact her first experiments with rock 'n' roll took place at poetry readings, where she would declaim over an improvised rock 'n' roll guitar backing provided by a friend, the rock critic Lenny Kaye, in an update on the poetry-and-jazz routines of the beatniks. A perfervid imaginer — with the talent and sometimes the skill to make it real for her and us both — she had also imagined herself a playwright (beatnik, avant-garde) and an actress (James Dean), cowriting with her then-boyfriend, the playwright Sam Shepard, a one-act psychodrama called *Cowboy Mouth* (1971), in which Shepard and she (under the pseudonym "Johnny Guitar") starred alongside Shepard's wife. Somewhere in the same period she further found time to imagine herself Edith Piaf, the French chanteuse, slipping into a black boa and evening gown to parade her chanteuse chops at the piss-elegant Reno Sweeney boîte in downtown Manhattan and — according to her — at cafés and nightclubs throughout Paris, too. But somehow, remarkably, Edith Piaf didn't quite work out, which is when Patti Smith turned her full attention to rock 'n' roll.

When I say that Smith imagined herself a rock 'n' roll star, I mean it quite literally. Even when she became a star, she was never much more than an inspired amateur. She never learned to play an instrument — though she would still plug in a guitar at a climactic moment in the act and madly scratch and pummel it to some expressionistic effect — and her anguished and uncontrolled vocal mannerisms suggested a parody of the girl groups, which were themselves parodistic (of girls) to begin with. She formed her band around the nucleus of her amateur musician friend Kaye, and the nucleus of the first album and early concerts would remain their improvisatorial expressions, after the fashion perhaps of jazz beboppers, on trash–rock standards like "Gloria" and "Land of a Thousand Dances." But, as opposed to the beboppers, such a point of departure was no doubt a necessity for Smith, who was only beginning to develop a songwriting craft she would never master.

Smith was not unaware, however, of her technical shortcomings — when she declared that "This is the era in which *everybody* creates!" she clearly meant herself as a prime example — and neither was her audience. To many, in fact, technical shortcomings were the best part. Smith's amateurism, and her resultant musical primitivism, represented not only an implicit encouragement to those of her public who imagined *themselves* rock stars but an assault on the seasoned-pro aesthetic of mainstream, corporate rock 'n' roll. With her tough-guy image and frequent calls to a kind of rock 'n' roll solidarity — i.e., the frothing, epileptic version of the Who's "My Generation" with which she used to close her shows — Smith went on to demonstrate her determination to take the assault even further, against establishments wherever they might nestle, reversing at last the Abbie Hoffman strategy in order to make rock 'n' roll as revolution. And never mind that Smith herself was eventually signed to a corporate label — in the way that she was just a little bit off, unapprehendable, in the way that she embodied the mad laughter which was always at the heart of rock 'n' roll, it all seemed that much more dangerous and so plausible, indeed just the sort of thing that might make Roy Cohn cross the street, if not surrender.

If Patti Smith's primitivism was not entirely born of choice, it jibed well enough with the rock 'n' roll essence, as well as with her own essentially romantic nature, that she knew to nurture it. Through her efforts, first realized on *Horses*, and the example of the hopelessly amateurish and happily primi-

236.

tive New York Dolls before her, and the Stooges, among others, before them, amateurism and primitivism would become snot-encrusted hallmarks of the punk style — and its biggest joke. But there was more: back early in 1976, a brief, first dispatch reached these shores describing an apparently typical engagement by a new band called the Sex Pistols. The group was slogging through an excruciatingly loud and inept set, all the while spitting and generally spewing hostility in the direction of their audience, who spat and tossed bottles and generally spewed hostility back, according to the dispatch — but all in the jolly spirit of the thing — when at one point between numbers, one of the more restrained members of the audience called out mockingly to neophyte bassist Sid Vicious, "You can't play!" To which Vicious promptly replied, "So what?" and, as the barroom barrage renewed itself, desultorily resumed proving it. All of which suggested that one punchline of the punk joke might be that an amateurist aesthetic rapidly evolves, by way of devolving, toward nihilism.

While Smith, too, was drawn by what she called the "sea of possibilities" in destruction and death and nothingness, at the same time she maintained a large, personal stake in the durability of things: ". . . only history (gentle rocking mona lisa) seals," she versified in her liner notes for *Horses*, adding expectantly, ". . . as for me i am truly totally ready to go . . ." The best part of this dead-serious joke for Patti Smith, then, may well have lain in the juxtaposing of her musical amateurism with her semipro literary abilities. And the full extent of her intensions may have been summed up in the early advertising on her behalf, the big, black headlines proclaiming, probably in her words: "Rock 'n' roll and the power of the word." Patti Smith was out to shoot up the classical with the vulgar, the intellectual with the antiintellectual, the unpopular with the popular, the sublime with the ridiculous. She would be the noble savage of literature and the "poet priestess," as one review tagged her, of rock 'n' roll; the writer as

.237

jukebox hero, the artiste as teen queen. It was a consummately democratic aspiration for an American artist — and more or less the shared aspiration of all American poets, at least since Whitman. And while many rock 'n' rollers before her had harbored squalid little aspirations toward Art — and for most it was not only in vain, but the ruin of their rock 'n' roll — with *Horses*, Patti Smith nearly achieved it — only to be tripped up short by a surfeit of that paradoxical self-absorption common to visionaries, be they democratic and utopian, Walt Whitman or otherwise. Nevertheless, the reaching itself, its *near* grasping, described an alternate direction for this new music, opening other possibilities, if not quite a "sea," in rock 'n' roll and in democracy, too. It was hysterical.

But for sheer punch line, it didn't have nothing on the Ramones:

> Beat on the brat
> With a baseball bat,
> Oh, yeah.

Or:

> Now I wanna sniff some glue,
> Now I wanna have something to do,
> All the kids wanna sniff some glue . . .

(Reconsidered on the next album, in the song "Carbona [cleaning fluid], Not Glue.")

Or:

"Hey, ho, let's go/Doin' the Blitzkrieg Bop . . ." All of it delivered over unremitting, uptempo, on-the-beat, metal sludge guitars by a guy with a half-octave range and a New York accent pretending to make believe he is British.

Autistic melodies, delinquent words, numbing volumes, amphetamine rhythms, absolutely no guitar solos — and absolutely no one capable of playing them if there were —

238.

absolutely no mercy: all musical transactions to be completed in under three minutes, if not under two, without once cracking a smile; monolithic, monochromatic sound matched by the look: sixties Beatles haircuts atop fifties leather jackets atop some favorite ripped-up jeans and holey sneakers held over from junior high; invented brothers and back-of-the-class, *Blackboard Jungle* greaseballs, Joey, Johnny, Dee Dee, and Tommy: the Ramones — they were everything that bona fide punks (hard core division, one must now specify) should be, and that was only right because they were the first.

While Patti Smith was sketching out her broad canvas at poetry readings on Second Avenue, the Ramones were hunkered down in a dive on the Bowery filling in their single-panel cartoon with a broken black crayon. Naturally, the overarching theme, as it were, of the Ramones and their music was adolescence — but here of the most pimply, ungainly, narrow, infantile, basically amoral, and modern American sort; adolescence not as metaphor but as its own stupid, solipsistic fact. In pursuit of that theme, having first disposed of just about all that was supposed to be meaningful and artful and enduring in rock 'n' roll — and, in the process, disposing of much that was pretentious and artsy and otherwise tediously self-conscious, the kind of fat, corporate rock 'n' roll that comes out of those endless studio sieges only "superstar" money can buy — the Ramones subsumed all that was supposed to be ephemeral and mindless and just plain bad into a juggernaut of pure, bad noise. And from the eponymous first album — thrust onto an unwitting world in the spring of 1976 — onward, and in concert as well, such would remain the aesthetic formula of the Ramones.

It was an amateurist aesthetic, to be sure. And while the Ramones could play as pros within the limits of their rather severely circumscribed musicianship, could deliver a pro-style *Ramones* show or record, there was never much danger that they would forfeit their basic integrity as amateurs. In

.239

the same way, while their image veered perilously close to sophisticated campness — and would later be adopted by certain segments of the chic — they retained their integrity as primitives because they remained congenitally unique, fundamentally original in stance and sound even when they were trying, by way of homage, to revive what they thought to be their roots. They had their antecedents, of course: the guitar sound from heavy metal; the vocals — or at least that clipped and strangely phony accent — from some low ebb of the mid-sixties British invasion, from Herman's Hermits, perhaps — with maybe that dollop of oleaginous angst thrown in by the Ronettes; the rushed beat from their beloved surf music, from the early Beach Boys and the Surfaris and Jan and Dean — not forgetting the Trashmen, whose one and only record, the immortal "Surfin' Bird" ("Poppa-oom-maow-maow . . . the bird is the word"), could well have served alone as inspiration for the entire Ramones oeuvre. Basically, wherever rock 'n' roll trash might be found, there is likely to be found as well something of the substance and something more of the spirit of the Ramones.

For all the intrinsic humor of the Ramones, however, there was also something about them in those early days that was not funny, something frightening even. But then new things usually are. It began with the not so new, with the simple iconographic element of menace in their black-leather-jacketed image. Then of course there was the simple impact of their sound on the human nervous system, an impact like that of heavy metal, but *more:* heavy metal without the relief of solos or portentous pauses, without dynamics, without texture. A sound beyond hearing, beyond ears, a pile-driver-in-fast-forward sound, it hit you in the chest, which could make it hard to breathe, which could make it hard to think. Which was part of the high — and part of the side effect. And in an anxious, panic-prone world, this was a dangerous sound. Beyond that there were the inescapable questions. Was this

240.

parody? Was it irony? Was it in fact humorous? Was it in fact music? In the possible answers — and the inevitable lack thereof — lurked further menace, and finally, above all, one arrived at the Ramones themselves . . . nothing. Their intentions were as secret as their real names. Take it or leave it. Like the new anticomedians — Andy Kaufman, for example — who came up in the seventies, who seemed to aim at provoking confusion, discomfort, boredom, even hate, rather than laughs, the Ramones obsessively blurred all lines between performance and reality. And no matter how funny and winsome you found them, you eventually had to ask yourself: *are there people like this?*

Where the Ramones came on inscrutably dumb, Television and Talking Heads came on smart. Where the Ramones portrayed an average Joe psychopathy, Television and Talking Heads portrayed neurosis. Where the Ramones were a robust antiart, Television and Talking Heads were arty to a rarefied and tubercular extreme. This was the other pole of the punk joke — "new wave," as it would become known, rather than hardcore punk — and these two bands were its originals. Actually, it was Tom Verlaine (né Miller), sometime Patti Smith protégé and leader of Television, who first discovered that Bowery dive called CBGB&OMFUG (owner Hilly Krystal's abbreviation of his original musical intentions for the place: country, bluegrass, blues & other music for uplifting gourmandizing) where the Ramones started and which gave birth to the whole punk movement. And while all the early punk bands to a certain extent shared an offbeat sense of humor and an amateur aesthetic and do-it-yourself ethos set in opposition to the capital-intensive, high-tech, professional values of mainstream corporate rock 'n' roll, what they mostly had in common was CBGB's, the place that would have them.

In other words, in a blindfold test one would never confuse the songs of the Ramones with those of Television or Talking

.241

Heads. In contrast to the Ramones' metal sludge, Television offered a clean, shimmering wash of guitar arpeggios, a very bright, thin sound with not much midrange, distinctly separated from the slightly jerky rhythms of its bottom. Not since the Byrds' electric twelve-string recordings circa "Mr. Tambourine Man" had there been such irrefutably pretty rhythm guitars, over which Verlaine would weave his deliberate, linear, almost modal or Eastern-sounding lead runs. Likewise, Talking Heads preferred the undistorted guitar sound, but with a generally sparer and more discrete band sound and choppier rhythms. Where lead guitarist Verlaine at times recalled the brittle lyricism of the Dead's Jerry Garcia or John Cippolina from Quicksilver Messenger Service (another of San Francisco's psychedelic-era originals), Heads' lead guitarist Byrne was pure frazzle. Accordingly, while lead singer and composer Verlaine invoked the dreamy ether in a song like "Glory," lead singer and composer Byrne invoked his own sweaty palms in "Psycho Killer" — though not without some amusement: "I'm tense and nervous/And I don't know why . . ." And then there were the voices: both of them weak, quavering, nonsingerly instruments, distant relatives of Bryan Ferry's and, some twenty years before, sobbing Johnny Ray's. But Verlaine mixed his in with the rest of the instruments almost as coloring, while with his, Byrne twitched forward, clenching and yelping and wheedling, to take control like a rock 'n' roll Norman Bates.

Again, the look matched the sound — and was just about as alien: Verlaine, gangly, in his crepe-soled creepers and too-short Levi's and clingy, polyester-knit sports shirt; Byrne, ganglier, in preppy penny loafers and khakis and a LaCoste alligator shirt. And perhaps most radically for rock 'n' rollers of the time, both of them with short hair. To the Ramones' latter-day greasers, Verlaine and Byrne played the "wimps," the "dinks," the "nerds" — certainly Talking Heads looked to be what they said they were. But there was an element of danger here too. If the Ramones were the glue sniffers in the back of the class, these guys — and one girl, Heads' bassist Tina Weymouth — were the A students in the front, of whom "stunned neighbors" would say to reporters, "But they were such *nice* kids . . ." after the nice kids had snapped, taking a family of four with them. "I hate people when they're not polite," fumed Byrne in "Psycho Killer." Indeed. And though it seemed that this overagitated preppy must be acting a character, one could never quite be sure — at the very least, one would hesitate, if one were Roy Cohn, before writing the lad a recommendation to Harvard. The danger was in the deadpan out-of-synch poses and in the verging on out-of-synch music; in the hopeless yearnings and wide-eyed apprehensions of Verlaine's elliptical word pictures, in the demonstrative nervous-breakdownism of Byrne's; and especially in those voices, voices lost enough and fearful enough and powerless enough to have to lash out eventually, if only, in the case of the somnambulistic Verlaine, to do itself in.

Like pearl divers, the Ramones gave a little jump at the edge of the abyss and, with head-first abandon, plummeted in, while Tom Verlaine, standing and watching, had a tragic accident, and David Byrne was pushed — and Patti Smith tried to get it all down for her own posterity. Much of it was exhilarating — a cool, death-defying spectacle that would serve as an example (and a warning) to all who would yet huddle safely; a continuing, chicken-dare triumph for the anarchy. But it had some obvious limits — like the bottom. Early on, in a voice more jangled than the rest, over jangled, falling-down-stairs guitar and bass, Richard Hell (né Myers), who broke off from Television to front his own group, the Voidoids, seemed to have reached it, on everyone's behalf, in a song called "Blank Generation." Courted by Susan Sontag (where Patti Smith had had to throw herself at Burroughs), touted by the news weeklies, when they finally descended on CBGB's, as the anthemizer of punkdom, Hell had announced:

"I belong to the blank generation/I can take it or leave it each time." And in its raw, wounded way his song was indeed stirring and anthemic. But stirring to what? A vision of the anthemizer from his first album cover comes to mind: Hell laid out as if crucified and under his ragged leather jacket, on his bare, hairless chest, *blank generation,* as brazen as Hester Prynne's embroidered *A,* but here scratched out in blood. And though Hell has protested that he did not mean *blank* generation, as in vacant, but meant instead _____ generation, as in a generation with no causes or characteristics, and so no name to call its own, *nameless* is only negligibly less bleak than *blank,* and anyway it was blank that stuck and, more than Hell may have realized, it was blank that was right.

Last time I was in Washington my hair was halfway to my waist and I had a hangover you don't forget. I can even give you exact time and date: January 20, 1973; all the livelong day. By one of those freaks of Einsteinian space, my hangover, which coincided with my District of Columbia debarkation, also coincided, as I was to find out, with a day of investiture for the new president of the United States, Richard M. Nixon.

Washington???

I had momentarily panicked when I awoke somewhere past Philly, but enough of the Old Grand Dad was still with me that the panic passed with barely a cold sweat. Just-post-teenage, lovesick and semiliterary, I was at the nadir of a drunken jag that had led from the Greenwich Village bar where the poet Dylan Thomas had once fallen from his last barstool into his last coma to this long, lonesome highway south. But I wasn't actually being Dylan Thomas when I packed a duffle and poked my thumb out on Seventh Avenue near the tunnel; I was being Jack Kerouac. But then I wasn't actually going to Washington; I was going to Arizona. Not only did I not know anybody in Washington, I wasn't even political anymore.

Hence, panic.

The two hippies who gave me a ride, *they* were going to Washington. They were going to be in the big demo protesting the investiture of Richard Nixon as president of the United States, and when the residual sedative flow had restored me to some semblance of woozy equilibrium, I decided so was I. A Kerouacian detour, I told myself, on the road to El Dorado. Go. Frankly, there wasn't a lot of choice.

The cops wouldn't let me walk off to the side, so I did my best to straggle behind. It was a paltry turnout — strictly made-for-TV-movie scale compared to the boffo Cinerama demos of a few years earlier. A lot of other people, it seemed, weren't political anymore either, having retired to one or another real world and quiet residency in the anti-Nixon demonstration of their minds. And after being in Washington that afternoon, I understood better why. It was a little embarrassing — which is why I took pains to imagine myself a poet-journalist, neutral and detached, notwithstanding this burgeoning case of the night-into-morning-after creeps.

You could tell by looking at the patched-elbow lefties who not only made up the lead but the bulk of the march, too, that everything had been hashed out with the cops well in advance and that all permits were in order here. The plan, as the organizers had explained it to us (them), was for the line of demonstrators to work its way around from the back to the front of the Capitol, where the inauguration would actually be taking place. For ten minutes all proceeded apace and with strictest, patched-elbow discipline, then suddenly a cop with a bullhorn announced that the march would not be permitted to turn the corner to the front after all but instead must immediately turn around. Some defiant shouts were raised, followed by a moderately heated exchange between protest leaders and the chief cop. But in a few more minutes resignation — spurred no doubt by a general realization of the nigh-pathetic dimensions of this righteous band — seemed to gain sway, and the roughly four hundred (plus one) commenced to column-rear — albeit somewhat uncrisply. "Off the grass," commanded the cop with the bullhorn. Some complied; some didn't; some probably didn't understand. The "grass" consisted of some modest brown patches on either side of the narrow road. "Off the grass!" he repeated, louder. Some more complied. Without further ado, the cop with the bullhorn unleashed his troops.

Somewhere not too far away around the corner of the Capitol building, the American (not to mention the world) press corps sucked en masse at the spectacle of Richard Nixon. Here, just out of sight of the TV eye — which had evidently decided that protest wasn't news anymore — just out of earshot, too, the DCPD held their own inauguration-(literally)-behind-the-inauguration. A tradition, perhaps. A little ritual slaughter of the innocents to propitiate the gods. And maybe, as slaughters go, it wasn't worth the mention — indeed, no one was really killed, nor, one can only presume, was anyone gravely, permanently injured. But not a word? Looking back, I wonder if I wasn't hallucinating. I wasn't.

They went at it with relish, and it was over almost before you could believe it had begun. I scuttled sideways and then backward with the crowd, hot fear in my chest. Two, three dozen police sliced into the fleshy ranks, the dispirited fleshy ranks. With big, stiff-wristed slugs of the club, they struck men down. Bloody scalps. I sidestepped some more. The rest of the crowd seemed to move slower now. I saw a policeman's club strike a young woman. I had to think about it. Did I see it? I saw another strike a woman already down. More bloody scalps. Did anyone else see it? Cops closing the distance, my heart throbbing in my neck — and then it was over. People crying, most dazed. The cops lined up at parade rest. "This demonstration is over," the bullhorn called out. No one argued. Blood here and there, but even those who were down eventually got up by themselves. I don't remember any ambulance or medic. Not so bad maybe, maybe *not* worth a mention, but I kept backing away, and soon I turned, my throat still pounding. I couldn't walk very fast on legs of gelatin, but I didn't look around. Some people see much worse every day. But it wasn't so much the violence as the violent injustice. Then again, some people see much worse every day.

"Tin soldiers and Nixon's coming" — and me with a hangover. Somewhere I lost my duffle, and the hippies with it. But I had just enough cash for the train back home, and I took it, and I never have hitchhiked to Arizona and didn't go back to Washington for nearly nine years, until today.

My hair is neatly clipped, and I'm wearing a jacket and tie, and I arrive in town like any commuter on the eight A.M. shuttle. I'm married now, settled down, more or less, and sober as a senator. And today I have an appointment in Washington, at Catholic University, to talk about the prophets.

Stepping onto the campus of the Catholic University of America in northeast Washington and into the munificent shadow of the National Shrine of the Immaculate Conception — "Largest Catholic Church in the United States," according to the brochure, and "7th largest church in the world" — I am unexpectedly riven somewhere between gut and frontal lobe by a certain sense of iniquity and general unworthiness I thought to have been expunged, along with my belief, a long time ago. Straightening up my bearing, as well as my motives, finally I am forced to submit to the obvious, but rather doomy, notion that the parochial school boy can never stray far. And, indeed, here I am. But what is most troubling is that concurrent with this clamminess of conscience, I am visited by a certain sense of warmth, a sense of being home.

Directly beneath the eaves of one of the ivy-shrouded, original buildings on campus is the cluttered, closet-size office of Dr. William E. May, Associate Professor of Moral Theology. A married layman, one of many who teach alongside the Marian brothers here, author of numerous Catholic press books and articles on moral and ethical issues — especially on issues of sex and the nature of human existence as they have been called into question by the practices of modern medicine and modern sex — May recently gained some national notice, and first caught my eye, as point man for the American Catholic governing body, the US Conference of Bishops, who had charged him with the sticky task of clarifying Pope John Paul II's latest broadside against contraception. A teacher of canon law, among other subjects, at the university, May is as down-the-line dogmatic as one would expect and yet, to a degree, remains persuasive, even to a dogmatically fallen-away type such as myself. After reading his anticontraception apologia and his more general, book-length study of "Christian ethics," *Becoming Human,* I decided to contact him for an appointment to talk about the Sex Pistols.

· · ·

"Rrrright . . . *now!*" says the cackling boy. A bass throbs. A drum snaps. The boy spits:

> I am an anti-Christ,
> I am an anarchist,
> Don't know what I want,

248.

But I know how to get it,
I wanna destroy passersby,
And I wanna be
Anarchy . . .
— *Sex Pistols,*
"*Anarchy in the UK*"

· · ·

William May is fiftyish, heavy, of average height, with shaggy gray hair, a shaggy gray suit and shirt, and shaggy gray orthopedic space shoes, none of which is necessarily gray, all of which lends him every aspect of the absentminded professor he sort of is. Except that in his aviator spectacles he also looks a little like Billy Carter, and in his speaking mannerisms — careening from loud and clear declaiming one moment to significant mumbling the next — he resembles the actor Sterling Hayden.

It would have been unfair to this genial and generous man to try and talk specifically about the Sex Pistols. Worse than that, it would have been useless — he wouldn't have had a clue. Nor, I'd guess, would the Ramones or Patti Smith or Richard Hell have been any more in his line. So what we talked about was death and sex and love and power and how to be moral in a quaking, cataclysmic age, about faith, and then I passed along to him a question my father had some time ago passed along to me, asking in effect: what is going *on?*

Same difference.

I would argue that it is, that the basic concern of punk, even at its amoral, faithless worst, represented here by the mung-mouthed Sex Pistols, was actually *theological* and that the faithless wild boys and girls were actually the faithful, just as elsewhere in our inverted century the sinners have been the saints.

· · ·

We descend from his musty garret to the lovely, wood-paneled cafeteria for lunch and order beer all around. William May tells me he first came to Washington in 1969, involved in the antiwar effort, and then, at my request, draws for us an agenda of the major issues of the last decade and a half in America, annotated with some of his personal experiences and expectations.

"I think that the crucial issue, first of all, would be the dignity of the person and the sanctity of life," he begins, not unpredictably perhaps. "There was an editorial in the *Journal of the California Medical Society* in nineteen seventy that showed very clearly what was happening in the early seventies. That our society was moving away from an older ethic of the sanctity of life to a new ethic of the quality of life and that this would effect significant changes.

"They pointed out that this was a shift from the traditional view related to the Declaration of Independence, in which it was said that 'All men are created equal, endowed by their Creator with certain inalienable rights, such as life, liberty, and the pursuit of happiness,' et cetera; the traditional view that the purpose of the society is to serve the needs of its members and that each member is equal under the law — all of which was predicated upon the assumption that the human being is different in *kind* from other animals, at least before the law.

"And I see this new intellectual model of society which has come about as a result of a lot of cultural changes — television, the impact of science and technology — a deterministic hypothesis that a human being is different from animals only in degree and that ultimately the difference is that we have a larger brain, that there's little difference between the mind and the brain, and that there's nothing to the person *in addition* to the brain that is required for us to think. The idea is that we're really not free and that the best way to get a good society is through control over the environment, both internal

250.

and external. That's what I saw emerging during the early seventies."

But there is more. He tips his beer mug and then resumes, with a mumble: ". . . A book that would illustrate this is B. F. Skinner's *Beyond Freedom and Dignity*. What Skinner's saying is that once you have people born, you shape their lives by shaping their environment. Of course the ones who are shaping the environment are simply the ones who know how to do this, human beings who are *superior* to others in their degree of development." He leans back, checking to make certain I've caught his irony, and then plunges ahead.

"Now what happened in the biological revolution is we developed the ability not only to modify the external environment, but to modify the *internal* environment through genetic manipulation. What we also have now — and this is related to the abortion issue — is the monitoring of the beginning of life, through amniocentesis and so forth, and if it doesn't meet certain standards, you can kick it out. This model of society says that the way to get a good environment is to have those who know how to control it in charge. This would be an intellectual elite — well motivated; for a utopia, as it were — but . . ." He trails off, concluding the thought in his head, now returning cheerily: "This was somewhat the direction I saw things going."

Not forgetting the original query, he adds, *"But . . ."* and raises his finger, *"I* was hoping the seventies would be an era in which there would be greater, I would say, *decentralization* and an endeavor to help individuals become more free, in the sense of being responsible for their own actions." Finishing off his conversational groundwork, he now lays out for me the fundamental "goods" of human existence: "life, life itself, friendships, the ability to make friends, justice, peace, truth, and so forth." And while I tick them off, wondering vaguely about the so forth, he continues: "But the presumption is that human beings are free, and that in the making of

.251

a good human person and a good human society the chief ingredient is free choices intelligently made."

. . .

LONDON (*Rolling Stone* magazine, 10/20/77; by Charles M. Young) ... One of the regulars at Sex was a kid named John Lydon, who was distinguished on three counts: 1) his face had the pallor of death; 2) he went around spitting on poseurs he passed on the street; and 3) he was the first to understand the democratic implications of punk — rather than pay ten pounds for an ugly T-shirt with holes in it, he took a Pink Floyd T-shirt, scratched holes in the eyes and wrote I HATE over the logo. McLaren stood him in front of the jukebox, had him mouth Alice Cooper's "I'm Eighteen" and declared him their new lead singer. Jones noticed the mung on Lydon's never-brushed teeth, and christened him Johnny Rotten ...

. . .

William May and I order our lunch — and two more beers. He picks right back up: "Another issue would be the relationship of the rulers to the ruled. I think Watergate illustrated that perfectly. I think some very good people thought that Nixon had broken faith with them, which I think is quite true. There is a special relationship between the representatives and the people, and there has to be a living bond between the two. But still, your representatives, your legislators, are not just rubber stamps of public opinion. This is an aspect of this keeping of faith: the representatives can resist the people, but in resisting must always make them aware of what holds them together as a people. I don't think Nixon was interested in doing that. I was hoping we would have some kind of leadership at the national level of that kind in the seventies."

"You're talking about government," I say. He listens intently. "But what about the idea that it's not so much government that rules anymore, it's, say, the large corporations . . ."

"Also the media, I think, too," he interjects.

"And the media."

"If you talk about large corporations," he points out, "you also talk about CBS, NBC, and ABC."

"But, for instance," I continue, "when the oil companies are seen to dictate energy policy, that's when people perceive a loss of control and maybe they have . . ."

"They *have* . . ." he says, now lapsing into significant mumbles. ". . . There's a theologian, Bernard Lonergan. He speaks of a movement of persons from *experience* to *understanding* to *critical reflection* to *responsible action*. He points out that our *understanding* is mediated to us. We don't have to discover everything for ourselves. We have a lot of meanings mediated to us by others. And these mediations can be either false or true, partial or apt — but," May declaims, "you have to ask *questions*."

Evenly, he goes on: "As I see here in our society today, it seems that the role of mediating meanings to people growing up . . . well, it used to be that meaning was mediated primarily through families. Of course those meanings could have been erroneous or partial, but that could be corrected later on through the challenge of others. But the biggest instrument today in mediating meaning would be the media, particularly television, because everybody grows up on it."

And what values does TV foster?

"I think television mediates all kinds of values, depending on what you're watching. But one of the obvious ones that can be developed through watching advertising — and advertisements in general — would be an individualistic and hedonistic value system . . . TV certainly can accomplish some tremendous things. Take *Roots*. I think there were much different values mediated through *Roots*.

"Of course, this isn't just television — it's the people who *own* the television sets. After all, they could turn them off. . . .

But it has, I think, deadened the sensitivity of people. That's one thing it's done. Another thing it does, of course, is it destroys the art of conversation." He pauses, dissatisfied, grasping for a better handle on his subject.

"In many ways," he says, taking another crack at it, "it's predicated on a principle that is destructive of the intelligence of the viewer. That attitude that 'You've got a bunch of morons out there looking at it' is part of that . . . I do think there are some very good things on television, but since so much of our information is given, particularly to the younger generation, through television, and is given to *them* at an age when all that comes through is this rugged individualism kind of idea, and that wealth, influence, ease, big cars, and so on are the desirable things to have, I think the general image that's mediated through television is contrary to the human good. A lot of truths get distorted through it. Take sex, for example. I think sex is a big question, an important part of human lives. But the biggest thing that television communicates about why we are sexual persons is that we have a need to release sexual tensions in the experience of orgasmic pleasure. This is a somewhat distorted version of what it means to be a sexual being. Communication of affection is involved in sex too."

I mention *The Mary Tyler Moore Show, All in the Family,* and *MASH,* all of which he more or less favors. "The one's you're talking about are, I think, quite superior to so many others," he says, "like *Soap* and *Three's Company* and all, though I couldn't really tell you what *they're* about, because whenever they go on in the house, the set goes off. I'm pretty upset about it. They have such banality about them. That's the problem: they're utterly *banal.*"

• • •

I've got no reason,
It's all too much,

You'll always find me
Out to lunch;
We're so pretty,
Oh, so pretty
We're vacant —
And we don't care . . .
    — *Sex Pistols, "Pretty Vacant"*

. . .

A dispute now arises over the ownership of a basket of french fries just delivered to the table. They are mine, in fact, but they've been set down at May's place. Absently, he begins to pick at them. I churn. Suddenly: "Oh! Are these yours? I'm sorry . . ." "No, no, no," I insist. Eventually, the basket lands in a DMZ at center table, where it goes mostly untouched.

My next question, however, refers to an earlier comment by the professor. "Given the size of this country," I ask, "and the nature of our economic system, is centralization — of bureaucracy, of capital — just inevitable? Do we perhaps need a basic restructuring?"

"I don't know," May replies, producing a handkerchief and blowing his nose loudly, in the manner of the older generation. "Seems to me that one of the basic problems is that most ordinary people have a feeling of hopelessness and impotence because there's so *much* of their lives that is covered by forces over which they have absolutely no control. Urban Renewal would be an example of this. Because as the cities were built up, they were built up more for the convenience of traffic than of individuals. . . . How you go about changing it, I don't know."

"What is the place of religious faith in this kind of economic system," I want to know, "and in a country that was founded basically to be anticlerical, even in a way anti-God . . ."

"It was individualistic, too . . ." he tosses in.

". . . and individualistic," I continue, "and proscience, pro-rational. . . . In *Becoming Human* you talk about being in community with others, but is that contradictory in a country founded on, as you say, rugged individualism?"

"Of course, you've had those strains in American thought all along," he says, by way of agreeing. "I think that's why I like this philosopher Jacques Maritain — because he makes a keen distinction between an individual person and a member of society. There's nothing wrong in being an individual. But as individuals we are replaceable. For example, if you have a football team and your tackles get injured, you get two more tackles. As *individuals* we are, in a sense, still subordinate to the whole society in which we live, and can be compelled to contribute to the common good, and so forth. But as *persons*, which is something else we are too, we are unique.

"This has to do with these goods of human life. The real goods of human life are *personal* goods. As personal goods, they are in some way shareable with others; we can communicate these goods . . ." He stops. I must be looking perplexed. "Let me illustrate this," he says, "I take a truth — or a joke or an aesthetic experience. Now I can develop my skills in this, but in order to exercise them I would really like to do it with people who have the same kind of skills. If you're a skilled chess player, you can play with yourself — but it's much more fun playing with another good chess player. If you're good at telling jokes, you like to tell them to other people. This is an aspect of these goods, sharing and communicating them.

"Even life itself. You can share it with other people. Parents can give life to their children, and so forth. And knowledge . . . only *you* can learn something, that's true, only the individual *person* can learn something. But once you learn it, you can communicate it to another, and after you share it, you *don't* lose possession of it."

· · ·

DALLAS (*Creem* magazine, 4/78; by Patrick Goldstein)
... In Dallas a tough young punkette punched Sid in the
face. She said she drove all the way from L.A. to do it. Vicious, surprised to find blood gushing from his nose and
mouth, took a couple of seconds to compose himself. Then
he spit it back in the girl's face. He proudly massaged the
rest of the blood on his chest ...

• • •

"So to accomplish and preserve and foster the human goods,
we have to be a community, act in concert," I try to sum
up. "But is there a contradiction of that in the American
ethos?"

"I don't know if it's actually a contradiction. You have conflicting tendencies, of rugged individualism, on the one hand
— that 'Devil take the hindmost' attitude, or that perverted
version of the golden rule, 'Do unto others before they do
unto you' — and on the other hand, you have the fact that
the American people have always been a rather generous people. Even in wars — in World War One and World War Two
there was always that aspect of saving the world for democracy, warding off what are portrayed as the forces of evil.
And in floods and earthquakes and in other areas the American people have always been somewhat generous. So what
you have is conflicting tendencies. And I think what you want
to get is a society that attempts to respect the individual —
and that's what this rugged individualism is about — but, at
the same time, a society where persons recognize they cannot
fulfill themselves unless they're ready to share. But the forces
of today that make policy *ignore* this aspect of human existence, the sharing."

"But our measure of success has very little to do with sharing — the big house, the cars," I say.

"You want to be left alone with your private pleas-
ures ..." says May, decaying again into mumbles, pondering.

"If you look at the motto 'E Pluribus Unum,' you realize our society is pluralistic, which in many ways is good. But in some way there has to also be that unity among the people. And I think that's what's really been missing in the past decade. In other words, what is it that unites us as a people?" He reaches for yet another text. "Walter Lippman put it this way: civilization was like an argument — which is different from being a quarrel. Because when you have an argument there's an acceptance of certain premises in terms of which you can convince others of the truth of what you are presenting. Whereas a quarrel is settled by the *argumentum baccum,* or the use of a stick. It may be that at one time in American life you had a consensus as to what pulled people together as one people, but maybe that's dissolved."

"Do you see that it has dissolved?"

"It's been eroded. And what's eroding it, I think, is the viewpoint that we really aren't free, that that's merely an illusion, that our lives are determined by forces over which we have no personal control, and that the way you get your utopian society is simply to use effective controllers. That the two forces of environment and heredity are all that matters."

.   .   .

Bo-dies — I'm not an animal,
Mom-my — I'm an abortion . . .
— *Sex Pistols, "Bodies"*

.   .   .

"Do you think there has been a loss of faith, then?"

"There has definitely been a loss of faith. This subject of human freedom, I see a lot of trends in Roman Catholic moral theology that to me simply accept *verbally* the question of human freedom but don't really cause the presumption that we are free to control our own lives. They are saying that you have to compromise to be realistic, that compromising is the

258.

best thing you can do here and now. I see that as a lack of a firm faith in God. In fact, Saint Augustine — well, this is very interesting because the Council of Trent" — convened by the pope in the sixteenth century to counter the Reformation — "uses his very words: 'God never commands us to do the impossible.' That is, in our *moral* lives. So what we have to do is do what we can and pray for what we cannot, in the faith that it will be given to us. And I think that has had an eroding effect."

"Because people will stop short, saying, 'That's the best I can do'?"

"Yeah. There's a book called *Principles for a Catholic Morality* which illustrates this. The author takes a statement by Saint Thomas establishing the first principle of natural law, the 'Harmony of Good Reason,' in which he said, 'Good is to be done, and evil is to be avoided.' But this author maintains that was simply a general maxim, and what it means is that you do the most good you can and the least evil you can, that this maxim of Saint Thomas's is an unrealistic, unachievable ideal. But I think that's predicated on a lack of faith — not only a lack of faith, but a lack of intelligence." May relates this ethic of accommodation to contraception — which "takes away from the person's responsibility for pregnancy," he says. ... "In other words, 'It wasn't my fault I got pregnant, I was taking a contraceptive.'" He also relates it to abortion, to which he is likewise, of course, opposed. He denies that contraception and abortion might actually represent the *accepting* of responsibility rather than its shirking. No, William May stands firm. "I would disagree that you have to accommodate," he says, adding, in the language of pop, where these things come down in the first place, "it's a cop-out."

· · ·

LONDON (*Rolling Stone*, 10/20/77; Charles M. Young)
... "John, wouldn't you make yourself look like a cunt for a million dollars?"

"How could you make me look like a bigger cunt than I am?" says Rotten. "The joke's on you."

.   .   .

We fight over the check. I win — which is only fair considering that it is I who have descended on him — and we repair upstairs.

"What would you say is the gravest threat to the common good?" I ask, trying to round it all up. "Is it really something like television? Is it the sanctioning of abortion?"

"I wouldn't see those as the biggest threats," he answers quietly. "Somehow or other I see them as manifestations of what must be underneath that somehow."

"Relating to what you mentioned before, the sanctity of life?"

"Right," he says, speaking up, "in some way related to that. I think maybe the biggest threats I see are cynicism and skepticism. And I see the television as reflecting the cynicism and skepticism, the idea that what's one man's meat is another man's poison, which is symptomatic of cynicism and skepticism." Subdued again, matter-of-fact, he admits, "Where that's rooted, I don't know."

"What do you mean by skepticism?"

"No one can tell you what's true."

"It's an inability to believe?"

"An inability to believe, agnosticism . . ."

"Cynicism being . . ."

"The cynicism that everybody's out for himself . . . suspicion of other persons, suspecting their motives."

"But considering only the pervasiveness of *official* lying by industry and government today," I suggest, "can a person afford to be anything but skeptical and cynical?"

"Sort of a protective device, huh?" says May.

"In fact," I go on, "to be completely unskeptical today would seem to be stupid, possibly even suicidal."

"What's it called, 'street wise'?" he asks, with what I take to be rhetorical deference. Is he making a point?

Does he see hope? "Do you think we've reached some sort of dead end?"

"I'm not a doomsayer, no. Or a coming apocalypse — I don't believe that. I do think that you have all these erosive factors operating, but there are still an awful lot of possibilities. First of all, I do think that human beings have a natural inclination toward the good. To become consciously aware of this inclination to the good is where our society has a great role to play. Our lives becoming human are full of enabling and disabling factors. I would say that cynicism and skepticism would be *dis*abling factors. But you do have enabling factors. There are a lot of dedicated public officials — there must be some, certainly, in the educational system, out there in the classrooms attempting to open up minds and raise these questions. And there are still a lot of families and people who are doing things, and there's always a possibility . . .

"But maybe the problem today would be that this feeling of despair would come, this feeling of impotence, this feeling of 'What can we do in the face of the power those corporate directors have?' and so forth, this feeling of 'What can we possibly do?' This feeling of defeat.

"Well, what we *can* do is give some sort of structure to it, a societal structure. Obviously, that's part of what the Church is supposed to do, a building up of support systems. Maybe the great molders of public opinion, like TV, could focus attention on some of these things," he says hopefully — finally sounding a little too unskeptical even to himself. "I guess it gets to the economic factor there . . . so maybe the economic push could be restored to the families and other small groupings. Maybe that could be effected through legislation."

• • •

No future,
No future,
No future,
For you . . .
We're the future,
Your future.
— *Sex Pistols,*
"*God Save the Queen*"

. . .

"Is it possible, for instance, that the antiwar movement was such a support system, a community?" I speculate. "And that its dissolution was finally as devastating to the American spirit as the war itself had been in the first place?"

"I think that's instructive," replies May. But ultimately, it seems, he doesn't. In fact, you might even say this erstwhile antiwarrior is skeptical. "I think that in a lot of the opposition to the Vietnam War there was a great deal of manipulation, though, by a lot of people whose opposition was not that great, not that motivated.

"Let me make a comparison," he continues, now tracing out a new subdivision within the boundaries of the old sixties generation gap. "I think there was a certain spirit in the civil rights movement, in the *early* sixties. There you had a cause that united diverse groups with great ideological differences. But this was a clear-cut issue of justice. That was quite central to it. And it did have a remarkable cohesiveness. Of course, you always have to accept *some* manipulation. But as a whole I think it had a remarkable effect. The leadership effected by a man like Martin Luther King was quite a catalyst for that. But once that cause was lost, then Vietnam and Watergate led to a lot of these other things."

. . .

LONDON (*Rolling Stone,* 10/20/77; by Charles M. Young)
... "Punks and niggers are almost the same thing," says Rotten ...

• • •

"Maybe there's some other kind of crucial issue that could draw out the people. Maybe the abortion issue. I think the abortion issue is fundamentally one of justice and not a matter of imposing morality on others — and I would say here that you have a lot of manipulation on this by what you call the New Right — it has to do with the protection of the lives of the innocent, protection of *all* the members of the society. If you had someone like Martin Luther King to take that issue and transcend, to get by some of the narrow goals of, say, the Moral Majority, that might be an issue to draw people out."

• • •

We got noise,
It's our choice,
It's what we wanna do
— *Sex Pistols, "I'm a Lazy Sod"*

• • •

"And I think another issue, a *real* big one, is nuclear weapons. I'm not a pacifist, but as long as you have those blasted nuclear weapons, sooner or later somebody's going to be using them. I don't see how we can go through another century — or another twenty years even — without some of these tremendous weapons actually being used. I would think the world leaders would realize that's the case and that there has to be a sane policy of nuclear disarmament. This would be another kind of point to get people together again, if good solid leadership were exerted."

• • •

DALLAS (*Creem*, 4/78; by Patrick Goldstein)
[Rotten:] "You won't see me writing any love songs. I wouldn't know what it's about" . . .

. . .

But there was one more thing that was bothering me.

"Is masturbation really a mortal sin?" I ask May.

"I would say that for an adult, if it's a fully free and deliberate act, with full consent, and so forth . . ." Pause. "Yes."

"It's *still* a mortal sin?"

"Yes, it would constitute a serious move."

"Could there be mitigating circumstances? Say, you were on a desert island alone? . . ."

"No, I don't think so."

"There are *no* mitigating circumstances?"

"I would say your mitigating circumstances might be teenagers going through adolescence, that growth process, and not understanding what they're doing. They're perplexed over it and everything else. That would be one mitigating circumstance."

"But why?"

"Well, I guess, with males, at least, you're exercising your genital sexual powers in isolation from another human being, for one thing. And this relation can end up with no possibility of the prospective, procreative, *meaningful* human sexuality. I think that would be the best reason. It's abuse of your body."

I call a cab.

. . .

I got no emotion for anybody else,
You gotta understand
I'm in love with myself,
My beautiful self.
     — *Sex Pistols, "No Feelings"*

. . .

264.

Wounded elephant guitars and the mad urban elephant boy croaks a death rattle song. Jump back, barrister. *These* unknown children, they mean *only* to destroy. Not even a faith based in love of oneself: they mean also to destroy themselves. And they do — and finally Walter Cronkite does the Sid Vicious obit on *The CBS Evening News*. Not even a faith: just "I HATE" and those scratched-out, savage eyes.

● ● ●

NEW YORK (*Creem,* 4/78; by Susan Whitall)
... So the band *has* split up?
Rotten: "Yes. It was the perfect time, really. We'd achieved just what we wanted to do: fuck up the media! We'd gone as far as that particular unit could go"...

● ● ●

Can there be a faith in no faith?

There's the question I really wanted to ask William May, Associate Professor of Moral Theology, the sixty-four-thousand-dollar question, the question of the nuclear, postwar era, the question of the century — young F. Scott Fitzgerald asked it of himself and *his* generation, which in 1920 was already "grown up to find all Gods dead, all wars fought, all faiths in man shaken." It's the question of America, maybe of the whole post-Declaration planet (and the Iranians, for one, answered it no and tossed their Western puppet in favor of a hell-fire theocrat). It's the question, of course, of the sons and daughters.

I hate, too, and sometimes I hate the sons and daughters. Sometimes I think we're a generation of faithless, worthless scum. Spoiled, indeed rotten, gluttonous, hedonistic, narcissistic, nihilistic, utterly corrupt, completely manipulated and, in turn, manipulating, invidious, insidious, wasted, wasteful; too stupid perhaps to be truly evil, but perhaps too evil to be much else; the festering boil to which the whole modern idea, if not the whole American idea, has come and from which the future (or is that presumptuous?) will be a long time recovering. But I especially think it when I am burying a young friend, as I am doing tomorrow. Again. Yet I know, too, it could have been even worse — Karen Ann Quinlan, the unmourned, the undead. At times like this, when the breaking down of all walls and standards breaks through to the darkness, when the morbid embrace is returned and the imitating of death becomes the real thing — and death itself is bereft of meaning, hope — and a guy I know is lying gray and naked and ruined on a tray in the New York City morgue, I think it. At times like this, I think the answer is no, you fool. And I hate those savage eyes: they almost always turn to tears.

And sometimes I think the answer is yes. Spoiled, yes, but to an omnivorous awareness of the riches of existence and the human possibilities. Stupid, yes, but in the time of the all-too-knowing. Evil, yes, in the midst of upside-down good. Gluttonous and hedonistic and narcissistic — but who exactly would have us be otherwise? And how much does he profit by it, this nouvelle cuisine–belching, jackbooted glutton himself? Nihilistic, yes — and so frighteningly effective. Yes, corrupt, and so incorruptible. Manipulated, yes: wily and adaptable. Manipulating, yes: enthusiastic. Yes, break down those walls and standards — everything is everything; we *are* all one; higher and higher; the sky's the limit. Break down seeing and hearing and thinking and fucking — and, yes, break down life itself. And if death is death and has no meaning, life then fills to overflowing. And all of the dead are martyrs. Hate, yes, all that's against you. Hate, and be sinful and human. Most of all, hate so that you can love. Ah, those noble savage eyes, I think sometimes, I'm so proud of my generation. I'm proud that we're brave, and I'm proud that we still live here at home. And I have hope. And faith.

. . .

266.

The King is gone, but he's not forgotten,
This is the story of Johnny Rotten,
It's better to burn out
Than it is to rust,
Hey, hey, my, my . . .
   — *Neil Young, "My My, Hey Hey*
   (Out of the Blue)"

• • •

And then I think of my friend, who loved William Burroughs
and lived most assiduously a life of rock 'n' roll. Why *this*
martyr? And I think of your friends. And of *our* children.

• • •

By plane, car, horse, camel, elephant, tractor, bicycle and
steam roller, on foot, skis, sled, crutch and pogo-stick the
tourists storm the frontiers, demanding with inflexible authority asylum from the "unspeakable conditions obtaining
in Freeland," the Chamber of Commerce striving in vain to
stem the debacle: "Please to be restful. It is only a few
crazies who have from the crazy place outbroken."
   — *William Burroughs,* Naked Lunch

• • •

And then I know the answer lies in between.
Can there be a faith in no faith? Yes.
Is there a choice? No.

Epilogue:
Do the Noise, Part 2

I suppose the punch line here should be Frank Sinatra and the return of melody. Which is just a slightly less tired way of saying Ronald Reagan and the swing to the right. The joke of course is that the rock 'n' roll generation fell on its ass.

And, indeed, open up the *New York Times,* and this week it's the eminent author, teacher, New York intellectual, American socialist, *Dissent* editor, and political wildman-when-he-was-young-you-should-have-seen-us-then Irving Howe standing up for despair. Oh, there's hope yet, a ray — *A Margin of Hope,* in fact, is the title of the Howe autobiography from which the *Times* article is adapted. But then the article itself is entitled "The Decade That Failed," which more or less puts us right back on well-trod ground. It's not that Irving Howe has actually gone over to the bad guys, but his message about the future — as well as about the past — of social progress in America, is not much more encouraging than theirs and, for all its elder statesman magnanimity, not much less nasty. Look at Jerry Rubin, mocks Howe (the *Times* providing a suitably silly-looking old photo): "Jerry Rubin ended up working on Wall Street." In other words, the sixties flopped; hippies copped; change stopped. Now there's practically no amount of this taunting that could compel me to defend the character of Jerry Rubin — like I said, I thought he and Abbie were assholes from the git. But it does make me wish that guys like Irving Howe could meet my dad.

Dad still blames the rock 'n' roll. (As a matter of fact, I do too.) He's a stubborn man, a real diehard. (But then so, obviously, am I.) Sometimes, however, he surprises me these days.

My dad first surprised me about two years back, when he was called for jury duty in the redneck Florida town where he lives and was eventually assigned to be foreman for the trial of a young man charged with possession of an ounce of pot. Pot — which he rightly interprets as coming from rock 'n' roll — makes my father nuts. That is, people using it. Unalterably and forever convinced of the *Reefer Madness* thesis, my father believes that all "hopheads" are also "pushers," and marijuana is the gateway to dope addiction, degeneracy, disease, and squalid death. Like I said, my father's not stupid — he is, however, a bit extreme when it comes to marijuana. On the face of it, then, the young defendant in that Florida courtroom had about as much chance as a snowball out in the parking lot.

How my father surprised me was by arguing for acquittal, voting for acquittal, and then, after reading the "not guilty," and securing permission from the judge, turning to the boy and first warning him gently and then encouraging him heartily and carrying on in general as if this were not a hophead but a son — even though they all knew, but the state, said Dad, failed to prove, the boy in fact was guilty. And the hope in it for me was not only that, like any good father, he cared, but that, like any good democrat, he had changed.

My father surprised me again last year. Fair and compassionate though he might be, on matters of feminism, while a long way from neanderthal, he's not yet Alan Alda. Although

270.

now, who knows? As he casually let drop one evening during a recent visit, he's hired a woman to help run the business — not a secretary, mind you, but a genuine female executive. What is going *on*? Indeed, that's what *I* thought as I pressed him for the clarifying detail. "But did any men apply for the job?" Yes. "More than one?" Yes. "High school graduates?" Yes. "Hopheads?" No. "Did the government make you hire her?" No. "Do you get a big tax break?" No. "Was she cheap, then?" No — in fact, more expensive. "So what's the angle?" With perhaps the barest sliver of pride showing beneath his irritation, my father replied curtly, "She was the best."

We still don't often see eye to eye, Dad and I, but then that would take all the fun out of things. I love too much this getting surprised by my father. But my fondest wish is that some time I might surprise him back.

. . .

Get with it, Irving Howe. The cargo has arrived. In fact, it's all around us. It's in the hair dryers and hot combs of the ex-jocks who tell us the local scores on TV and in the new wave discos. It's in the young women with their attaché cases lined up for the Boston shuttle plane; it's in the young women with the astronaut insignia lined up to fly the space shuttle. Not to mention the space program's first black pilot. It's in the politicians, from Tom Hayden and the socialist administration of Santa Monica, California, to former McGovern aide and presidential hopeful Senator Gary Hart, to the graduates of Nader and even, somewhere, the fallen-away liberal mophead David Stockman, somehow. And it's in the guttersnipe faith of hardcore punks still slogging away in Los Angeles, struggling finally to supplant the sixties and seventies, perhaps, but *not* to turn time back. It's in pasty city dwellers eating health food; it's in farmers doing cocaine. It's in kids dropping out of schools; it's in adults dropping out of

.271

jobs. It's in adults postponing having those kids, and then learning the violin with them when they turn three. It's in No Nukes and Nuke Freeze, too. It's in more than five hundred thousand not signing up for the draft — half a million strong.

It's a change that's of a piece and that's across the board — if it's not yet clearly cataclysmic. But give it twenty years like the Manus. There's a small triumph for change every day, someone's father ever so slightly, ever so tremendously, transformed. Sometimes there's even triumph in the thud, in the despair and the decay and the defeat. . . . Handsome Dick Manitoba called the other day, wanted us to go to CBGB's to check out Scott Kempner's new band, the Del-Lords, which he is trying to manage. It must have been another six months since I'd spoken with Manitoba, over a year since I'd last seen Scott, and the idea of going to CBGB's sounded like nostalgia. We went at the last minute, out of obligation, expecting not much — or less. But there at the door was Handsome Dick Manitoba in rockabilly pompadour, tweed jacket, and jeans with suspenders, trim, but not wasted, beaming — and really handsome. He's moved out of his parents' and in with an old friend from New Paltz who's recently divorced. He's working as a messenger on Wall Street for minimum wage during the day and at night for free (for now) for Scott, and he tells me not to be discouraged about having to get a day job. He tells me: "It's *not* surrender. It's only temporary." Manitoba is also at the same time full of fun and daring and outrage once more, and it dawns on me that he'll be doing his infamous spit trick over *all* our graves. And furthermore, if CBGB's is nostalgia, Scott's band is fresh and hot. These boys are thinking big again, like true-blue Americans should, and I walk out of that Bowery dump (and home to Mary) feeling a little bigger myself.

It's on nights like that — stone-cold sober, I should add —

that I know Dad and I are right to blame the rock 'n' roll. I know that ultimately the joke's on those who see in these times only the grief and the failure. And I know the punch line: *womp-baba-loo-bomp-a-lomp-bam-boom.*